Stud
Hall and Taylor's
MACROECONOMICS
Third Edition

Study Guide
Hall and Taylor's
MACROECONOMICS
Third Edition

David H. Papell
University of Houston

W. W. Norton & Company
New York   London

Acknowledgments

At all stages of writing the study guide, I have benefited greatly from the editorial comments and suggestions made by Drake McFeely. I am also grateful to Cheryl Holsey and Stephen Kerman for their careful reworking of the problems, to Tina Phillips for her painstaking review of the third edition, and to Kelly Nusser for her post-it notes. The feedback on the first two editions that I have received from students at the University of Houston and the University of Virginia has been very helpful in preparing the third edition.

Copyright © 1991, 1988, 1986 by W. W. Norton & Company, Inc.
All rights reserved.
Printed in the United States of America.

Third Edition

ISBN 0-393-96046-3

W. W. Norton & Company, Inc., 500 Fifth Avenue, New York, N.Y. 10110
W. W. Norton & Company Ltd., 10 Coptic Street, London WC1A 1PU

3 4 5 6 7 8 9 0

Contents

Preface

Part I. Fundamentals of Macroeconomics

Chapter 1. The Macroeconomy 3
Chapter 2. Measuring Economic Performance: Output and Income 14
Chapter 3. Monitoring the Economy: Inflation and Employment 26
Chapter 4. The Long-Run Growth Model 41
Chapter 5. Fiscal and Monetary Policies in a Full-Employment Economy 50
Chapter 6. Short-Run Fluctuations 60
Chapter 7. The IS-LM Model 73
Chapter 8. The Complete Model 88
Chapter 9. Macroeconomic Policy: A First Look 104

Part II. The Micro Foundations of Aggregate Demand

Chapter 10. Consumption Demand 121
Chapter 11. Investment Demand 135
Chapter 12. Foreign Trade and the Exchange Rate 146
Chapter 13. The Government's Budget Deficit and Aggregate Demand 157
Chapter 14. The Monetary System 168

Part III. The Micro Foundations of Output Determination and Price Adjustment

Chapter 15. The Labor Market and Flexible-Price Theories of Fluctuations 183
Chapter 16. The Firm and the Labor Market with Price and Wage Rigidities 198
Chapter 17. Aggregate Dynamics and Price Adjustment 208

Part IV. Macroeconomic Policy

Chapter 18. Designing and Maintaining a Good Macro Policy 223
Chapter 19. The World Economy 236

Preface

The purpose of this study guide is to help you learn the material in Hall and Taylor's *Macroeconomics*, Third Edition. It isolates the major learning objectives, reviews the major terms and concepts, and provides self-tests and problem sets for every chapter in the text. A word of caution before you continue, however: The study guide will help you to learn the material more easily, but it is not a substitute for reading the textbook.

Each chapter in the study guide opens with a section called *Main Objectives*, which highlights the basic topics covered in the text chapter. This is followed by a section called *Key Terms and Concepts*, which reviews and explains the chapter's most important concepts. Next comes the *Self-Test*. Here, there are three types of questions: fill in the blank, true-false, and review. You will find answers to the Self-Test at the back of each chapter. Finally, each chapter includes a *Problem Set*, where *Worked Problems* that include step-by-step solutions precede *Review Problems* that you work yourself. Answers to the Review Problems are also found at the back of each chapter.

While every student studies differently, you might use the study guide in the following way. First, read the chapter in the textbook without worrying too much about understanding everything. Second, read the Main Objectives and Key Terms and Concepts sections in the study guide. If you come across a concept that you do not understand, go back to the text. Third, take the Self-Test as if you were taking an exam. Write down your answers, and be sure to provide an explanation for the true-false questions. Refer back to the text or to the study guide to make sure that you understand the questions that you missed. Fourth, work through the Problem Set, using the Worked Problems to learn how to solve the different types of numerical problems. Finally, re-read the chapter in the text to make sure that you understand it completely. You should now be well prepared to answer the questions and problems in the back of each text chapter.

PART I

Fundamentals of Macroeconomics

CHAPTER 1   The Macroeconomy

Main Objectives

Following the turbulence of the 1970s and early 1980s, when fluctuations in gross national product, employment, inflation, and interest rates were larger and more erratic than at any time since the Great Depression of the 1930s, the United States enjoyed a continuous expansion from 1982 to 1990. Historical experience, however, warns us that expansions do not last forever, and the U.S. economy went into recession during the last quarter of 1990. In order to explain both how the economy grows and why it fluctuates over time, macroeconomists construct models. Chapter 1 introduces the basic properties and terminology of macroeconomic models.

Key Terms and Concepts

Macroeconomics is the study of economic growth and fluctuations. While the long-run growth of the economy is largely determined by factors such as population growth and technological progress, this growth is irregular. The economy undergoes both **recessions**, periods of contracting economic activity, and **recoveries**, periods of above-average economic growth following a recession. The top of a recovery is a **peak** and the bottom of a recession is a **trough**.

Real gross national product (GNP) is the most comprehensive measure of total production in the United States. It adjusts the dollar value of goods produced for changes in prices. The **rate of inflation** is the percentage change in the average price of all goods in the economy from one year to the next.

The **employment rate** is the ratio of employed workers to the working-age population. The **unemployment rate** is the percentage of workers who are looking for work and have not yet found it. The **rate of interest** is the amount charged by lenders per dollar per year, expressed as a percent. The **real interest rate** is the rate of interest minus the expected rate of inflation. The **money supply** consists of currency and deposits at banks. The money supply divided by the price level is called **real money**.

Potential GNP (or **potential output**) is the amount of output that would have been produced had the economy been in neither boom nor recession. Over time, real GNP fluctuates from its long-run, or potential, growth path. Other economic variables also fluctuate. Employment is highly correlated with GNP, and therefore falls during recessions. Inflation tends to be higher when the economy is near its peak, and lower when it is in a trough. Interest rates are procyclical; they rise during recoveries and fall during recessions.

Describing macroeconomic behavior in complete detail would prove unwieldy—there is too much going on. So economists construct **macroeconomic models**, simplified descriptions of how consumers and firms behave and interact, to explain fluctuations. In this way, they can test their theories against observation, or note how different theories interact, without extraneous detail. We pay a great deal of attention in this course to macroeconomic models with **flexible** and **sticky prices**. Models with flexible prices assume that wages and prices adjust rapidly according to traditional supply-and-demand analysis. In this way, workers and machines are kept fully employed, so that the economy always operates at its long-run potential output. Models with sticky prices postulate that this adjustment takes time and explain fluctuations by bottlenecks in the adjustment process.

The **long-run growth model** with flexible prices is illustrated in Figure 1–1. Potential output is depicted as a vertical line. In Chapter 4 we will see why potential output does not depend on the price level. The **aggregate demand curve**, which slopes downward, is the total amount of demand throughout the economy. In Chapter 7 we will see how the aggregate demand curve is derived. With flexible prices, changes in aggregate demand affect the price level. While they do not affect GNP, they cause important **shifts in production** from one type of good to another.

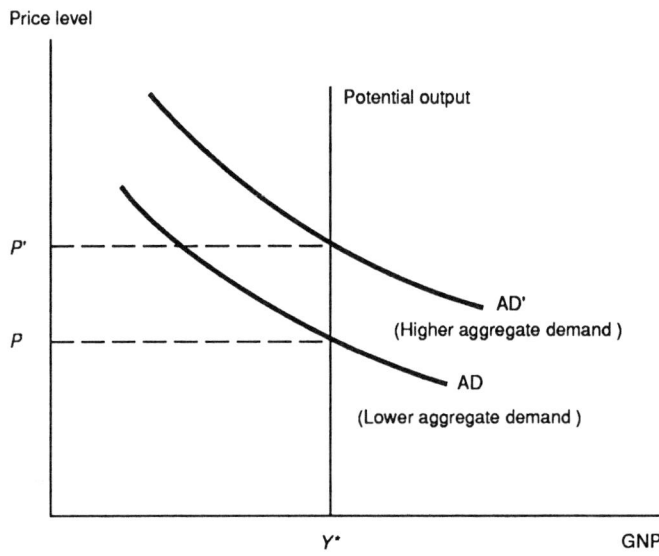

Figure 1-1

According to the long-run growth model with flexible prices, real GNP can only change if potential output changes. The Great Depression of the 1930s saw real GNP fall by so much that an explanation based on a drop in potential output seemed inadequate. During the depression, John Maynard Keynes, the great British economist, created a new macroeconomic model, the model with fixed prices, where shifts in aggregate demand could affect GNP. The model with fixed prices is illustrated in Figure 1-2, where the price level is depicted as a horizontal line. Changes in aggregate demand affect GNP while leaving the price level unchanged.

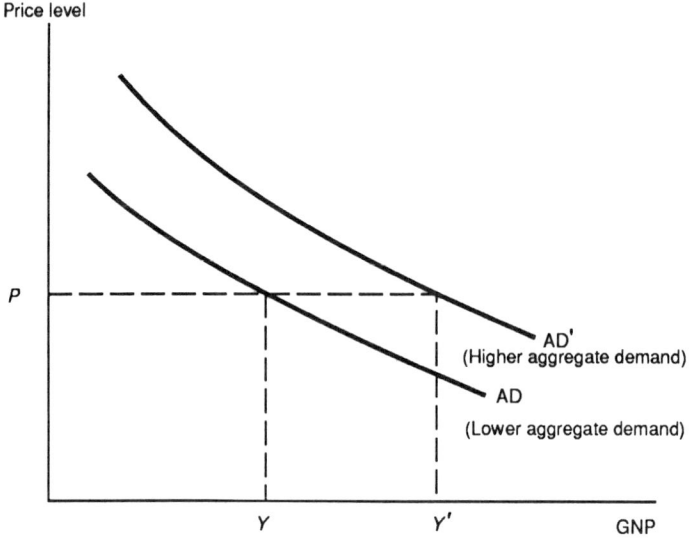

Figure 1–2

Neither the long-run growth model nor the model with fixed prices provides a complete description of the economy. The model with fixed prices can account for short-run fluctuations in output and employment, but cannot explain inflation. The long-run growth model can explain inflation, but not short-run fluctuations.

Gradual price adjustment bridges the gap between the model with fixed prices and the long-run growth model. In its simplest form, the idea of price adjustment is that when output is less than potential GNP there is pressure on prices to adjust downward. When output exceeds potential GNP, there is pressure on prices to adjust upward. Sticky prices, fixed in the short run but flexible in the long run, are explained by the process of price adjustment.

When we examine the behavior of individual firms and consumers, we will discover that expectations of the future play an important role. The theory of **rational expectations** is that firms and consumers, in forming their expectations, use whatever information is available to them in the most effective manner. While this seems innocuous, it has far-reaching implications for the study of consumption, investment, and price adjustment.

One of the most important goals of macroeconomic policy-making is maintaining a steady growth of aggregate demand. There is considerable controversy, however, about how this should be accomplished. **Monetarists** such as Nobel laureate Milton Friedman, formerly of the University of Chicago and now of the Hoover Institute at Stanford

THE MACROECONOMY

University, believe that steady money growth will best stabilize the growth of aggregate demand. **New classicals** such as Robert Lucas of the University of Chicago and Thomas Sargent of Stanford University, who maintain that wages and prices adjust very quickly, also advocate steady money growth. **Keynesians** such as Nobel laureates James Tobin of Yale University and Franco Modigliani of M.I.T. favor the active use of monetary policy to offset other sources of instability in the economy.

The **complete model**, the macroeconomic model developed in the remainder of the book, incorporates the concepts presented above. The model assumes sticky prices—fixed in the short run to explain fluctuations in output and employment, and flexible in the long run to explain inflation. Price adjustment explains the transition from short-run to long-run potential GNP. Rational expectations are assumed throughout.

Self-Test

Fill in the Blank

1. The economy is in a _____ if production and employment are falling.

2. When production and employment are increasing rapidly, the economy is in a _____.

3. During the 1970s and early 1980s, fluctuations in the United States economy were larger and more erratic than at any time since _____.

4. The _____ is the percentage change in the price level from one year to the next.

5. _____ is the most comprehensive measure of total production in the United States.

6. The nominal interest rate minus the expected rate of inflation is the _____.

7. If prices were _____ workers and machines would be fully employed.

8. Shifts in demand influence output if prices are _____.
9. If firms and consumers make the most of the information available to them, they are said to form their expectations _____.
10. _____ output is the amount of output that will be produced if the economy is in neither boom nor recession.
11. _____ GNP adjusts the dollar value of goods produced for changes in prices.
12. The money supply divided by the price level is called _____ money.

True-False
13. A peak is the bottom of a recession.
14. Economic fluctuations are regular and can be anticipated with great accuracy.
15. Interest rates are procyclical.
16. With perfectly flexible prices, shifts in demand cannot explain recessions and booms.
17. Macroeconomists are very successful at predicting interest rates.
18. The economy is in a recovery if production and employment are increasing rapidly.
19. Economic fluctuations have increased since World War II.
20. Fluctuations in employment follow closely the fluctuations in real GNP.
21. With sticky prices, output always equals potential GNP.
22. Declines in inflation usually occur during recessions.
23. The recession in the early 1980s was the largest in the last 75 years.
24. The employment rate is the ratio of employed workers to unemployed workers.

THE MACROECONOMY

Review Questions

25. What is the long-term pattern of economic fluctuations in the United States?
26. Explain why macroeconomists are concerned about economic fluctuations.
27. What other economic variables fluctuate along with GNP?
28. What determines potential output?
29. How are the price level and output determined in the long-run growth model and the model with fixed prices?
30. How are economic fluctuations explained in the long-run growth model and the model with fixed prices?
31. Why did Keynes reject the model with flexible prices?
32. Why is the model with fixed prices inappropriate for the long run?
33. What is the difference between Keynesians and monetarists?
34. What is a simple expression of the idea of price adjustment?
35. What is meant by rational expectations?
36. In the long-run growth model, what effect, if any, do changes in aggregate demand have on GNP?
37. What is assumed about prices in the complete model?

Problem Set

Worked Problems

1. Suppose the aggregate demand curve is given by the expression $Y = 4,000 + 2,000/P$, where Y is output and P is the price level. Potential output is $Y^* = \$5,000$ billion.

   a. Draw potential output and the aggregate demand curve on a diagram with the price level P on the vertical axis and output Y on the horizontal axis.

   b. What is the price level P if prices are flexible?

   c. Suppose that prices are fixed and $P = 1$. What is the level of actual output? Is actual output Y above or below potential output Y^*? Is there pressure on the price level to move upward or downward?

d. Suppose that prices are fixed and P = 3. What is the level of output now? Is it above or below potential output? What pressure is there on prices?

   a. *Potential output is a vertical line where output = potential output = $5,000 billion. The aggregate demand curve is downward sloping because output demanded is lower if prices are higher.*

   b. *If prices are flexible, output equals potential output. Thus 4,000 + 2,000/P = $5,000 billion, which can only hold if P = 2.*

   c. *If prices are fixed and P = 1, actual output Y = 4,000 + 2,000/1 = $6,000 billion. Since potential output Y* = $5,000 billion, actual output is above potential, putting pressure on the price level to move upward.*

   d. *If prices are fixed and P = 3, actual output Y = 4,000 + 2,000/3 = $4,667 billion. Since potential output Y* = $5,000 billion, actual output is below potential, putting pressure on prices to fall.*

2. The price level was 54 in 1950, 69 in 1960, 92 in 1970, and 178 in 1980. What was the rate of inflation for the 1950s, 1960s, and 1970s? Why would models with sticky prices be more appropriate for the 1950s and 1960s than for the 1970s?

   The rate of inflation was 28 percent for the 1950s, 33 percent for the 1960s, and 93 percent for the 1970s. Models with sticky prices are more appropriate for the 1950s and 1960s than for the 1970s because inflation was much lower.

Review Problems

3. Suppose the aggregate demand curve is given by the expression Y = 5,000 + 3,000/P, where Y is output and P is the price level. Potential output Y* = $6,500.

   a. Draw potential output and the aggregate demand curve.

   b. What is the price level P if prices are flexible?

   c. Suppose that prices are fixed and P = 3. What is the level of actual output? Is actual output Y above or below potential output Y*? Is there pressure on the price level to move upward or downward?

THE MACROECONOMY 11

4. Suppose the aggregate demand curve is still given by $Y = 5{,}000 + 3{,}000/P$, but potential output $Y^* = \$8{,}000$.

   a. Draw potential output and the aggregate demand curve.

   b. What is P if prices are flexible? Compare your answer with Problem 3b.

   c. Suppose that prices are fixed and $P = 3$. What is the level of output now? Is it above or below potential output? What pressure is there on prices?

5. Suppose that the aggregate demand curve is now given by $Y = 6{,}500 + 3{,}000/P$, with potential output $Y^* = \$8{,}000$.

   a. Draw potential output and the aggregate demand and supply curves.

   b. What is P now if prices are flexible? Compare your answer with Problem 4b.

   c. Suppose that prices are fixed and $P = 2$. What is the level of output now? Is it above or below potential output? What pressure is there on prices?

6. The price level was 107.9 in 1984, 111.5 in 1985, and 114.5 in 1986. What were the rates of inflation for 1985 and 1986? If people expect the rate of inflation to be the average rate of inflation in the previous two years, what was the expected rate of inflation for 1987? If the interest rate in 1987 was 6 percent, what was the real interest rate?

Answers to the Self-Test

1. Recession
2. Recovery
3. The Great Depression of the 1930s
4. Inflation rate
5. Real gross national product
6. Real interest rate
7. Flexible
8. Fixed or sticky
9. Rationally
10. Potential
11. Real
12. Real
13. False. A peak is the top of a recovery.
14. False. They are irregular and cannot be predicted well.
15. True. They fall during recessions and rise during recoveries.

16. True. With perfectly flexible prices, shifts in demand cannot affect output. They can only affect prices.
17. False. Macroeconomists are no more successful at predicting interest rates than anyone else.
18. True. That is the definition of a recovery.
19. False. They have decreased in magnitude.
20. True. Employment falls during recessions and rises during recoveries.
21. False. With sticky prices, output can diverge from potential GNP.
22. True. In the past 20 years, almost all of the significant declines in the rate of inflation occurred during recession periods.
23. False. The Great Depression was much larger.
24. False. The employment rate is the ratio of employed workers to the working-age population.
25. Economic fluctuations were very large during the 1920s and 1930s, decreased during the 1950s and 1960s, and increased, although not back to their pre–World War II levels, during the 1970s and 1980s.
26. Macroeconomists are concerned about fluctuations because people can be adversely affected, an example being unemployment and layoffs during recessions.
27. Employment, inflation, interest rates, and exchange rates also undergo fluctuations.
28. Potential output is determined by the productive capacity of the economy, which in turn is determined by the volume of productive factors—capital and labor. It is unrelated to the price level.
29. In the long-run growth model, output is determined by potential output, and the price level is determined by aggregate demand. In the model with fixed prices, the price level is fixed by assumption, and output is determined by aggregate demand.
30. In the long-run growth model, since output is determined by potential output, economic fluctuations can only occur when potential output changes. In the model with fixed prices, shifts in aggregate demand can cause fluctuations.
31. During the Great Depression, the decrease in real GNP was too large, 30 percent from 1929 to 1933, to be explained by shifts in potential output.
32. In the long run, an economic model should be able to explain inflation, which the model with fixed prices cannot do.
33. Monetarists believe that steady money growth will best stabilize the growth in aggregate demand. Keynesians believe in a more active use of policy. They feel that changes in the money supply should be used to offset other sources of instability in the economy.
34. When output is less than potential GNP, there is pressure on prices to adjust downward. When output exceeds potential GNP, there is pressure on prices to adjust upward.
35. Rational expectations means that consumers and firms, when forming their expectations about the future, make the most of the information available to them.
36. In the long-run growth model, changes in aggregate demand cause shifts in production from one type of good to another, but do not affect the level of GNP.

THE MACROECONOMY

37. Prices are assumed to be sticky, fixed in the short run but flexible in the long run.

Solutions to Review Problems

3. a. The aggregate supply curve is a vertical line where output = potential output = $6,500. The aggregate demand curve is downward sloping.
   b. If prices are flexible output equals potential output. Thus $5,000 + 3,000/P = \$6,500$, and $P = 2$.
   c. If prices are fixed and $P = 3$, actual output $Y = 5,000 + 3,000/3 = \$6,000$. Since potential output $Y^* = \$6,500$, actual output is below potential, putting downward pressure on the price level.
4. a. The new aggregate supply curve is a vertical line with $Y^* = \$8,000$. The aggregate demand curve is unchanged.
   b. If prices are flexible, $5,000 + 3,000/P = \$8,000$, so $P = 1$. The price level is lower than in Problem 3b. This shows that, if prices are flexible, an increase in potential output with unchanged aggregate demand will lower prices.
   c. $Y = 5,000 + 3,000/3 = \$6,000$. Since $Y^* = \$8,000$, output is still below potential, and there is still downward pressure on prices.
5. a. The aggregate demand curve has a higher intercept but the same slope as before. The aggregate supply curve is the same as in Problem 4.
   b. If prices are flexible, $6,500 + 3,000/P = \$8,000$, so $P = 2$. The price level is higher than in Problem 4b. This shows that, if prices are flexible, an increase in aggregate demand with unchanged potential output will raise prices.
   c. If prices are fixed and $P = 2$, $Y = 6,500 + 3,000/P = \$8,000$, which is also equal to potential output. There is no pressure on prices to either rise or fall.
6. The rate of inflation was 3.3 percent in 1985 and 2.7 percent in 1986. The expected rate of inflation for 1987 was 3 percent. The real interest rate was 3 percent.

CHAPTER 2

Measuring Economic Performance: Output and Income

Main Objectives

Economic fluctuations are movements in real gross national product around its long-run, potential level, as we saw in Chapter 1. In Chapter 2 we see how gross national product is defined and measured. Three different ways to measure GNP, as spending, production, and income, are discussed and we see how each adds up to the same thing. Beyond mastering the definitions of GNP, you should become familiar with the concepts of saving and investment, and how transactions with the rest of the world relate to domestic GNP.

Key Terms and Concepts

Gross national product (GNP) can be measured in terms of production, income, or spending. **Production GNP** is the dollar value of the goods and services produced during a period of time. **Income GNP** is wages and interest paid by firms, plus profits earned by owners of firms. **Spending GNP** is the amount of goods and services bought by consumers, other firms, and the government, plus **inventories** (goods produced but not yet sold). Through two accounting rules—including inventories in spending and computing profits as sales minus expenses—production GNP, income GNP, and spending GNP are always the same. This is an identity—simply a matter of definition.

It will most often prove useful to define GNP in terms of spending. **Consumption** is spending by households. It includes purchases of durable goods such as automobiles, nondurables goods such as food, and services such as medical care. **Investment** is the sum of spending by firms on plant, equipment, and inventories and spending by households on housing. **Nonresidential fixed investment** is spending on structures such as office buildings and on equipment for use in business such as computers. **Residential fixed investment** is spending on construction of new houses and apartment buildings. Note that spending on new houses is included in investment, not in consumption. **Inventory investment** is the value of goods that are produced, but not sold, during a given period. If more goods are sold than produced, inventory investment is negative for the period. **Government purchases** is spending on goods and services by state, local, and federal governments.

For a country with a closed economy, one that does not trade with other countries, this would exhaust our categories of spending. Goods produced could be either consumed (except for new houses) if sold to households, invested if sold to firms or added to inventories, or counted as government purchases if sold to the government, so that spending would equal production. We could then say that GNP is equal to consumption plus investment plus government purchases.

Since countries trade with other countries, these categories are incomplete. Some of the goods that we produce are purchased by foreigners. These are our **exports** and are included in our GNP. On the other hand, part of our consumption, investment, and government purchases are of goods produced by foreigners. These are our **imports** and should not be counted as part of our GNP. Exports minus imports is called **net exports**. For an open economy, GNP is equal to consumption plus investment plus government purchases plus net exports. When net exports are positive, there is a **trade surplus**. When net exports are negative, there is a **trade deficit**.

The **capital stock** is the total amount of productive capital—factories, equipment, and houses—in the economy. **Investment** is the flow of new capital that is added during the year to the stock of capital. Since part of the capital stock is always wearing out, or **depreciating**, part of investment goes to maintain the existing level of the capital stock. Net investment is equal to investment minus depreciation. **Net national product (NNP)** includes only net investment. GNP includes gross investment.

GNP can increase either if the physical amount of goods and services produced increases or if prices rise. GNP adjusted for changing prices is called **real GNP**, and measures the physical amount of production. To clarify the distinction between real GNP and GNP, sometimes the term **nominal GNP** is used for the dollar value of goods and services produced. Nominal GNP is synonymous with GNP.

In order for gross national product to measure the value of production, it is necessary to avoid double counting. Thus only new purchases are counted in spending. Purchases of old houses and used cars are not included because they contributed to GNP when new. Furthermore, only goods purchased at the end of the production line, as final goods, are counted in spending. If General Motors purchases steel to produce an automobile, the steel is an **intermediate good,** and is not counted. When the car is sold, the value of the steel is included as part of the final good.

The concept of **value added** is used to prevent double counting when GNP is computed by production. The value added by a firm is the difference between the revenue a firm earns by selling its products and the amount it pays for intermediate goods produced by other firms. If Goodyear buys rubber and steel to produce steel-belted radial tires, the value added is the difference between what it earns from the tires and what it pays for the rubber and steel. GNP is the sum of the value added by all firms in the economy.

GNP can also be computed as the sum of all incomes in the economy. In the actual statistical accounts, there is no measure of income that is exactly comparable to GNP. The closest is **national income**, which is approximately equal to net national product minus sales and excise taxes. **Personal income** equals national income plus government and business **transfer payments** (social security and other benefits) plus interest on the government debt and from other nonbusiness sources minus social security taxes minus corporate retained earnings. **Disposable personal income**, often just called **disposable income**, is personal income minus income taxes. Disposable income is equal to GNP plus government transfers plus interest on the government debt minus taxes.

Saving is income minus consumption. We can use this definition to analyze saving for various sectors of the economy. **Private saving** is disposable income minus consumption. **Government saving** equals the income received by the government (tax receipts minus government transfers minus interest on the government debt) minus government spending on goods and services. A positive value for government saving is also called a **government budget surplus**. A negative value is a **government budget deficit**. **Rest of world saving** refers to the income that other countries receive from our purchase of their goods and services (our imports) minus their spending on our goods and services (our exports).

Money and bonds are financial liabilities of the government and financial assets of the private sector. The term **government budget identity** means that negative government saving, or the government budget deficit, must be financed either by issuing money or by issuing bonds.

The basic measure of our transactions with the rest of the world is the **merchandise trade balance**, which is our exports of goods minus our imports of goods. The **balance on goods and services** adds net interest payments on foreign investments to the trade balance. The **current account**, which is the most comprehensive measure of our transactions with the rest of the world, adds net international transfers and remittances to the balance on goods and services.

The other side of the rest of the world accounts is the **capital account**, which measures international borrowing and lending. When an American borrows from a foreigner, either by taking out a loan or by selling a bond, it is a capital inflow or a **capital account surplus**. An American lending to a foreigner falls into the category of a capital outflow or a **capital account deficit**. When the United States imports more than it exports, it runs a current account deficit. In order to finance the deficit, it has to borrow from the rest of the world, creating a capital account surplus. Thus the negative current account is matched by the positive capital account. Put another way, the sum of the current and capital accounts is equal to zero.

The **exchange rate** is the price of dollars in terms of foreign currency, and measures how much foreign currency, say 150 Japanese yen, one can buy with one dollar. When the exchange rate rises, say to 200 yen, foreign goods become cheaper compared to home goods. The **trade-weighted average exchange rate** is an average of the exchange rates between the dollar and several different currencies.

Self-Test

Fill in the Blank

1. Gross national product can be computed by measuring _____, _____, or _____.
2. Consumption is spending by _____.
3. The two types of fixed investment are _____ and _____.
4. Net investment is gross investment minus _____.
5. _____ investment consists of goods produced but not yet sold.
6. Net exports equal _____ minus _____.
7. To avoid double counting, we include only purchases of _____ goods when computing GNP.
8. Personal income minus income taxes is _____ personal income.

9. If government saving is negative, there is a government budget _____.

10. The measure of our transactions in goods, services, and transfers with the rest of the world is the _____ account.

11. When net exports are positive, there is a trade _____.

12. When net exports are negative, there is a trade _____.

True-False

13. We know that measuring GNP by either production, spending, or income each adds up to the same thing because of long experience with macroeconomic theories.

14. Spending on new houses is the only type of household spending that is not included in consumption.

15. The capital stock increases by the total amount of investment spending.

16. GNP is both the dollar value of all final goods and services produced in this country during a given period of time and the sum of all the value added by firms during the same period.

17. Both nominal and real GNP measure the dollar volume of production.

18. GNP increases if you buy either a new or a used car.

19. If Ford sells more automobiles, GNP will increase whether they are purchased by Americans or foreigners.

20. If you buy 100 shares of IBM stock, it is investment and adds to GNP.

21. If a firm replaces an old typewriter with a new one, it does not add to GNP because the total number of typewriters remains unchanged.

22. If General Motors produces more cars than it sells, this causes a smaller increase in GNP than if it sold all the cars it produced.

23. When the exchange rate rises, foreign goods become cheaper compared to home goods.

24. The exchange rate has been nearly constant during the last ten years.

Review Questions

25. How is GNP computed when measured through spending?
26. What are the components of consumption?
27. What is the relationship between the stock of capital and investment?
28. What happened to real GNP from 1981 to 1986? How does this illustrate an economic cycle?
29. Suppose that the economy is closed and that there is no government. Show that saving must equal investment.
30. Is there any necessity for saving to equal investment in an open economy with a government?
31. Why must a government budget deficit be financed by issuing money or bonds?
32. What is the difference between the merchandise trade balance, the balance on goods and services, and the current account balance?
33. Why does the sum of the current and capital accounts equal zero?
34. How does the current account deficit help finance the government budget deficit?
35. What does the trade-weighted average exchange rate measure?
36. How have fluctuations in the exchange rate been associated with movements in U.S. output?

Problem Set

Worked Problems

1. Consider a closed economy without a government with expenditure totals given by

    $C = \$1,200$ billion (Consumption)
    $I = 400$ (Investment)

    a. What is gross national product?
    b. Show that saving equals investment.

    a. *GNP = Consumption + Investment.*
       Using Y to denote GNP, Y = C + I = 1,200 + 400 = $1,600 billion.
    b. *Saving = Income − Consumption = GNP − Consumption.*

Using S to denote saving,
$$S = Y - C$$
$$= 1{,}600 - 1{,}200 = \$400 \text{ billion, which equals investment.}$$

2. Consider a closed economy with expenditure totals given by

   C = \$1,200 billion (Consumption)
   I = 400 (Investment)
   G = 300 (Government spending)
   F = 200 (Government transfers)
   N = 100 (Interest on the government debt)
   T = 400 (Taxes)

   a. What is GNP?
   b. What is private saving?
   c. What is government saving?
   d. What is total saving? Show that it equals investment.

   a. GNP = Consumption + Investment + Government spending.
   $$Y = C + I + G$$
   $$= 1{,}200 + 400 + 300 = \$1{,}900 \text{ billion.}$$

   b. Private saving = Disposable income − Consumption.
   Disposable income = GNP + Government transfers + Interest on the government debt − Taxes.
   Using S_p to denote private saving,
   $$S_p = (Y + F + N - T) - C$$
   $$= (1{,}900 + 200 + 100 - 400) - 1{,}200 = \$600 \text{ billion.}$$

   c. Government saving = Taxes − Government transfers − Interest on the government debt − Government spending.
   Using $S_g = T - F - N - G$
   $$= 400 - 200 - 100 - 300 = -\$200 \text{ billion.}$$

   d. Total saving = Private saving + Government saving.
   $$S = S_p + S_g$$
   $$= 600 - 200 = \$400 \text{ billion, which equals investment.}$$

3. Consider an open economy with expenditure totals given by

   C = \$1,200 billion (Consumption)
   I = 400 (Investment)
   G = 300 (Government spending)
   X = −100 (Net exports)
   F = 200 (Government transfers)
   N = 100 (Interest on the government debt)
   T = 400 (Taxes)

a. What is GNP?
b. What is private saving?
c. What is government saving?
d. What is rest of world saving?
e. What is total saving? Show that it equals investment.

a. GNP = Consumption + Investment + Government spending + Net exports.
Y = C + I + G + X
= 1,200 + 400 + 300 − 100 = $1,800 billion.

b. Private saving = Disposable income − Consumption.
Disposable income = GNP + Government transfers + Interest on the government debt − Taxes.
S_p = (Y + F + N − T) − C
= (1,800 + 200 + 100 − 400) − 1,200 = $500 billion.

c. Government saving = Taxes − Government transfers − Interest on the government debt − Government spending.
S_g = T − F − N − G
= 400 − 200 − 100 − 300 = −$200 billion.

d. Rest of world saving = −Net exports.
Using S_r to denote rest of world saving,
S_r = −X
= $100 billion.

e. Total saving = Private saving + Government saving + Rest of world saving.
S = $S_p + S_g + S_r$
= 500 − 200 + 100 = $400 billion, which equals investment.

Review Problems

4. Consider an economy with expenditure totals given by

C = $1,700 billion (Consumption)
I = 600 (Investment)

a. What is GNP?
b. What is saving?
c. How much does the capital stock increase during the period?

5. Consider the economy in Problem 4, but with depreciation equal to $200.

a. What is net investment?

b. What is GNP?

c. How much does the capital stock increase during the period?

6. Consider an economy with expenditure totals given by

C = $1,500 billion (Consumption)
I = 600 (Investment)
G = 500 (Government spending)
F = 300 (Government transfers)
N = 100 (Interest on the government debt)
T = 1,000 (Taxes)

a. What is GNP?

b. What is private saving?

c. What is government saving?

d. What is total saving? Show that it equals investment.

7. Consider an open economy with the same expenditure totals as in Problem 6, except for

X = $100 (Net exports)

a. What is GNP?

b. What is private saving?

c. What is government saving?

d. What is rest of world saving?

e. What is total saving? Show that it equals investment.

8. Consider an economy with expenditure totals given by

C = $2,300 billion (Consumption)
I = 700 (Investment)
G = 800 (Government spending)
F = 100 (Government transfers)
N = 100 (Interest on the government debt)
T = 800 (Taxes)

a. What is GNP?

b. What is private saving?

c. What is government saving?

d. What is total saving? Show that it equals investment.

e. What is the government budget deficit?

f. Suppose that money equals $600 and government bonds $800 at the start of the year. If 80 percent of the government deficit is financed by issuing bonds, calculate the new levels of bond and money holdings.

9. Consider an open economy with the same expenditure totals as in Problem 8, except for

$$X = -\$200 \qquad \text{(Net exports)}$$

a. What is GNP?

b. What is private saving?

c. What is government saving?

d. What is rest of world saving?

e. What is total saving? Show that it equals investment.

f. What percentage of the government budget deficit is financed by the current account deficit?

Answers to the Self-Test

1. Spending, production, or income
2. Households
3. Nonresidential and residential
4. Depreciation
5. Inventory
6. Exports minus imports
7. Final
8. Disposable
9. Deficit
10. Current
11. Surplus
12. Deficit
13. False. We know they are the same simply because of an accounting identity.
14. True. It is included in residential investment.
15. False. It increases by net, not gross, investment.
16. True. The two ways of calculating GNP are equivalent.
17. False. Real GNP measures the physical volume of production.
18. False. It is unchanged if you buy a used car.
19. True. Both domestic consumption and exports add to GNP.
20. False. Investment is spending that adds to or maintains the capital stock. Buying shares of stock is not investment in the sense used by macroeconomists, and does not add to GNP.
21. False. Purchases of new equipment by firms are investment whether they add to or maintain their capital stock.

22. False. The unsold cars constitute inventory investment, which adds to GNP just like consumption.
23. True. When the exchange rate rises, one dollar can buy more foreign currency, making foreign goods cheaper.
24. False. The exchange rate has had large fluctuations during the last ten years.
25. When measured through spending, GNP is equal to consumption plus investment plus government purchases plus net exports.
26. The components of consumption are durable goods, nondurable goods, and services.
27. Investment is the flow of new capital during the year that is added to the existing stock of capital.
28. Real GNP fell from 1981 to 1982, and then rose again in 1983 through 1986 above the 1981 value. This illustrates an economic cycle because it began with a contraction in real GNP (a recession), reached a trough, and continued with an expansion (a recovery).
29. For a closed economy with no government, GNP is equal to consumption plus investment. From the definition of saving, national income equals consumption plus saving. Since spending on GNP is equal to national income, saving equals investment.
30. In an open economy with a government, total saving, the sum of private, government, and rest of world saving, equals investment.
31. When the government spends more than it collects, it runs a deficit and must borrow to cover the difference. Issuing bonds and money, which are liabilities of the government, is how the government borrows.
32. The merchandise trade balance measures trade in goods. The balance on goods and services adds interest payments on foreign investments, and the current account adds remittances and transfers.
33. When there is a current account deficit, it must be financed by borrowing from the rest of the world, resulting in a matching capital account surplus. The two sum to zero.
34. Both the government budget deficit and the current account deficit are financed by borrowing. When there is a current account deficit, some of the borrowing is from foreigners.
35. The trade-weighted average exchange rate measures the average of the exchange rates between the dollar and several different currencies. The more that a country trades with the United States, the more weight it receives.
36. The dollar fell during the boom of the late 1970s and rose during the recession of the early 1980s. Other fluctuations in the exchange rate, however, have not been associated with movements in U.S. output.

Solutions to Review Problems

4. a. $Y = C + I = 1{,}700 + 600 = \$2{,}300$.
   b. $S = Y - C = 2{,}300 - 1{,}700 = \$600 = I$.
   c. The capital stock increased by $600, the amount of investment.

5. a. Net investment = Investment (gross) − Depreciation
      = 600 − 200 = $400.
   b. GNP is still equal to $2,300 because gross, not net, investment is used to calculate it.
   c. The capital stock increases by $400, the amount of net investment.
6. a. $Y = C + I + G$
      = 1,500 + 600 + 500 = $2,600.
   b. $S_p = (Y + F + N + T) - C$
      = (2,600 + 300 + 100 − 1,000) − 1,500 = $500.
   c. $S_g = T - F - N - G$
      = 1,000 − 300 − 100 − 500 = $100.
   d. $S = S_p + S_g$
      = 500 + 100 = $600 = I$.
7. a. $Y = C + I + G + X$
      = 1,500 + 600 + 500 + 100 = $2,700.
   b. $S_p = (Y + F + N - T) - C$
      = (2,700 + 300 + 100 − 1,000) − 1,500 = $600.
   c. $S_g = T - F - N - G$
      = 1,000 − 300 − 100 − 500 = $100.
   d. $S_r = -X = -\$100$.
   e. $S = S_p + S_g + S_r$
      = 600 + 100 − 100 = $600 = I$.
8. a. $Y = C + I + G$
      = 2,300 + 700 + 800 = $3,800.
   b. $S_p = (Y + F + N - T) - C$
      = (3,800 + 100 + 100 − 800) − 2,300 = $900.
   c. $S_g = T - F - B - G$
      = 800 − 100 − 100 − 800 = −$200.
   d. $S = S_p + S_g$
      = 900 − 200 = $700 = I$.
   e. The government budget deficit is $-S_g$, which equals $200.
   f. The change in bonds is 80 percent of the 200 government budget deficit, or 160, so the new level of bonds is 960. The change in money is 20 percent of 200, or 40, so the new level of money is 640.
9. a. $Y = C + I + G + X$
      = 2,300 + 700 + 800 − 200 = $3,600.
   b. $S_p = (Y + F + N - T) - C$
      = (3,600 + 100 + 100 − 800) − 2,300 = $700.
   c. $S_g = T - F - N - G$
      = 800 − 100 − 100 − 800 = −$200.
   d. $S_r = -X = \$200$.
   e. $S = S_p + S_g + S_r$
      = 700 − 200 + 200 = $700 = I$.
   f. Since the current account deficit, $200, is the same as the government budget deficit, the entire budget deficit is financed through the current account deficit. This means that foreigners have acquired $200 in United States bonds or money.

CHAPTER 3 Monitoring the Economy: Inflation and Employment

Main Objectives

Inflation and unemployment are the two most visible symbols of the economy's performance. Added up, the two have been popularized in presidential campaigns as the "misery index." In the late 1970s, when we had double-digit inflation, rates above 10 percent per year, it was considered imperative that inflation be reduced, even at the cost of provoking a recession. The flip side of the misery index, high unemployment, is the single most important indicator of economic distress. The battle against inflation in the late 1970s drove the unemployment rate above 10 percent in the early 1980s, the largest recession since the Great Depression. In this chapter, you will learn how inflation and unemployment are measured. Also important is the relationship between unemployment and gross national product.

Key Terms and Concepts

The **rate of inflation** is the percentage rate of change in the general price level from one period to the next. There are two ways to measure inflation. The first, **price indexes**, is calculated directly from data on the prices of thousands of goods and services. The best-known price index, the **consumer price index (CPI)**, measures the cost of living for a typical urban family. The weights on the individual prices in the CPI are based on a survey of consumer buying habits. Another widely used index is the **producer price index (PPI)**, which measures the prices charged by producers at various stages in the production process.

The second way to measure inflation is to deflate nominal values by dividing them by the real values they represent. For instance, the ratio of nominal to real GNP is called the **GNP implicit price deflator**, or often just the **GNP deflator**. There are deflators for each component of

GNP. The **consumption deflator**, for example, is the ratio of nominal to real consumption.

People are classified as employed if they are working. **Employment** in the United States is measured by two surveys, one of households and one of establishments where people work. In the long run, employment grows with potential GNP: To create more output firms require more workers. Employment falls with output during recessions, and rises during recoveries. Employment is not a complete measure of the input of labor in production because the average number of hours worked each week also falls during recessions and rises during recoveries. **Total hours of work**, employment multiplied by average hours worked, is a better measure.

If people are not working and are looking for work, they are classified as **unemployed**. The **labor force** is defined as the number of persons sixteen years of age or over who are either working or are unemployed. The **unemployment rate** is the percentage of the labor force that is unemployed. There are many people who are not working who are not counted as unemployed, including students, those at home taking care of their own children, and people who have become so discouraged about their job prospects that they have stopped looking. People who are not working but who are not looking for work are classified as **out of the labor force**. The **labor force participation rate** is the percentage of the working-age population that is in the labor force.

Unemployment is never equal to zero. There are always people entering the labor force (just turning sixteen, graduating from school, or starting to look for work again), in between jobs, or in professions with high job turnover. Unemployment of such people is called **frictional unemployment**. There are also people with so few skills that they are chronically unemployed. The rate of unemployment that prevails even in normal times, when real GNP equals potential output, is called the **natural rate of unemployment**. It is now usually estimated to be about 6 percent, rising from about 5 percent in the 1960s.

Okun's law is a useful approximation of the cyclical relationship between unemployment and real GNP. It says that for each percentage point by which the unemployment rate is above the natural rate, real GNP is 3 percent below potential GNP. Okun's law is given by

$$\frac{(Y - Y^*)}{Y^*} = -3(U - U^*), \tag{3-1}$$

where U is the unemployment rate, U^* is the natural rate of unemployment, Y is GNP, and Y^* is potential GNP. It is named after the late Arthur Okun of the Brookings Institution. The percentage departure of GNP from potential is called the **GNP gap**.

The **real wage** is the nominal wage divided by the price level. For workers concerned about the real purchasing power of their earnings, the appropriate price level is the CPI or the consumption deflator. Workers who wish to protect themselves against inflation can negotiate **cost-of-living adjustments (COLAs)** to have their payment rise in proportion to the increase in the CPI. The purpose of this is to fix one's real, instead of nominal, wage. Social security payments and many collective-bargaining agreements now incorporate COLAs.

Productivity is the amount of output per unit of input. When economists talk about productivity, they generally mean **labor productivity**, output per hour of labor. A broader measure, **total factor productivity**, is output per generalized unit of input. Productivity is procyclical, rising during booms and falling in recessions. Productivity growth has been slow since 1973. It has declined in each recession and has not increased enough in each recovery to return to the normal trend.

Self-Test

Fill in the Blank

1. The index that measures the cost of living for a typical urban family is the _____.

2. The _____ measures prices charged by producers at various stages of the production process.

3. The ratio of nominal GNP to real GNP is the _____.

4. The ratio of nominal consumption to real consumption is the _____.

5. The _____ is the number of persons sixteen years of age or over who are either working or unemployed.

6. The _____ is the percentage of the labor force that is unemployed.

7. The _____ is the percentage of the working-age population that is in the labor force.

8. The unemployment rate that prevails in normal times is the _____ of unemployment.

9. Unemployment of people in between jobs is an example of _____ unemployment.

10. The percentage departure of GNP from potential is called the _____.

11. The nominal wage divided by the price level is the _____ wage.

12. Output per hour of labor is called _____.

True-False

13. If the rate of inflation falls, prices decrease.
14. The consumer price index and the consumption deflator are not exactly identical.
15. The producer price index measures the prices actually paid by consumers.
16. Employment is procyclical.
17. People sixteen years of age or older are classified as either employed or unemployed.
18. If an unemployed person enrolls in school, the unemployment rate decreases.
19. If a student graduates from college and begins to look for a job, the unemployment rate increases.
20. One example of frictional unemployment is when a worker quits one job to search for another.
21. There is no unemployment when real GNP equals potential GNP.
22. The natural rate of unemployment is constant.
23. Real wages decline when oil prices rise.
24. Productivity growth has increased since 1973.

Review Questions

25. What are the two ways that the general price level can be measured?
26. Why might you expect cost-of-living adjustments (COLAs) to have become less popular in the 1980s than in the 1970s?

27. Explain why total hours of work is a better measure of labor input to the economy than employment.

28. What is the difference between being unemployed and being out of the labor force?

29. What has happened to the labor force participation rate for women in the last few decades?

30. Why has the natural rate of unemployment increased since the 1960s?

31. What has happened to the labor force since the 1960s that should have contributed to lowering the natural rate of unemployment?

32. What is Okun's law?

33. What is the GNP gap? Is it possible for the GNP gap to be positive as well as negative?

34. How has the real wage fluctuated since 1973?

35. What is the difference between labor productivity and total factor productivity?

36. Describe some of the possible reasons for the slowdown in productivity growth since 1973.

Problem Set

Worked Problems

1. Looking into our crystal ball, we see the following data from the early 2000s:

Year	Unemployment Rate
2001	.05 (5 percent)
2002	.04 (4 percent)
2003	.05 (5 percent)
2004	.06 (6 percent)

   a. Assuming that the natural rate of unemployment is 6 percent ($U^* = .06$), calculate the GNP gap for each of the unemployment rates from 2001 to 2004.

   b. What is the relationship between GNP and potential GNP for these years?

   c. If GNP is $2,000 billion in 2003, calculate potential GNP.

a. According to Okun's law, the GNP gap is $-3(U - U^*)$. For 2001, with $U = .05$ and $U^* = .06$, $-3(U - U^*) = .03$ (3 percent). The answers for the other years are

2002	.06 (6 percent)
2003	.03 (3 percent)
2004	.00 (0 percent)

b. GNP is above or equal to potential GNP for all four years.

c. Okun's law states that $(Y - Y^*)/Y^* =$ GNP gap. To calculate potential output, rearrange terms so that $Y^* = Y/(1 + $ GNP gap$)$. For 2003, if $Y = 2,000$ and the GNP gap (previously calculated) $= .03$, then $Y^* = 2,000/1.03 = \$1,941.7$ billion.

2. We also see the following data on prices from the early 2000s:

Year	CPI
2001	400
2002	440
2003	462
2004	462

a. Calculate the rate of inflation for 2002, 2003, and 2004.

b. Suppose that the increase in the wage rate for a group of workers that sign an employment contract for the 2-year period starting in 2003 is $\Delta W/W = .1$. What happens to the real wage measured in terms of the CPI?

c. Suppose instead that the wage rate is partially indexed to the CPI according to the formula

$$\Delta W/W = .05 + .5\, \Delta CPI/CPI.$$

What now happens to the real wage?

d. Finally, suppose that the wage rate is completely indexed to the CPI according to

$$\Delta W/W = \Delta CPI/CPI.$$

What happens to the real wage?

e. If, when these contracts were negotiated, workers and employers believed that inflation for 2003 and 2004 would be the same as it was in 2002, was there any reason for either to prefer one formula over the others? Did these preferences change over time once inflation became known?

a. The rate of inflation is

2002	.10 (10 percent)
2003	.05 (5 percent)
2004	.00 (0 percent)

b. Wages increase by 10 percent each year. Prices increase by 5 percent in 2003 and stay the same in 2004, so real wages increase.

c. Wages increase by 7.5 percent in 2003 and 5 percent in 2004. Real wages still increase, although by less than in Part b.

d. The real wage is constant when the nominal wage is completely indexed to the CPI.

e. If inflation had remained at 10 percent in 2003 and 2004, real wages would have been constant with any of the three formulas, so there was no reason for either workers or employers to prefer one over the others. Since the inflation rate declined, workers ended up better off with less indexation (b) while employers would have been better off with more (d).

Review Problems

3. The following unemployment rate (U) data are from the early 1960s:

Year	U
1960	.054 (5.4 percent)
1961	.065 (6.5 percent)
1962	.054 (5.4 percent)
1963	.055 (5.5 percent)

a. Assuming that the natural rate of unemployment was 5 percent ($U^* = .05$), calculate the GNP gap for each of the unemployment rates from 1960 to 1963.

b. Using the theory of price adjustment discussed in Chapter 1, what pressure was there on prices during these years?

c. Real GNP was $832.5 billion in 1963. Calculate potential GNP.

4. These data come from the late 1960s:

Year	U
1966	.037 (3.7 percent)
1967	.037 (3.7 percent)
1968	.035 (3.5 percent)
1969	.034 (3.4 percent)

a. Assuming that the natural rate of unemployment was 5 percent ($U^* = .05$), calculate the GNP gap for each of the unemployment rates from 1966 to 1969.

b. Using the theory of price adjustment discussed in Chapter 1, what pressure was there on prices during these years?

c. Real GNP was $1,087.6 billion in 1969. Calculate potential GNP.

5. Now we can examine the late 1970s:

Year	U
1976	.076 (7.6 percent)
1977	.069 (6.9 percent)
1978	.060 (6.0 percent)
1979	.058 (5.8 percent)

a. Assuming that the natural rate of unemployment had risen to 6 percent ($U^* = .06$), calculate the GNP gap for each of the unemployment rates from 1976 to 1979.

b. Using the theory of price adjustment discussed in Chapter 1, what pressure was there on prices during these years?

c. Real GNP was $1,479.4 billion in 1979. Calculate potential GNP.

6. We now consider the 1980s:

Year	U
1982	.095 (9.5 percent)
1983	.095 (9.5 percent)
1984	.074 (7.4 percent)
1985	.071 (7.1 percent)

a. Assuming that the natural rate of unemployment is 6 percent ($U^* = .06$), calculate the GNP gap for each of the unemployment rates from 1982 to 1985.

b. Using the theory of price adjustment discussed in Chapter 1, what was the pressure on prices during these years?

c. Real GNP was $1,480 billion in 1982. Calculate potential GNP.

7. These data come, once again, from the early 1960s.

Year	CPI
1960	88.7
1961	89.6
1962	90.6
1963	91.7

a. Calculate the rate of inflation for 1961, 1962, and 1963.

b. Suppose that the increase in the wage rate for a group of workers that sign an employment contract for the 2-year period starting in 1962 is $\Delta W/W = .01$. What happens to the real wage measured in terms of the CPI?

c. Suppose instead that the wage rate is partially indexed to the CPI according to the formula

$$\Delta W/W = .005 + .5 \, \Delta CPI/CPI.$$

What happens to the real wage?

d. Finally, suppose that the wage rate is completely indexed to the CPI according to

$$\Delta W/W = \Delta CPI/CPI.$$

What happens to the real wage?

e. If, when these contracts were negotiated, workers and employers believed that inflation for 1962 and 1963 would be the same as it was in 1961, was there any reason for either to prefer one formula over the others? Did these preferences change over time once inflation became known?

8. Now use the following data from the late 1960s:

Year	CPI
1966	97.2
1967	100.0
1968	104.2
1969	109.8

a. Calculate the rate of inflation for 1967, 1968, and 1969.

b. Suppose that the increase in the wage rate for a group of workers that sign an employment contract for the 2-year period starting in 1968 is $\Delta W/W = .029$. What happens to the real wage measured in terms of the CPI?

c. Suppose instead that the wage rate is partially indexed to the CPI according to the formula

$$\Delta W/W = .014 + .5 \, \Delta CPI/CPI.$$

What happens to the real wage?

d. Finally, suppose that the wage rate is completely indexed to the CPI according to

$$\Delta W/W = \Delta CPI/CPI.$$

What happens to the real wage?

e. If, when these contracts were negotiated, workers and employers believed that inflation for 1968 and 1969 would be the same as it was in 1967, was there any reason for either to prefer one formula over the others? Did these preferences change over time once inflation became known?

9. The following data are from the late 1970s:

Year	CPI
1976	170.5
1977	181.5
1978	195.4
1979	217.4

a. Calculate the rate of inflation for 1977, 1978, and 1979.

b. Suppose that the increase in the wage rate for a group of workers that sign an employment contract for the 2-year period starting in 1978 is $\Delta W/W = .065$. What happens to the real wage measured in terms of the CPI?

c. Suppose instead that the wage rate is partially indexed to the CPI according to the formula

$$\Delta W/W = .032 + .5\, \Delta CPI/CPI.$$

What happens to the real wage?

d. Finally, suppose that the wage rate is completely indexed to the CPI according to

$$\Delta W/W = \Delta CPI/CPI.$$

What happens to the real wage?

e. If, when these contracts were negotiated, workers and employers believed that inflation for 1978 and 1979 would be the same as it was in 1977, was there any reason for either to prefer one formula over the others? Did these preferences change over time once inflation became known?

10. We now consider the 1980s:

Year	CPI
1982	289.1
1983	298.4

Year	CPI
1984	311.1
1985	322.2

a. Calculate the rate of inflation for 1983, 1984, and 1985.

b. Suppose that the increase in the wage rate for a group of workers that sign an employment contract for the 3-year period starting in 1983 is $\Delta W/W = .10$. What happens to the real wage measured in terms of the CPI?

c. Suppose instead that the wage rate is partially indexed to the CPI according to the formula

$$\Delta W/W = .05 + .5 \, \Delta CPI/CPI.$$

What happens to the real wage?

d. Finally, suppose that the wage rate is completely indexed to the CPI according to

$$\Delta W/W = \Delta CPI/CPI.$$

What happens to the real wage?

e. If, when these contracts were negotiated, workers and employers believed that inflation for 1983 through 1985 would be the same as the average for 1980 through 1982, 10.0 percent, was there any reason for either to prefer one formula over the others? Did these preferences change over time once inflation became known?

Answers to the Self-Test

1. Consumer price index
2. Producer price index
3. GNP deflator
4. Consumption deflator
5. Labor force
6. Unemployment rate
7. Labor force participation rate
8. Natural rate
9. Frictional
10. GNP gap
11. Real
12. Labor productivity
13. False. The rate of inflation is the percentage change of the price level. If inflation falls from 10 to 5 percent, prices are still rising.
14. True. They are measured differently.

15. False. The producer price index measures the prices charged by producers at various stages in the production process.
16. True. Employment rises during expansions and falls during recessions.
17. False. They can also be out of the labor force.
18. True. You are counted as out of the labor force if in school full time.
19. True. You are counted as unemployed when you begin to look for a job.
20. True. Others are workers looking for a first job or reentering the labor force.
21. False. The unemployment rate that prevails in normal times is the natural rate of unemployment.
22. False. While it changes only very slowly, it has increased from 5 to 6 percent since the 1960s.
23. True. Oil and labor are both inputs to production. When the price of oil rises, the nominal wage (the price of labor) cannot rise as much as the general price level. Thus the real wage declines.
24. False. The growth of productivity has decreased since 1973.
25. The general price level can be measured either by constructing price indexes or by calculating deflators.
26. COLAs protect workers against inflation. With the slowdown of inflation in the 1980s, there was less need for protection.
27. Total hours of work is employment multiplied by the hours of work of the average worker. It is a better measure of labor input than employment because it incorporates how many hours people work.
28. Being unemployed means you are not working and are looking for work. Being out of the labor force means you are neither working nor looking for work.
29. The labor force participation rate for women has increased considerably in the last few decades.
30. The natural rate of unemployment has increased because the baby boom after World War II added more young workers, who have higher unemployment rates than older workers, to the labor force.
31. The labor force has become better educated.
32. Okun's law states that for each percentage point by which the unemployment rate is above the natural rate, real GNP is 3 percent below potential GNP.
33. The GNP gap is the percentage departure of GNP from potential. It can be positive (GNP can be above potential) if unemployment is below the natural rate.
34. The real wage fell after the oil price increase in 1974, rose during the late 1970s, fell again after the second oil price shock in 1979–80, and rose sharply when oil prices declined in 1986.
35. Labor productivity is output per hour of labor. Total factor productivity is output per generalized unit of input, which includes capital, energy, and materials as well as labor.
36. Increases in oil prices, reduction in expenditures on research and development, and insufficient investment in new machines and factories are some of the possible reasons for the slowdown in productivity since 1973.

Solutions to Review Problems

3. a. The GNP gap is $-3(U - U^*)$. With $U^* = .05$, the gap was

1960	−.012 (−1.2 percent)
1961	−.045 (−4.5 percent)
1962	−.012 (−1.2 percent)
1963	−.015 (−1.5 percent)

   b. With the gap between −1.2 and −4.5 percent, GNP was below potential and there was pressure on prices to fall, although, for three of the four years, the gap was quite small.

   c. Rearranging Okun's law, $Y^* = Y/(1 + \text{GNP gap})$. For 1963, with $Y = \$832.5$ and the gap $= -.015$, $Y^* = \$845.2$.

4. a. The GNP gap is $-3(U - U^*)$. With $U^* = .05$, the gap was

1966	.039 (3.9 percent)
1967	.039 (3.9 percent)
1968	.045 (4.5 percent)
1969	.048 (4.8 percent)

   b. With the gap between 3.9 and 4.8 percent, GNP was above potential and there was pressure on prices to rise.

   c. Rearranging Okun's law, $Y^* = Y/(1 + \text{GNP gap})$. For 1969, with $Y = \$1,087.6$ and the gap $= .048$, $Y^* = \$1,037.8$.

5. a. The GNP gap is $-3(U - U^*)$. With $U^* = .06$, the gap was

1976	−.048 (−4.8 percent)
1977	−.027 (−2.7 percent)
1978	.000 (0 percent)
1979	.006 (.6 percent)

   b. With the gap between −4.8 and −2.7 percent during 1976 and 1977, GNP was below potential and there was pressure on prices to fall. There was very little pressure on prices during 1978 and 1979.

   c. Rearranging Okun's law, $Y^* = Y/(1 + \text{GNP gap})$. For 1979, with $Y = \$1,479.4$ and the gap $= .006$, $Y^* = \$1,470.6$.

6. a. The GNP gap is $-3(U - U^*)$. With $U^* = .06$, the gap was

1982	−.105 (−10.5 percent)
1983	−.105 (−10.5 percent)
1984	−.042 (−4.2 percent)
1985	−.033 (−3.3 percent)

   b. With the gap between −3.3 and −10.5 percent, GNP was below potential and there was pressure on prices to fall.

   c. Rearranging Okun's law, $Y^* = Y/(1 + \text{GNP gap})$. For 1982, with $Y = \$1,480$ and the gap $= -.105$, $Y^* = 1,480/.895 = \$1,654$.

7. a. The rate of inflation was

1961	.010 (1.0 percent)
1962	.011 (1.1 percent)
1963	.012 (1.2 percent)

b. Wages increase by 1 percent each year. Prices increase by 1.1 percent in 1962 and 1.2 percent in 1963, so real wages fall very slightly.
   c. Wages increase by 1.05 percent in 1962 and 1.1 percent in 1963. Real wages fall very slightly in both 1962 and 1963.
   d. The real wage is constant when the nominal wage is completely indexed to the CPI.
   e. If inflation had remained at 1.0 percent in 1962 and 1963, real wages would have been constant with any of the three formulas, so there was no reason for either workers or employers to prefer one over the others. Since the inflation rate was so close to 1.0 percent, the choice of one formula over another would not have made much difference.
8. a. The rate of inflation was

1967	.029 (2.9 percent)
1968	.042 (4.2 percent)
1969	.054 (5.4 percent)

   b. Wages increase by 2.9 percent each year. Prices increase by 4.2 percent in 1968 and 5.4 percent in 1969, so real wages fall.
   c. Wages increase by 3.5 percent in 1968 and 4.1 percent in 1969. Real wages fall, but by less than in Part b.
   d. The real wage is constant when the nominal wage is completely indexed to the CPI.
   e. If inflation had remained at 2.9 percent in 1968 and 1969, real wages would have been constant with any of the three formulas, so there was no reason for either workers or employers to prefer one over the others. Since the inflation rate increased, workers ended up better off with more indexation (d) while employers would have been better off with less (b).
9. a. The rate of inflation was

1977	.065 (6.5 percent)
1978	.077 (7.7 percent)
1979	.113 (11.3 percent)

   b. Wages increase by 6.5 percent each year. Prices increase by 7.7 percent in 1978 and 11.3 percent in 1979, so real wages fall.
   c. Wages increase by 7.1 percent in 1978 and 8.9 percent in 1979. Real wages fall, but by less than in Part b.
   d. The real wage is constant when the nominal wage is completely indexed to the CPI.
   e. If inflation had remained at 6.5 percent in 1978 and 1979, real wages would have been constant with any of the three formulas, so there was no reason for either workers or employers to prefer one over the others. Since the inflation rate increased, workers ended up better off with more indexation (d) while employers would have been better off with less (b).

10. a. The rate of inflation was

1983	.032 (3.2 percent)
1984	.043 (4.3 percent)
1985	.036 (3.6 percent)

  b. Wages increase by 10.0 percent each year. Prices increase by an average of 3.7 percent, so real wages increase.
  c. Real wages increase, but by less than in Part b.
  d. Real wages are constant.
  e. With expected inflation equal to 10 percent, there was no reason for either workers or employers to prefer one over the others. Since inflation was actually below 10 percent, workers ended up better off with less indexation (b) while employers would have been better off with more (d).

CHAPTER 4 THE LONG-RUN GROWTH MODEL

Main Objectives

The first three chapters have given us much to consider: economic growth, fluctuations, inflation, unemployment, and productivity. These are the central concerns of macroeconomists, and they are all related to one another. In Chapter 4, we assemble the first part of the complete model, called the long-run growth model, to explain the growth path of potential GNP. It simplifies away short-run fluctuations by looking at an economy that is always in full employment because wages and prices are perfectly flexible, and focuses on the labor force, capital stock, and technology.

Key Terms and Concepts

The **long-run growth model**, also called the **neoclassical growth model**, is designed to explain the general upward path of potential GNP over time. It describes the economy in a state where supply and demand for both goods and workers are in balance, and does not consider short-run economic fluctuations around potential GNP.

The determinants of the long-run growth path of output are **labor**, the people available for work; **capital**, equipment, structures, and other productive facilities; and **technology**, the knowledge about how to use labor and capital to produce goods and services.

The **production function** is a description of the technology which shows how much output can be made from given amounts of labor and capital. In symbols,

$$Y = F(N, K), \qquad (4\text{-}1)$$

where Y is output, N is employment, and K is the stock of capital. In order to determine potential GNP, we must calculate the long-run capital stock and labor force.

The stock of capital, as we will see in Chapter 11, is predetermined by past investment and savings decisions. The **marginal product of labor**, the additional output that is produced by one additional unit of work, declines as the amount of employment increases. Firms choose the level of employment so that the marginal product of labor equals the real wage. The **demand for labor** is a negative function of the real wage because the marginal product of labor declines with increased labor input.

The **supply of labor** depends on the real wage in two contrasting ways. The **substitution effect** is that, at higher real wages, the incentive to work is stronger and people will want to work more. This increases the labor supply. The **income effect** is that higher real wages, by increasing people's income, make them better off. People who are better off choose to spend more time at home and less time in the labor market, which decreases the labor supply. Research indicates that these two effects offset each other. The net effect of the real wage on labor supply is approximately zero.

Equilibrium employment, N^*, is the volume of employment at the intersection of the labor supply and demand schedules, as shown in Figure 4–1. It is the amount people want to work given the real wage that employers are willing to pay. **Potential GNP**, Y^*, is the amount of output produced at equilibrium employment. Y^* is also called the full-employment level of output. Potential GNP is not influenced by the price level.

The **natural rate of unemployment** is the amount of unemployment when the labor market is in equilibrium. The natural rate is positive

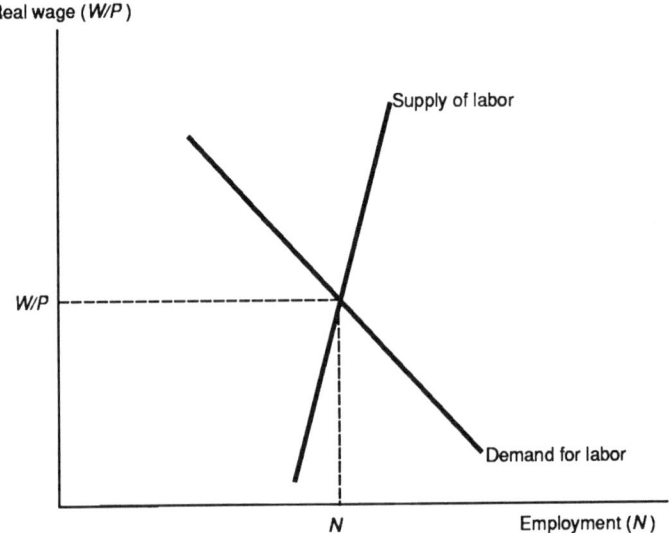

Figure 4–1

THE LONG-RUN GROWTH MODEL

for three reasons. Frictional unemployment occurs when people leave one job to look for another, finish school and look for employment, or look for a job after having been out of the labor force. Another reason is that there may be unemployment in some sectors even when the economy as a whole is at full employment. A third reason is that some disadvantaged groups—young people, members of racial minorities, and the unskilled—spend a large fraction of each year out of work. Economists differ on numerical estimates of the natural rate, but 5–6 percent seems to be a good approximation.

Potential output grows rather steadily from year to year. We can model the sources of growth of potential output using the following production function:

$$Y_t = A_t F(N_t, K_t), \tag{4-2}$$

where A_t is a measure of total factor productivity. A modification of this production function, the **economic growth formula**, says that the rate of growth of output equals the rate of growth of productivity plus the weighted rates of growth of labor and capital:

$$\Delta Y/Y = \Delta A/A + .7\Delta N/N + .3\Delta K/K, \tag{4-3}$$

where .7 is the share of labor and .3 is the share of capital in national income.

Policies to stimulate growth can be directed toward productivity, capital formation, or labor input. Policies to increase productivity include tax incentives, such as those passed in 1981 to encourage research and development. Since the process of productivity growth is not well understood by economists, it is hard to evaluate these policies. Investment tax credits give firms tax breaks for investment. They are an example of policies to stimulate capital formation. The investment tax credit appears to increase output growth for a few years, after which investment declines to more normal levels.

Policies to increase labor supply have focused on tax cuts and tax reform. Tax cuts, such as President Reagan's 1981 tax cut, have both substitution and income effects. If, as the evidence suggests, the labor supply schedule is steep, the effect on labor supply of tax cuts will be quite small. Tax reforms that are revenue neutral, such as the Tax Reform Act of 1986, do not have income effects. The labor supply schedule should shift by the full amount of the substitution effect, and the impact on the growth of output is potentially quite substantial.

The **real business cycle school** argues that economic fluctuations are better described by movements in potential GNP than by departures from potential GNP. Real business cycle models emphasize shocks to technology, which cause shifts in the labor demand schedule and movements in potential GNP. While these shocks are certainly important, an increase in the world oil price being one example of an adverse shock, many economists are skeptical that exogenous contractions in productivity are large enough to explain recessions.

Self-Test

Fill in the Blank

1. The _____ model is designed to explain the path of potential GNP.
2. The long-run growth model is also called the _____ growth model.
3. The _____ relates total output to total labor and capital inputs.
4. The additional output that is produced by one additional unit of work is the _____.
5. The two effects of higher real wages on labor supply are the _____ effect and the _____ effect.
6. The _____ is the amount of unemployment when output is equal to potential GNP.
7. A measure of overall productivity is _____ productivity.
8. The three sources of economic growth are growth in _____, _____, and _____.
9. A tax reform is _____ if it keeps tax receipts constant.
10. The volume of employment at the intersection of the supply of labor and demand for labor schedules is called _____ employment.
11. The amount of output produced at equilibrium employment is called _____ GNP.

THE LONG-RUN GROWTH MODEL 45

12. The _____ school argues that economic fluctuations are best described by movements in potential GNP.

True-False

13. An economy in which wages and prices are perfectly flexible is always exactly at full employment.
14. Higher real wages unambiguously increase the supply of labor.
15. With perfectly flexible prices and wages, the level of output in any one year is determined solely by the labor market.
16. Unemployment is zero when the labor market is in equilibrium.
17. The natural rate of unemployment is constant.
18. Tax cuts unambiguously increase the supply of labor.
19. The Tax Reform Act of 1986 increased labor supply.
20. The share of labor is greater than the share of capital in national income.
21. According to the economic growth formula, output growth is completely determined by growth in labor and capital.
22. Potential GNP rises with the price level.
23. Shocks to technology can cause movements in potential GNP.
24. According to the real business cycle model, monetary policy is of central importance in explaining economic fluctuations.

Review Questions

25. What determines output in the long-run growth model?
26. Why is the demand for labor a negative function of the real wage?
27. Describe the empirical evidence regarding the effect of the real wage on labor supply.
28. Why is the natural rate of unemployment not equal to zero?
29. What types of policies can the government use to stimulate economic growth?
30. Why can a tax cut and a tax reform have different effects on labor supply?

31. According to the economic growth formula, what determines output growth?
32. What determines equilibrium employment?
33. Why is potential GNP not influenced by the price level?
34. What, according to the real business cycle model, determines economic fluctuations?
35. How do shocks to technology affect potential GNP?
36. Why are many economists skeptical about the ability of the real business cycle model to explain recessions?

Problem Set

Worked Problems

1. a. Suppose that the growth rate of total factor productivity is 5 percent, the growth rate of employment is 8 percent, and the growth rate of capital is 4 percent. What is the growth rate of real output?

   b. If the growth rate of productivity increases by 2 percentage points, what happens to the growth rate of real output?

   a. According to Equation 4-3, the growth rate of real output equals the growth rate of productivity plus the weighted growth rates of labor and capital:

   $$\Delta Y/Y = .05 + .7(.08) + .3(.04)$$
   $$= .118 (11.8 \text{ percent}).$$

   b. The growth rate of real output will also increase by 2 percentage points to 13.8 percent.

2. Consider the following long-run growth model:

   $N = 800 + 20(W/P)$ (Labor supply)
   $N = 2,000 - 10 (W/P)$ (Labor demand)
   $Y = 125 \sqrt{N}$ (Production function)

   a. What is the equilibrium level of employment N and the real wage W/P?

   b. What is the equilibrium level of output Y?

a. We first use the labor supply and demand schedules to solve for the real wage.

$$800 + 20(W/P) = 2{,}000 - 10(W/P)$$
$$30\,(W/P) = 1{,}200$$
$$(W/P) = 40$$

We then substitute the value for the real wage back into either the labor supply or the labor demand schedule to solve for equilibrium employment.

$$N = 800 + 20(40) = 1{,}600$$
$$N = 2{,}000 - 10(40) = 1{,}600$$

b. We solve for output using the production function.

$$Y = 125\sqrt{1{,}600} = 125(40) = 5{,}000.$$

Review Problems

3. a. Suppose that the growth rate of total factor productivity is 5 percent, the growth rate of employment is 4 percent, and the growth rate of capital is 3 percent. What is the growth rate of real output?

   b. If the growth rate of employment increases by 2 percentage points, what happens to the growth rate of real output?

4. a. Suppose that the growth rate of total factor productivity is 3 percent, the growth rate of employment is 6 percent, and the growth rate of capital is 6 percent. What is the growth rate of real output?

   b. If the growth rate of capital increases by 3 percentage points, what happens to the growth rate of real output?

5. Consider the following long-run growth model:

   $N = 300 + 20(W/P)$ (Labor supply)
   $N = 1{,}500 - 20\,(W/P)$ (Labor demand)
   $Y = 100\,\sqrt{N}$ (Production function)

   a. What is the equilibrium level of employment N and the real wage W/P?

   b. What is the equilibrium level of output Y?

6. Consider the following long-run growth model:

$$N = 525 + 20(W/P) \quad \text{(Labor supply)}$$
$$N = 1{,}575 - 10\,(W/P) \quad \text{(Labor demand)}$$
$$Y = 100\sqrt{N} \quad \text{(Production function)}$$

a. What is the equilibrium level of employment N and the real wage W/P?

b. What is the equilibrium level of output Y?

Answers to the Self-Test

1. Long-run growth
2. Neoclassical
3. Production function
4. Marginal product of labor
5. Substitution and income
6. Natural rate of unemployment
7. Total factor
8. Labor, capital, and technology
9. Revenue neutral
10. Equilibrium
11. Potential
12. Real business cycle
13. True. Wages and prices can adjust instantaneously to offset the effect of disturbances.
14. False. The supply of labor increases because of the substitution effect but decreases because of the income effect.
15. True. With the stock of capital predetermined, the level of output in any one year depends only on employment, which is determined in the labor market.
16. False. It is equal to the natural rate.
17. False. It has increased slowly since the 1950s.
18. False. Tax cuts have both substitution and income effects.
19. True. The Tax Reform Act of 1986 lowered marginal tax rates and was revenue neutral, which increased labor supply.
20. True. The share of labor is .7 and the share of capital is .3.
21. False. Productivity also contributes to output growth
22. False. Potential GNP is not influenced by the price level.
23. True. Shocks to technology shift the labor demand schedule, affecting potential GNP.
24. False. Real business cycle models emphasize shocks to technology.
25. Output in the long-run growth model is determined by the capital stock and equilibrium employment.
26. The demand for labor is a negative function of the real wage because the marginal product of labor declines with increased labor input.

THE LONG-RUN GROWTH MODEL

27. Research indicates that the substitution and income effects offset each other, making the net effect approximately zero.
28. The natural rate is positive because of frictional unemployment, sector-specific unemployment, and high unemployment among disadvantaged groups.
29. The government can use policies designed to increase productivity, capital formation, or labor input.
30. A tax cut has both substitution and income effects, while a revenue-neutral tax reform has only substitution effects.
31. The economic growth formula says that the rate of growth of output equals the rate of growth of productivity plus the weighted rates of growth of labor and capital.
32. Equilibrium employment, the amount people want to work given the real wage that employers are willing to pay, is determined by the intersection of the demand for labor and supply of labor schedules.
33. Potential GNP is determined by equilibrium employment and the capital stock, neither of which is affected by the price level.
34. According to the real business cycle model, movements in potential GNP determine economic fluctuations.
35. Shocks to technology affect potential GNP by causing shifts in the labor demand schedule.
36. Many economists are skeptical that exogenous contractions in productivity, which are the central driving force of the real business cycle model, are large enough to explain recessions.

Solutions to Review Problems

3. a. The growth rate of real output $\Delta Y/Y = 8.7$ percent.
   b. $\Delta Y/Y$ increases to 10.1 percent.
4. a. $\Delta Y/Y = 9$ percent.
   b. $\Delta Y/Y$ increases to 9.9 percent.
5. a. The real wage $W/P = 30$.
      Equilibrium employment $N = 900$.
   b. Output $Y = 3,000$.
6. a. The real wage $W/P = 35$.
      Equilibrium employment $N = 1,225$.
   b. Output $Y = 3,500$.

CHAPTER 5 FISCAL AND MONETARY POLICIES IN A FULL-EMPLOYMENT ECONOMY

Main Objectives

In Chapter 4, we developed the long-run growth model to explain the path of potential GNP. In this chapter, we evaluate the effects of monetary and fiscal policy in the context of the long-run model. These results enable us to understand the effects of various policies over a period of three years or more, and are an important building block of the complete model.

Key Terms and Concepts

Fiscal policy, which is determined by the president and the Congress, involves changes in government purchases, taxes, transfer payments to the private sector, and interest payments on the government debt. The **federal budget deficit** is defined as total expenditures minus taxes,

$$\text{Budget deficit} = G + F + N - T, \qquad (5\text{--}1)$$

where G is government purchases, F is transfer payments, N is interest on the government debt, and T is taxes. **Monetary policy**, which is controlled by the Federal Reserve System (the Fed), involves changes in the money supply.

In the long-run growth model, actual GNP always equals potential GNP, which depends only on the supply of labor, capital, and technology. Changes in government spending have little effect on the supply of the three productive factors. While changes in tax rates

FISCAL/MONETARY POLICIES IN FULL-EMPLOYMENT ECONOMY 51

affect worker incentives, which in turn affect potential GNP, changes in tax revenues, the measure of fiscal policy which appears in Equation 5–1, do not. Changes in the money supply also will not affect the supply of the productive factors. Since neither monetary nor fiscal policy affects the supply of the three productive factors, neither policy will affect potential GNP, nor, over the period of time appropriate to the long-run growth model, three years or more, will they affect actual GNP.

According to the **income identity**, GNP equals the sum of consumption, investment, government spending, and net exports,

$$Y = C + I + G + X, \qquad (5-2)$$

where Y is GNP, C is consumption, I is investment, G is government spending, and X is net exports. Since fiscal policy does not affect GNP in the long run, an increase in government spending must cause a decrease in **nongovernment purchases**, $C + I + X$, of exactly the same amount. The term **crowding out** is used to describe this process.

Consumption, investment, and net exports all depend negatively on interest rates. When the interest rate rises, firms have to pay more to finance their investment of machines and equipment and consumers have to pay more to finance their consumption of automobiles and other durables, thus decreasing both consumption and investment. Net exports depend negatively on the interest rate because higher U.S. interest rates encourage foreigners to put their funds in dollars, raising the exchange rate. The higher exchange rate lowers exports and raises imports, decreasing net exports.

The **interest-rate sensitivity** of consumption, investment, and net exports determines how a decrease in nongovernment purchases, caused by an increase in government spending, is distributed among the three components. Consumption is less sensitive to interest rates than investment or net exports because a large percentage of consumption consists of nondurables and services, neither of which is much affected by interest rates. When government spending increases, causing interest rates to rise, investment and net exports fall more than consumption. This analysis also illustrates the close relation between the budget deficit, which is caused by an increase in government purchases if not matched by a tax increase, and the trade deficit, a fall in net exports.

Money is the sum of currency used by the Federal Reserve System and checking account balances held by the public. Money is the funds individuals want badly enough for transactions that they are willing to forgo the additional interest they might earn by keeping the funds in another form. The demand for money increases with income because, as income rises, people want to make more transactions. It increases with the price level because, as the price level increases, people need more money to make the same real transactions. It decreases with the interest rate because other alternatives for holding financial wealth, such as savings accounts and bonds, pay higher interest rates.

The **money demand function** is an algebraic expression of the above ideas,

$$M = (kY - hR)P, \qquad (5\text{--}3)$$

where M is the demand for money, Y is income, R is the interest rate, P is the price level, and k and h are positive coefficients.

Money market equilibrium occurs when the supply of money equals the demand for money. Since the money supply is determined by the Fed, the demand for money must adjust to achieve equilibrium. In the long-run growth model, with output equal to potential GNP and the interest rate equal to its equilibrium value, only the price level adjusts to equilibrate the money market.

Neutrality of money, also called the **classical dichotomy**, means that changes in the money supply have no influence on output or the interest rate. This can be illustrated using the money demand function,

$$M = (kY^* - hR^*)P, \qquad (5\text{--}4)$$

where Y^* is the potential GNP and R^* is the equilibrium interest rate. When the Fed increases the money supply, the price level increases in proportion while output and the interest rate are unchanged. Another implication from Equation 5–4 is that an increase in government spending, which raises the equilibrium interest rate, causes the price level to rise to offset the fall in money demand. A further implication is that an increase in potential GNP, holding the money stock constant, will cause the price level to fall.

Inflation is the rate of increase of the price level. If potential GNP and the equilibrium interest rate are constant, inflation is equal to the rate of growth of the money supply. In a growing economy, where potential GNP increases over time, the rate of inflation will be less than money supply growth. Empirical evidence indicates that, since 1973, money growth has been about 2 percentage points above inflation for a sample of industrialized countries.

Self-Test

Fill in the Blank

1. _____ policy involves changes in government purchases and taxes.

2. _____ policy involves changes in the money supply.

3. Total expenditures minus taxes is the _____.
4. According to the _____, GNP equals the sum of consumption, investment, government spending, and net exports.
5. Consumption, investment, and net exports all depend _____ on interest rates.
6. _____ is the sum of currency used by the Fed and checking account balances held by the public.
7. The demand for money depends positively on _____ and the _____.
8. Money demand depends negatively on the _____.
9. The money supply is determined by the _____.
10. _____ occurs when the demand for money equals the supply of money.
11. The property that changes in the money supply do not affect output or the interest rate is called _____ or the _____.
12. _____ is the rate of increase in the price level.

True-False
13. Fiscal policy is determined by the president and the Congress.
14. Monetary policy is determined by the president and the Congress.
15. The term "the Fed" is shorthand for "the federal government."
16. In the long run, an increase in government spending causes an equal decrease in nongovernment purchases.
17. Consumption depends negatively on interest rates.
18. Investment depends negatively on interest rates.
19. Net exports depend negatively on interest rates.
20. The interest-rate sensitivity of consumption is greater than that of investment or net exports.

21. The supply of money depends on income, the price level, and the interest rate.
22. In the long-run growth model, interest rates adjust to equilibrate the money market.
23. Neutrality of money implies that, when the Fed raises the money supply, the price level increases in proportion.
24. Neutrality of money implies that inflation equals money supply growth.

Review Questions

25. Over what period of time is the long-run growth model applicable?
26. Why do fiscal and monetary policy have little effect on potential GNP?
27. In the long-run growth model, why do fiscal and monetary policy have little effect on actual GNP?
28. In the long-run growth model, what is the effect of an increase in government spending?
29. In the long-run growth model, what is the effect of an increase in the money supply?
30. What is the relation between the interest rate and the exchange rate?
31. Why is the interest-rate sensitivity of consumption less than that of investment or net exports?
32. What is the relation between the budget deficit and the trade deficit?
33. Why does the demand for, rather than the supply of, money adjust to achieve money market equilibrium?
34. In the long-run growth model, why does only the price level adjust to equilibrate the money market?
35. What is the neutrality of money?
36. What is the empirical evidence regarding the long-run relation between inflation and money supply growth?

FISCAL/MONETARY POLICIES IN FULL-EMPLOYMENT ECONOMY

Problem Set

Worked Problems

1. Consider the following long-run growth model:

   $Y^* = C + I + G + X$ (Income identity)
   $C = 3{,}000$ (Consumption)
   $I = 1{,}000 - 1{,}500R$ (Investment)
   $X = 500 - 1{,}000R$ (Net exports)

   with potential output $^* = \$5{,}000$ billion and government spending $G = \$750$ billion.

   a. What is the equilibrium interest rate R?

   b. What are the equilibrium levels of consumption C, investment I, and net exports X?

   c. If government spending G increases to $\$800$ billion, what is the new interest rate?

   a. We solve for the equilibrium interest rate by substituting the equations for consumption, investment, and net exports, as well as the values for potential output and government spending, into the income identity:

   $Y^* = C + I + G + X$
   $5{,}000 = 3{,}000 + 1{,}000 - 1{,}500R + 750 + 500 - 1{,}000R$
   $5{,}000 = 5{,}250 - 2{,}500R$
   $R = .1$ *(10 percent)*

   b. Substitute the equilibrium interest rate from Part a into the consumption, investment and net export equations:

   $C = 3{,}000$
   $I = 1{,}000 - 1{,}500(.1) = 850$
   $X = 500 - 1{,}000(.1) = 400$

   c. Substitute the new level of government spending into the income identity from Part a:

   $5{,}000 = 3{,}000 + 1{,}000 - 1{,}500R + 800 + 500 - 1{,}000R$
   $5{,}000 = 5{,}300 - 2{,}500R$
   $R = .12$ *(12 percent)*

2. Add the following equation for money demand to the long-run growth model of Problem 1:

   $$M = (.8Y^* - 5{,}000R)P,$$

with potential output $Y^* = \$5{,}000$ billion, government spending $G = \$750$ billion, and the money supply $M = \$2{,}800$ billion.

a. What is the price level P?

b. If the money supply M increases to $\$3{,}500$ billion, what are the new price level and interest rate?

a. Using the equilibrium interest rate from the solution to Part a of Problem 1, substitute the values of the money supply and potential output into the money demand equation:

$$2{,}800 = [.8(5{,}000) - 5{,}000(.1)]P$$
$$2{,}800 = (4{,}000 - 500)P$$
$$2{,}800 = 3{,}500P$$
$$P = .8$$

b. Substitute the new value of the money supply into the money demand equation:

$$3{,}500 = 3{,}500P$$
$$P = 1$$

The increase in the money supply of 25 percent (from $\$2{,}800$ to $\$3{,}500$ billion) causes the same 25 percent increase in the price level (from .8 to 1). The equilibrium interest rate is unchanged at 10 percent. This is an illustration of the neutrality of money.

Review Problems

3. Consider the following long-run growth model:

$$Y^* = C + I + G + X \quad \text{(Income identity)}$$
$$C = 2{,}000 \quad \text{(Consumption)}$$
$$I = 500 - 1{,}000R \quad \text{(Investment)}$$
$$X = 200 - 3{,}000R \quad \text{(Net exports)}$$

with potential output $Y^* = \$3{,}000$ billion and government spending $G = \$900$ billion.

a. What is the equilibrium interest rate?

b. What are the equilibrium levels of consumption, investment, and net exports?

c. If government spending decreases to $\$700$ billion, what is the new interest rate?

4. Add the following equation for money demand to the long-run growth model of Problem 3:

$$M = (1.2Y^* - 2{,}000R)P,$$

with potential output $Y^* = \$3{,}000$ billion, government spending $G = \$900$ billion, and the money supply $M = \$3{,}300$ billion.

a. What is the price level?

b. If the money supply decreases to $2,970 billion, what are the new price level and interest rate?

5. Consider the following long-run growth model:

$$Y^* = C + I + G + X \quad \text{(Income identity)}$$
$$C = 1{,}500 \quad \text{(Consumption)}$$
$$I = 500 - 1{,}000R \quad \text{(Investment)}$$
$$X = 100 - 1{,}250R \quad \text{(Net exports)}$$

with potential output $Y^* = \$2{,}200$ billion and government spending $G = \$280$ billion.

a. What is the equilibrium interest rate?

b. What are the equilibrium levels of consumption, investment, and net exports?

c. If government spending increases to $325 billion, what is the new interest rate?

6. Add the following equation for money demand to the long-run growth model of Problem 5:

$$M = (Y^* - 5{,}000R)P,$$

with potential output $Y^* = \$2{,}200$ billion, government spending $G = \$280$ billion, and the money supply $M = \$2{,}160$ billion.

a. What is the price level?

b. If the money supply increases to $2,340 billion, what are the new price level and interest rate?

Answers to the Self-Test

1. Fiscal
2. Monetary
3. Federal budget deficit
4. Income identity
5. Negatively
6. Money
7. Income and the price level
8. Interest rate
9. Federal Reserve System
10. Money market equilibrium

11. Neutrality of money or classical dichotomy
12. Inflation
13. True. Fiscal policy is determined by the executive and legislative branches of government.
14. False. Monetary policy is determined by the Federal Reserve System.
15. False. "The Fed" is shorthand for "the Federal Reserve System."
16. True. This is the definition of crowding out.
17. True. Increases in the interest rate raise the cost of borrowing, lowering spending on consumer durables.
18. True. Increases in the interest rate raise the cost of borrowing, lowering investment.
19. True. Increases in the interest rate raise the exchange rate, lowering net exports.
20. False. Both investment and net exports are more sensitive to interest rates than is consumption.
21. False. The supply of money is controlled by the Federal Reserve System.
22. False. In the long-run growth model, the price level adjusts to equilibrate the money market.
23. True. An increase in the level of the money supply, which affects neither potential GNP nor the equilibrium interest rate, causes the price level to increase in proportion.
24. False. In an economy where potential GNP is growing, inflation will be less than money supply growth.
25. The long-run growth model is applicable to situations of three or more years.
26. Neither fiscal nor monetary policy has much effect on the supply of the productive factors, labor, capital, and technology, that determine potential GNP.
27. In the long-run growth model, actual GNP always equals potential GNP. Since neither monetary nor fiscal policy has much effect on potential GNP, they have little effect on actual GNP.
28. An increase in government spending causes a decrease in nongovernment purchases of the same amount.
29. An increase in the money supply causes a proportional increase in the price level.
30. When interest rates in the United States are higher, the return on U.S. assets is greater, increasing their demand and raising the exchange rate.
31. Consumption is less sensitive to interest rates than are investment or net exports because a large proportion of consumption consists of nondurables and services.
32. Higher government spending, if not accompanied by tax increases, causes a budget deficit by definition. The higher government spending raises interest rates, causing the exchange rate to rise and net exports to fall, which is a trade deficit.
33. The money supply is controlled by the Fed, leaving only money demand free to adjust to achieve equilibrium.
34. In the long-run growth model, the other two variables which affect money demand, output and the interest rate, are always at their potential or equilibrium values.

35. Neutrality of money is the property that changes in the money supply have no influence on output or the interest rate.
36. Since 1973, money growth has been about 2 percentage points above inflation for a sample of industrialized countries.

Solutions to Review Problems

3. a. $R = .15$.
   b. $C = 2{,}000$
      $I = 500 - 1{,}000(.15) = 350$
      $X = 200 - 3{,}000(.15) = -250$.
   c. $R = .1$.
4. a. $P = 1$.
   b. $P = .9, R = .15$.
5. a. $R = .08$.
   b. $C = 1{,}500$
      $I = 500 - 1{,}000(.08) = 420$
      $X = 100 - 1{,}250(.08) = 0$.
   c. $R = .1$.
6. a. $P = 1.2$.
   b. $P = 1.3, R = .08$.

CHAPTER 6　Short-Run Fluctuations

Main Objectives

In Chapters 4 and 5, we developed the long-run growth model to show how potential GNP grows over time and to analyze the long-run effects of monetary and fiscal policy. In this chapter, we develop the aggregate demand model to begin consideration of short-run fluctuations. The key simplification of the aggregate demand model is to ignore interest rates. You should learn the consumption function and the income identity, and know how GNP is determined by combining the two of them through the concept of spending balance. You should also learn how government spending affects GNP through the multiplier, and how endogenous net exports affect the analysis of spending balance.

Key Terms and Concepts

Aggregate demand is the total of the spending demands by the various sectors in the economy. These include **consumption** by households, **investment** by firms, **exports** by foreigners, and **government spending**. The short-run model that incorporates these spending relationships is called the **aggregate demand model**. It describes the behavior of the economy out of equilibrium. The **aggregate demand curve** is the main relationship of the model. It will be algebraically derived in Chapter 7.

Shifts of the aggregate demand curve, which can be caused by changes in monetary policy, fiscal policy, consumption, investment, or net exports, cause short-run fluctuations in GNP from its growth path. Shifts in the price level, such as these caused by changes in the price of oil, also cause fluctuations.

The initial response by firms to changes in demand is to adjust production. Firms normally operate with some excess capacity. When there is an increase in spending demand, they increase production to meet the demand for their goods. If they need additional labor, they can increase the hours per week of their workers, recall laid-off workers, or hire additional workers.

Firms also adjust their prices to changes in demand, but there is a crucial difference between the adjustment of production and the

SHORT-RUN FLUCTUATIONS

adjustment of prices. Price adjustments are **sticky** compared to production adjustments. The adjustment of prices occurs gradually, while the adjustment of production and employment occurs almost instantaneously.

Recessions are short-run periods when the level of employment is lower than the equilibrium level needed to be at potential GNP. During recessions, the labor market is out of equilibrium and both firms and workers face **incentives** to expand employment. These incentives take time to operate; recessions generally occur every few years and last for a year or two.

The **income identity** says that income (Y) equals the sum of consumption (C), investment (I), government spending (G), and net exports (X),

$$Y = C + I + G + X. \tag{6-1}$$

It incorporates two important concepts. First, as shown in Chapter 2, income equals GNP. Second, as discussed above, aggregate demand determines GNP. We use the terms output, income, and GNP interchangeably, always represented by the symbol Y.

The **consumption function** states that consumption depends on disposable income (Y_d), which is equal to income minus taxes,

$$C = a + b Y_d. \tag{6-2}$$

There is a subsistence level of consumption, a, about which the individual has no choice. If the individual's income is less than a, he borrows. At income levels above a, he has a choice between consumption and saving. The coefficient b is the **marginal propensity to consume**. It measures how much of an additional dollar of disposable income is spent on consumption. For instance, if we set b equal to .8, we are saying that 80 cents of each additional dollar of disposable income is spent on consumption. The other 20 cents is saved.

If the tax rate is the constant t, total tax payments are the tax rate multiplied by income, tY. Disposable income Y_d = income – taxes = $Y - tY = (1 - t)Y$. By replacing disposable income Y_d with $(1 - t)Y$, the consumption function can be written

$$C = a + b(1 - t)Y. \tag{6-3}$$

Spending balance occurs at levels of consumption C and income Y that obey both the consumption function and the income identity. We substitute the consumption function into the income identity, $Y = C + I + G, + X$, and solve for income to obtain

$$Y = a + b(1-t)Y + I + G + X$$
$$Y[1 - b(1-t)] = a + I + G + X$$
$$Y = \frac{1}{1 - b(1-t)}(a + I + G + X). \quad (6\text{–}4)$$

To solve for consumption, substitute back into the consumption function the value of income when spending balance is attained. Because they can be determined inside the model in this case, income and consumption are called **endogenous variables**. Investment, government spending, and net exports cannot be determined inside the model—yet—so they are called **exogenous variables**, determined outside the model.

The **multiplier** measures how much a change in investment, government spending, or net exports changes income. The formula for the multiplier when investment, government spending, and net exports are exogenous is $1/[1 - b(1-t)]$. It is greater than 1 because both b and t are between 0 and 1, indicating that an increase in investment, government spending, or net exports will have a more than proportional effect on income.

The **net export function** relates net exports to income,

$$X = g - mY, \quad (6\text{–}5)$$

where g is a constant and m is a coefficient. Net exports depend negatively on income because, as income rises, spending rises. Since part of this rise in spending is on imported goods, imports rise and net exports fall. The coefficient m is called the **marginal propensity to import**, and measures how much of an additional dollar of income is spent on imports.

We now find the value of income at the point of spending balance in an open economy where net exports are endogenous by substituting the net export function, as well as the consumption function, into the income identity, $Y = C + I + G + X$, and solve for income to obtain

$$Y = a + b(1-t)Y + I + G + g - mY$$
$$Y[1 - b(1-t) + m] = a + I + G + g$$
$$Y = \frac{1}{1 - b(1-t) + m}(a + I + G + g). \quad (6\text{–}6)$$

The **open-economy multiplier**, which measures the impact of a change in government spending or investment on output in an open economy where net exports are endogenous, is $1/[1 - b(1-t) + m]$. The open-economy multiplier is smaller when the marginal propensity to import m is larger. If m were zero, so that increases in income did not affect imports, the open-economy multiplier would be the same as in Equation 6–4. With m greater than zero, the open-economy multiplier is smaller than the multiplier with exogenous net exports.

SHORT-RUN FLUCTUATIONS

In Chapter 4, we based our analysis of the relation between trade deficits and government budget or fiscal deficits on changes in interest rates. Changes in income provide an additional short-run channel for that relation. Increases in government spending G, if not matched by tax increases, cause fiscal deficits. According to the multiplier, increases in G also cause income Y to rise. When Y increases, imports rise and trade deficits occur.

Self-Test

Fill in the Blank

1. The total of the spending demands in all the sectors of the economy is _____ demand.
2. The _____ model is the short-run model that incorporates spending relationships.
3. _____ are short-run periods when the level of employment is lower than in equilibrium.
4. During recessions, firms and workers face _____ to expand employment.
5. The income identity says that income is the sum of _____, _____, _____, and _____.
6. The _____ is the fraction of an increase in disposable income that is consumed.
7. The _____ is the fraction of an increase in income that is spent on imports.
8. The _____ relates consumption to disposable income.
9. The _____ relates net exports to income.
10. The price level is called _____ because, in the short run, its value is determined by events that have occurred in previous years.

11. The _____ measures how much a change in investment, government spending, or net exports changes income.

12. The government budget deficit is also called the _____ deficit.

True-False

13. Firms normally operate at less than 100 percent capacity utilization.
14. If aggregate demand increases, firms will increase output before they increase prices.
15. Disposable income is equal to income minus saving.
16. Consumption will equal zero if disposable income equals zero.
17. Spending balance means that the government budget deficit is zero.
18. The income identity says that income is equal to consumption.
19. The multiplier is always greater than the marginal propensity to consume.
20. If the tax rate is zero, the multiplier would equal 1.
21. Net exports depend negatively on income.
22. The open-economy multiplier measures the impact of a change in government spending on exports.
23. The open-economy multiplier is smaller than the multiplier when net exports are exogenous.
24. Fiscal and trade deficits are unrelated.

Review Questions

25. What are the four components of aggregate demand?
26. What occurs in the labor market during recessions?
27. What does it mean for prices to be sticky?
28. What are the two concepts that are incorporated into the income identity?
29. Why does the consumption function depend on disposable, and not total, income?
30. When does spending balance occur?

31. If aggregate demand is less than output produced, how is spending balance achieved?
32. What is the difference between endogenous and exogenous variables?
33. What is the relation between the government spending and investment multipliers?
34. Why is the open-economy multiplier smaller than the multiplier when net exports are exogenous?
35. Why do increases in income cause trade deficits?
36. Why do trade and fiscal deficits occur together?

Problem Set

Worked Problems

1. Consider an economy described by the following equations:

$$Y = C + I + G + X \quad \text{(Income identity)}$$
$$C = 100 + .9\, Y_d \quad \text{(Consumption)}$$

   with investment $I = \$200$ billion, government spending $G = \$200$ billion, net exports $X = \$100$ billion, and the tax rate $t = .2$.

   a. What is the level of income when spending balance occurs? What is the multiplier?

   b. Suppose government spending increases to $300 billion. What is the new level of income?

   a. *From the income identity,*

   $$Y = C + I + G + X.$$

   Using the consumption function, $C = 100 + .9\, Y_d$, and the definition of disposable income, $Y_d = Y - .2Y$,

   $$Y = 100 + .9(Y - .2Y) + 200 + 200 + 100$$
   $$= 600 + .72Y.$$

   Subtract .72Y from both sides of the equation,

   $$Y - .72Y = 600,$$

   factor out Y,

   $$Y(1 - .72) = 600,$$
   $$.28Y = 600,$$

and multiply both sides by $1/.28 = 3.571$ to obtain the solution,

$$Y = 3.571(600) = \$2{,}143 \text{ billion}.$$

By solving for income, we automatically derive the multiplier. It is the number, 3.571, that multiplies the exogenous components of consumption, investment, government spending, and net exports, 600, to get income.

Alternatively, we can use the formula

$$\frac{1}{1-b(1-t)} = \frac{1}{1-.9(1-.2)} = \frac{1}{1-.72} = \frac{1}{.28} = 3.571$$

to find the multiplier. It is important that you learn how to derive the multiplier rather than just memorize the formula, which is correct only if investment, government spending, and net exports all do not depend on income.

b. This can be solved in two ways. One is to recalculate Y using the new level of G, 300.

$$\begin{aligned} Y &= 100 + .9(Y - .2Y) + 200 + 300 + 100 \\ &= 700 + .72Y \\ &= 3.571(700) = \$2{,}500 \text{ billion}. \end{aligned}$$

A second is to use the multiplier to calculate the change in Y,

$$\Delta Y = 3.571 \qquad \Delta G = 3.571(100) = 357,$$

and then add the change in Y, 357, to the original value of Y, 2,143, to get the new value, \$2,500 billion.

2. Consider an economy described by the following equations:

$$\begin{aligned} Y &= C + I + G + X & \text{(Income identity)} \\ C &= 100 + .9\, Y_d & \text{(Consumption)} \\ X &= 100 - .12Y & \text{(Net exports)} \end{aligned}$$

with investment $I = \$200$ billion, government spending $G = \$200$ billion, and the tax rate $t = .2$.

a. What is the level of income when spending balance occurs? What is the multiplier? Compare the multiplier to the multiplier when net exports are exogenous in Problem 1.

b. Suppose government spending increases to \$300 billion. What is the new level of income?

a. From the income identity,

$$Y = C + I + G + X,$$

and using the consumption function, $C = 100 + .9 Y_d$, the net export function, $X = 100 - .12Y$, and the definition of disposable income, $Y_d = Y - .2Y$,

$$Y = 100 + .9(Y - .2Y) + 200 + 200 + 100 - .12Y,$$
$$= 600 + .6Y.$$

Subtract .6Y from both sides of the equation,

$$Y - .6Y = 600,$$

factor out Y,

$$Y(1 - .6) = 600,$$
$$.4Y = 600,$$

and multiply both sides by 2.5 to obtain the solution,

$$Y = 2.5(600) = \$1{,}500 \text{ billion}.$$

By solving for income, we automatically derive the multiplier, 2.5. The open-economy multiplier, 2.5, is smaller than the multiplier with exogenous net exports, 3.571, for the same marginal propensity to consume and tax rate.
Alternatively, we can use the formula

$$\frac{1}{1 - b(1 - t) + m} = \frac{1}{1 - .9(1 - .2) + .12} = \frac{1}{.4} = 2.5$$

to find the multiplier.

b. This can be solved in two ways. One is to recalculate Y using the new level of G, 300.

$$Y = 100 + .9(Y - .2Y) + 200 + 300 + 100 - .12Y$$
$$= 700 + .6Y$$
$$= 2.5(700) = \$1{,}750 \text{ billion}.$$

A second is to use the multiplier to calculate the change in Y,

$$\Delta Y = 2.5 \qquad \Delta G = 2.5(100) = 250,$$

and then add the change in Y, 250, to the original value of Y, 1,500, to get the new value, \$1,750 billion.

Review Problems

3. Consider an economy described by the following equations:

$$Y = C + I + G + X \quad \text{(Income identity)}$$
$$C = 300 + .8 Y_d \quad \text{(Consumption)}$$

with investment $I = \$300$, government spending $G = \$100$, net exports $X = \$100$, and the tax rate $t = .2$.

  a. What is the level of income when spending balance occurs? What is the multiplier?

  b. Consider the same economy, except that investment depends positively on income, so that $I = 300 + .2Y$. What is the level of income and multiplier now?

  c. Returning to the investment equation in Part a, suppose that the tax rate is increased to .4. What happens to income and to the multiplier?

4. Consider an economy described by the following equations:

$$Y = C + I + G + X \quad \text{(Income identity)}$$
$$C = 400 + .9\, Y_d \quad \text{(Consumption)}$$

with investment $I = \$300$, government spending $G = \$100$, net exports $X = \$100$, and the tax rate $t = .5$.

  a. What is the level of income when spending balance occurs? What is the multiplier?

  b. Suppose government spending increases to $200. What is the new level of income?

5. Consider an economy described by the following equations:

$$Y = C + I + G + X \quad \text{(Income identity)}$$
$$C = 400 + .9\, Y_d \quad \text{(Consumption)}$$

with investment $I = \$200$, government spending $G = \$200$, net exports $X = \$100$, and the tax rate $t = .3333$.

  a. What is the level of income when spending balance occurs? What is the multiplier?

  b. Suppose government spending increases to $300. What is the new level of income?

6. Consider an economy described by the following equations:

$$Y = C + I + G + X \quad \text{(Income identity)}$$
$$C = 300 + .8\, Y_d \quad \text{(Consumption)}$$
$$X = 100 - .04Y \quad \text{(Net exports)}$$

with investment $I = \$200$, government spending $G = \$200$, and the tax rate $t = .2$.

a. What is the level of income when spending balance occurs? What is the multiplier? Compare your answer to the multiplier in Problem 3.

b. Consider the same economy, except that investment depends positively on income, so that $I = 200 + .2Y$. What is the level of income and multiplier now?

c. Returning to the investment equation in Part a, suppose that the tax rate is increased to .4. What happens to income and to the multiplier?

7. Consider an economy described by the following equations:

$$Y = C + I + G + X \quad \text{(Income identity)}$$
$$C = 400 + .9Y_d \quad \text{(Consumption)}$$
$$X = 100 - .05Y \quad \text{(Net exports)}$$

with investment $I = \$300$, government spending $G = \$100$, and the tax rate $t = .5$.

a. What is the level of income when spending balance occurs? What is the multiplier? Compare your answer to the multiplier in Problem 4.

b. Suppose government spending increases to $200. What is the new level of income?

8. Consider an economy described by the following equations:

$$Y = C + I + G + X \quad \text{(Income identity)}$$
$$C = 400 + .9Y_d \quad \text{(Consumption)}$$
$$X = 200 - .1Y \quad \text{(Net exports)}$$

with investment $I = \$200$, government spending $G = \$200$, and the tax rate $t = .3333$.

a. What is the level of income when spending balance occurs? What is the multiplier? Compare your answer to the multiplier in Problem 5.

b. Suppose government spending increases to $300. What is the new level of income?

Answers to the Self-Test

1. Aggregate
2. Aggregate demand
3. Recessions
4. Incentives

5. Consumption, investment, government spending, and net exports
6. Marginal propensity to consume
7. Marginal propensity to import
8. Consumption function
9. Net export function
10. Sticky
11. Multiplier
12. Fiscal
13. True. Firms normally operate with some excess capacity.
14. True. This is what it means for prices to be "sticky."
15. False. Disposable income is equal to income minus taxes.
16. False. The positive value of the coefficient a in the consumption function, $C = a + bY_d$, means that, rather than starve if disposable income is zero for one year, people will spend some of their savings.
17. False. Spending balance can occur with a positive, negative, or zero government budget deficit.
18. False. The income identity says that income is equal to the sum of consumption, investment, government spending, and net exports.
19. True. The multiplier is greater than 1 and the marginal propensity to consume is less than 1.
20. False. The multiplier would equal $1/(1-b)$ if the tax rate was zero.
21. True. Imports rise when income rises, lowering net exports.
22. False. The open-economy multiplier measures the impact of a change in government spending on income.
23. True. If the marginal propensity to import is positive, the open-economy multiplier is smaller than the multiplier when net exports are exogenous.
24. False. Increases in government spending cause both fiscal and trade deficits.
25. The four components of aggregate demand are consumption, investment, government spending, and net exports.
26. The labor market is out of equilibrium during recessions. While there exist incentives for firms and workers to expand employment, these incentives take time to operate.
27. Prices are called sticky because they adjust slowly, compared with adjustments in production, to changes in spending demand.
28. The two concepts incorporated into the income identity are that income equals GNP and that aggregate demand determines GNP.
29. The consumption function describes people's choices between consuming and saving. The income available to make such a choice is their after-tax, or disposable, income.
30. Spending balance occurs when the income identity, consumption function, and net export function are satisfied.
31. If a firm produces more output than it can sell, it must either store the additional output, which is costly, or let the output go to waste. The firm is better off by decreasing production, which achieves spending balance.
32. An endogenous variable is determined within the model. An exogenous variable is determined outside the model.
33. The government spending and investment multipliers are equal.

SHORT-RUN FLUCTUATIONS

34. The open-economy multiplier is smaller than the multiplier when net exports are exogenous because part of the induced increase in consumption is spent on imports, which do not add to GNP.
35. When income rises, part of the increase is spent on imports, causing trade deficits.
36. Increases in government spending, which cause fiscal deficits, also raise income, causing trade deficits.

Solutions to Review Problems

3. a. $Y = C + I + G + X$ for spending balance to hold.
    $= 300 + .8(Y - .2Y) + 300 + 100 + 100$
    $= 800 + .64Y$
    $= 2.777(800) = \$2,222.$

    The government spending multiplier is 2.777. In this case, since neither investment, government spending, nor net exports depend on income, the formula $1/[1 - .8(1 - .2)]$ will also give the correct answer.

    b. $Y = 300 + .8(Y - .2Y) + 300 + .2Y + 100 + 100$
    $= 800 + .84Y$
    $= 6.25(800) = \$5,000.$

    The multiplier is 6.25. In this case, since investment depends on income, the formula will not give the correct answer.

    c. $Y = 300 + .8(Y - .4Y) + 300 + 100 + 100$
    $= 800 + .48Y$
    $= 1.923(800) = \$1,538.$

    The multiplier, 1.923, decreases because higher taxes lower disposable income. Since the multiplier falls, and the exogenous variables are unchanged, income decreases.

4. a. $Y = 400 + .9(Y - .5Y) + 300 + 100 + 100$
    $= 900 + .45Y$
    $= 1.818(900) = \$1,636.$
    The multiplier is 1.818.

    b. $Y = \$1,818.$

5. a. $Y = 400 + .9(Y - .3333Y) + 200 + 200 + 100$
    $= 900 + .6Y$
    $= 2.5(900) = \$2,250.$
    The multiplier is 2.5.

    b. $Y = \$2,500.$

6. a. $Y = 300 + .8(Y - .2Y) + 200 + 200 + 100 - .04Y$
    $= 800 + .6Y$
    $= 2.5(800) = \$2,000.$

    The government spending multiplier is 2.5. It is smaller than the multiplier, 2.777, in Problem 3. In this case, since neither investment nor government spending depends on income, the formula $1/[1 - .8(1 - .2) + .04]$ will also give the correct answer.

    b. $Y = 300 + .8(Y - .2Y) + 200 + .2Y + 200 + 100 - .04Y$
    $= 800 + .8Y$
    $= 5(800) = \$4,000.$

The multiplier is 5. In this case, since investment depends on income, the formula will not give the correct answer.

c. $Y = 300 + .8(Y - .4Y) + 200 + 200 + 100 - .04Y$
    $= 800 + .44Y$
    $= 1.79(800) = 1,429.$

The multiplier, 1.79, decreases because higher taxes lower disposable income. Since the multiplier falls, and the exogenous variables are unchanged, income decreases.

7. a. $Y = 400 + .9(Y - .5Y) + 300 + 100 + 100 - .05Y$
        $= 900 + .4Y$
        $= 1.67(900) = \$1,500.$

    The multiplier is 1.67. It is smaller than the multiplier, 1.818, in Problem 4.

    b. $Y = \$1,667.$

8. a. $Y = 400 + .9(Y - .3333Y) + 200 + 200 + 200 - .1Y$
        $= 1,000 + .5Y$
        $= 2(1,000) = \$2,000.$

    The multiplier is 2. It is smaller than the multiplier, 2.5, in Problem 5.

    b. $Y = \$2,200.$

CHAPTER 7 The IS-LM Model

Main Objectives

In Chapter 6, we developed the concept of spending balance to show how income is determined in the aggregate demand model. In this chapter, we extend the model by adding financial variables (interest rates and the supply of money) to construct a complete, although simplified, picture of how the economy operates in the short run. You should understand how this model, called the IS-LM model, can be used to analyze monetary and fiscal policy, and how it is summarized by constructing the aggregate demand curve, one of the basic tools of analysis for the remainder of the book.

Key Terms and Concepts

The **investment function** describes the relation between investment and the interest rate,

$$I = e - dR, \qquad (7\text{--}1)$$

where I is investment and R is the real interest rate. The constant e measures the part of investment that does not depend on interest rates, while the coefficient d measures how much investment falls when the interest rate increases by 1 percentage point. The relationship is negative because most investment purchases are financed by borrowing. Higher interest rates increase the cost of borrowing, resulting in less investment spending.

The **real interest rate** R is the nominal interest rate minus the expected rate of inflation. Investment depends on the real interest rate because investors consider expected inflation when determining the cost of borrowing.

The net export function depends on the interest rate R as well as income Y,

$$X = g - mY - nR. \qquad (7\text{--}2)$$

Net exports depend negatively on the interest rate because higher U.S. interest rates encourage foreigners to put their funds in dollars, raising the exchange rate. The higher exchange rate lowers exports and raises imports. The coefficient n measures how much net exports fall when the interest rate increases by 1 percentage point.

In Chapter 5, we learned that the **demand for money** increases with income, increases with the price level, and decreases with the interest rate, as in the following algebraic expression,

$$M = (kY - hR)P, \qquad (7\text{–}3)$$

where M is the demand for money, Y is income, R is the interest rate, and P is the price level. The demand for money can also be written in terms of **real money**, money M divided by the price level P,

$$M/P = kY - hR. \qquad (7\text{–}4)$$

This says that the demand for real money depends positively on real income and negatively on the interest rate.

The economic model described by the income identity, consumption function, investment function, net export function, and money demand is called the **IS-LM model**. It has two exogenous variables (government spending and the money supply) and five endogenous variables (income, the interest rate, consumption, investment, and net exports). Since prices are sticky and adjust only gradually, they are neither exogenous nor endogenous. We call the price level **predetermined** because, in each period, its value is determined by events that have occurred in previous periods. Another way to think about the price level is as exogenous in the short run and endogenous in the long run.

The **money supply** is determined by the Federal Reserve System. In the long-run equilibrium model of Chapters 4 and 5, the price level adjusts to achieve money market equilibrium. In the short-run IS-LM model, with predetermined prices, the interest rate and, to a lesser extent, income adjust to keep the demand for money equal to its fixed supply. Since the supply of money and the demand for money are always equal, we also use M to represent the money supply.

The **IS curve** shows all the combinations of the interest rate and income that satisfy the income identity, the consumption function, the investment function, and the net export function. It is the set of points for which spending balance occurs. It is downward sloping because lower interest rates cause investment demand to increase, which is consistent with spending balance only if more output is produced. An increase in government spending shifts the IS curve to the right because, for any given level of the interest rate, the increase in G raises Y through the multiplier process. The IS curve is illustrated in Figure 7–1.

THE IS-LM MODEL

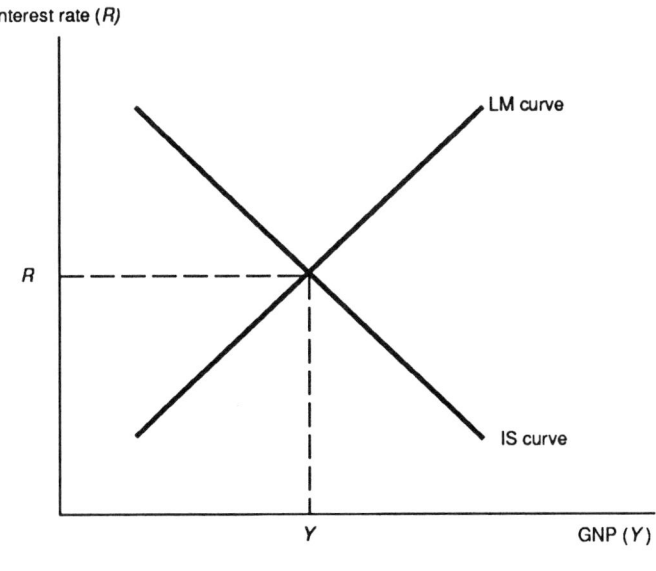

Figure 7-1

The **LM curve** shows all combinations of the interest rate and income that satisfy the money demand relationship for a fixed level of the money supply and for a predetermined value of the price level. It slopes upward because, with the nominal money supply fixed by the Fed and the price level predetermined, an increase in income, which increases the demand for money, must be accompanied by an increase in the interest rate, which decreases the demand for money, to keep the demand for money equal to its (fixed) supply. An increase in the money supply shifts the LM curve to the right because, for fixed P, an increase in M is an increase in real money. For any given level of the interest rate, income must rise so that the demand for money equals its new, higher, supply. The LM curve is also illustrated in Figure 7-1.

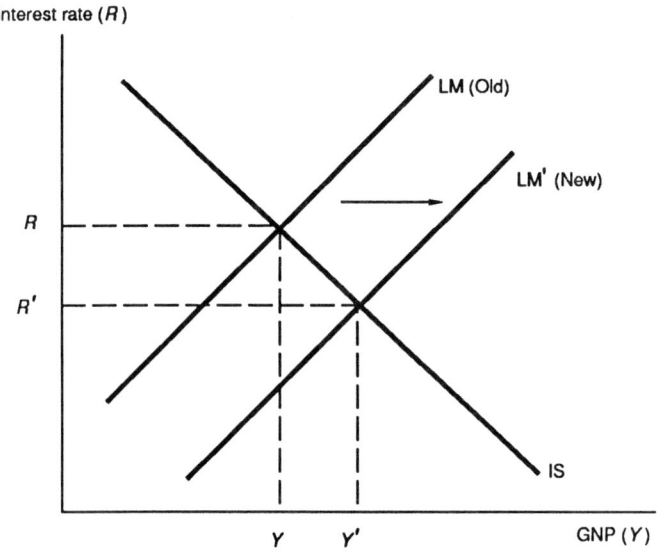

Figure 7–2

Changes in the money supply are called **monetary policy**. When the Fed increases the money supply, as shown in Figure 7–2, income rises and the interest rate falls. When the money supply is first increased, there is more money in the economy than people demand. Interest rates fall and investment increases, which raises GNP through the multiplier process.

Changes in government spending, taxes, and transfers are called **fiscal policy**. An increase in government spending, as in Figure 7–3, increases income and increases the interest rate. The increase in government spending increases income through the multiplier and raises the interest rate because, as GNP increases, the demand for money increases. The interest rate must rise to keep the demand for money equal to its fixed supply. With investment and net exports depending on the interest rate, increases in government spending do not have the full multiplier effect on income. The higher interest rate lowers investment and net exports, offsetting some of the stimulus to GNP caused by government spending. The offsetting negative effect is called **crowding out**.

THE IS-LM MODEL

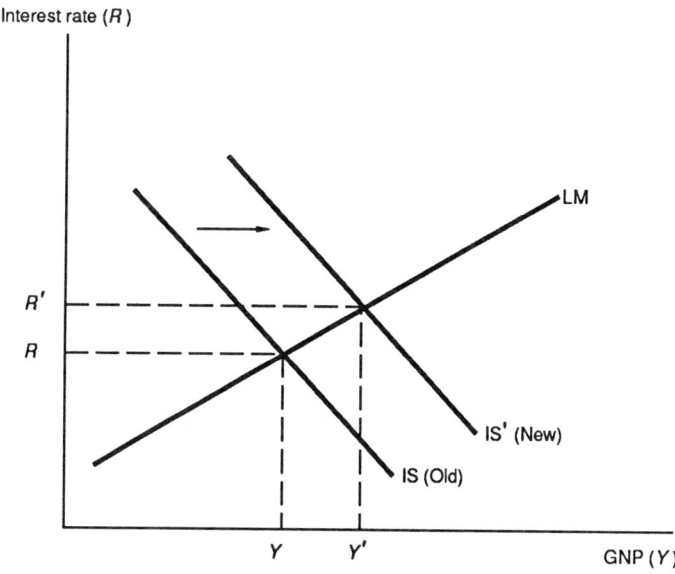

Figure 7–3

The coefficients that describe the response of investment (d), net exports (n), and money demand (h) to changes in the interest rate determine the relative effectiveness of monetary and fiscal policy in increasing aggregate demand. If investment and net exports are very sensitive to interest rates ($d + n$ is large), the IS curve is relatively flat. Fiscal policy is weak and monetary policy is strong. If money demand is very sensitive to interest rates (h is large), the LM curve is relatively flat. Fiscal policy is strong and monetary policy is weak. A high spending multiplier also increases the effectiveness of fiscal policy.

The **aggregate demand curve** shows the combinations of price levels and output where the IS and LM curves intersect, or where spending balance occurs and money demand equals money supply. It slopes downward because a decrease in prices increases real money, shifting the LM curve to the right, lowering interest rates, increasing investment, and increasing output. An increase in either the money supply or government spending, as in Figure 7–4, shifts the aggregate demand curve to the right.

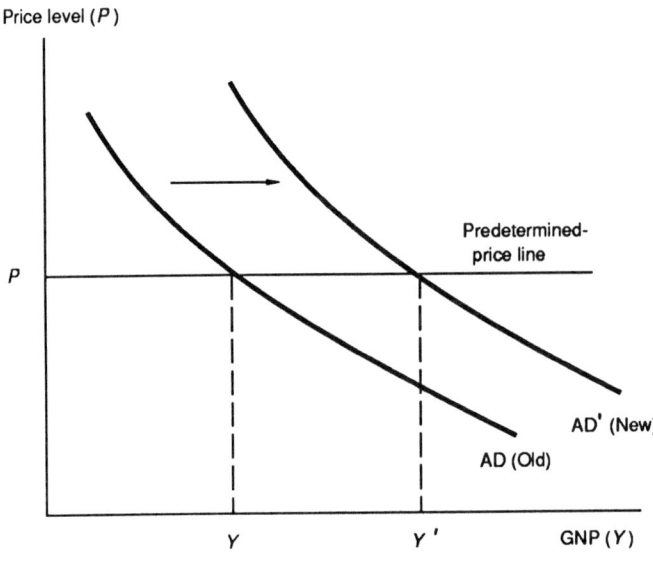

Figure 7–4

Self-Test

Fill in the Blank

1. The _____ describes the relation between investment and interest rates.
2. Net exports depend on _____ and _____.
3. The real interest rate is the nominal interest rate minus the _____ rate of inflation.
4. The money supply divided by the price level is called _____ money.
5. The demand for money _____ with income, _____ with the price level, and _____ with the interest rate.

THE IS-LM MODEL

6. The IS curve is the combination of _____ and _____ for which spending balance occurs.

7. The LM curve illustrates the condition that the demand and supply of _____ are equal.

8. Fiscal policy is made by the _____.

9. Monetary policy is made by the _____.

10. The offsetting negative effect on GNP, caused by higher interest rates following an increase in government spending, is called _____.

11. If investment and net exports are very sensitive to interest rates, fiscal policy is _____ and monetary policy is _____.

12. If money demand is very sensitive to interest rates, fiscal policy is _____ and monetary policy is _____.

True-False

13. Investment is negatively related to the interest rate.
14. Net exports are negatively related to the interest rate.
15. In the United States, monetary and fiscal policies are determined by different people.
16. Monetary policy shifts both the IS and LM curves.
17. An increase in government spending will always cause a more than proportional increase in GNP.
18. Increases in the money supply and in government spending have the same effects on income.
19. Increases in the money supply and in government spending have the same effects on interest rates.
20. Increases in the money supply and in government spending have the same effects on the aggregate demand curve.
21. Prices adjust to keep the demand for money equal to the supply of money in the IS-LM model.

22. The same variable can be exogenous for one model and endogenous for another.
23. If investment and net exports are very sensitive to interest rates, the LM curve is flat.
24. If the price level decreases, the aggregate demand curve shifts to the right.

Review Questions

25. Why does an increase in the interest rate decrease net exports?
26. What does it mean for the price level to be predetermined?
27. When interest rates rise so that the return on financial assets, such as bonds, is high, does this mean that investment is high?
28. What is the relationship between real and nominal interest rates?
29. What are the implications of crowding out for the effectiveness of government spending?
30. What are the three factors that determine the demand for money, and what are their effects?
31. Why does monetary policy shift the LM, but not the IS, curve?
32. Why does fiscal policy shift the IS, but not the LM, curve?
33. If the money supply and government spending both decrease, what happens to output and the interest rate?
34. What conditions are satisfied along the aggregate demand curve?
35. Can anything besides changes in the money supply or government spending shift the aggregate demand curve?
36. Since decreases in the price level and increases in the money supply both shift the LM curve to the right, why does the former cause a movement along the aggregate demand curve while the latter causes it to shift?

THE IS-LM MODEL

Problem Set

Worked Problems

1. Consider an economy described by the following equations:

   $Y = C + I + G + X$ (Income identity)
   $C = 100 + .9Y_d$ (Consumption)
   $I = 200 - 500R$ (Investment)
   $X = 100 - .12Y - 500R$ (Net exports)
   $M = (.8Y - 2{,}000R)P$ (Money demand)

   with government spending $G = \$200$ billion, the tax rate $t = .2$, the nominal money supply $M = \$800$ billion, and the predetermined price level $P = 1$.

   a. What is the IS curve?
   b. What is the LM curve?
   c. What are the values of income and the interest rate when spending balance occurs and the demand for money equals the supply of money?
   d. What are the values of consumption, investment, and net exports?

   a. We derive the IS curve using the same technique that was used to solve for income in Problem 2 of Chapter 6.

   $Y = C + I + G + X$
   $= 100 + .9(Y - .2Y) + 200 - 500R + 200 + 100 - .12Y - 500R$
   $= 600 + .6Y - 1{,}000R$
   $= 1{,}500 - 2{,}500R.$

   b. We derive the LM curve from the equation for money demand, given a fixed level for the money supply and a predetermined value of the price level (1 in this problem):

   $$800 = .8Y - 2{,}000R.$$

   Adding $2{,}000R$ to both sides of the equation,

   $$.8Y = 800 + 2{,}000R,$$

   and dividing both sides by .8, we obtain

   $$Y = 1{,}000 + 2{,}500R,$$

   which is the equation for the LM curve.

c. We compute the values for income and the interest rate by using the IS and LM curves, solving for R, and then solving for Y. Combining the two equations,

$$1{,}500 - 2{,}500R = 1{,}000 + 2{,}500R,$$

adding 2,500R and subtracting 1,000 from both sides,

$$500 = 500R,$$
$$R = .10 \text{ (10 percent)}.$$

Substituting the value for R into either the IS or LM curve, Y = $1,250 billion.

d. We determine the values for consumption, investment, and net exports by substituting the computed values of R and Y into the consumption, investment, and net export equations.

$$C = 100 + .9Y_d$$
$$= 100 + .9(1 - .2)1{,}250 = \$1{,}000 \text{ billion.}$$
$$I = 200 - 500R$$
$$= 200 - 50 = \$150 \text{ billion.}$$
$$X = 100 - .12Y - 500R$$
$$= 100 - 150 - 50 = -\$100 \text{ billion.}$$

2. Derive the aggregate demand curve and show by how much an increase in government spending or real money of $100 billion increases GNP in Problem 1. Compare your answer for government spending to the government spending multiplier in Problem 2 of Chapter 6.

To derive the effects of increases in government spending and real money on income, start with the equation for the LM curve, do not substitute a specific value for real money, and solve for output.

$$M/P = .8Y - 2{,}000R$$
$$Y = 1.25(M/P) + 2{,}500R.$$

Now use the income identity, substitute the consumption, investment, and net export equations, but not a specific value for government spending, and solve for 2,500 times the interest rate.

$$Y = 100 + .9(Y - .2Y) + 200 - 500R + G + 100 - .12Y - 500R$$
$$Y = 400 + .6Y - 1{,}000R + G$$
$$1{,}000R = 400 - .4Y + G$$
$$2{,}500R = 1{,}000 - Y + 2.5G.$$

Substitute the spending balance equation into the LM curve, and solve for Y.

$$Y = 1.25(M/P) + 1{,}000 - Y + 2.5G$$
$$2Y = 1.25(M/P) + 1{,}000 + 2.5G$$
$$Y = 625(M/P) + 500 + 1.25G.$$

THE IS-LM MODEL

An increase in government spending of 100 raises real GNP by 125. An increase in the money supply of 100, with the price level constant, raises real GNP by 62.5. These are illustrated in Figures 7–2 and 7–3.

In Problem 6.2, with the government spending multiplier equal to 2.5, an increase in government spending of $100 billion raised real GNP by $250 billion. The only difference between the two models is that investment and net exports now depend on the interest rate. This is an example of crowding out. Government spending, in this problem, is only half as effective when the effects of interest rates on investment and net exports are included.

Review Problems

3. Consider an economy described by the following equations:

   $Y = C + I + G + X$ (Income identity)
   $C = 300 + .8Y_d$ (Consumption)
   $I = 200 - 1,500R$ (Investment)
   $X = 100 - .04Y - 500R$ (Net exports)
   $M = (.5Y - 2,000R)P$ (Money demand)

   with government spending $G = \$200$, the tax rate $t = .2$, the nominal money supply $M = \$550$, and the predetermined price level $P = 1$.

   a. What is the IS curve?
   b. What is the LM curve?
   c. What are the values of income and the interest rate when spending balance occurs and the demand for money equals the supply of money?

4. Derive the aggregate demand curve and show by how much an increase in government spending or real money increases GNP in Problem 3. Compare your answer for government spending to the government spending multiplier in Problem 6 of Chapter 6.

5. Consider an economy described by the following equations:

   $Y = C + I + G + X$ (Income identity)
   $C = 400 + .9Y_d$ (Consumption)
   $I = 300 - 2,000R$ (Investment)
   $X = 100 - .05Y - 1,000R$ (Net exports)
   $M = (.4Y - 1,000R)P$ (Money demand)

   with government spending $G = \$100$, the tax rate $t = .5$, the nominal money supply $M = \$180$, and the predetermined price level $P = 1$.

a. What is the IS curve?
b. What is the LM curve?
c. What are the values of income and the interest rate when spending balance occurs and the demand for money equals the supply of money?

6. Derive the aggregate demand curve and show by how much an increase in government spending or real money increases GNP in Problem 5. Compare your answer for government spending to the government spending multiplier in Problem 7 of Chapter 6.

7. Consider an economy described by the following equations:

$$Y = C + I + G + X \quad \text{(Income identity)}$$
$$C = 400 + .9Y_d \quad \text{(Consumption)}$$
$$I = 200 - 1{,}800R \quad \text{(Investment)}$$
$$X = 200 - .1Y - 200R \quad \text{(Net exports)}$$
$$M = (.8Y - 3{,}000R)P \quad \text{(Money demand)}$$

with government spending $G = \$200$, the tax rate $t = .3333$, the nominal money supply $M = \$1{,}104$, and the predetermined price level $P = 1$.

a. What is the IS curve?
b. What is the LM curve?
c. What are the values of income and the interest rate when spending balance occurs and the demand for money equals the supply of money?

8. Derive the aggregate demand curve and show by how much an increase in government spending or real money increases GNP in Problem 7. Compare your answer for government spending to the government spending multiplier in Problem 8 of Chapter 6.

Answers to the Self-Test

1. Investment function
2. Income and the interest rate
3. Expected
4. Real
5. Increases with income, increases with the price level, and decreases with the interest rate
6. Interest rates and income
7. Money
8. The president and Congress
9. Federal Reserve System

THE IS-LM MODEL

10. Crowding out
11. Fiscal policy is weak and monetary policy is strong.
12. Fiscal policy is strong and monetary policy is weak.
13. True. Increases in the interest rate raise the cost of borrowing, lowering investment.
14. True. Increases in the interest rate raise the exchange rate, lowering net exports.
15. True. Monetary policy is determined by the Federal Reserve System. Fiscal policy is determined by Congress and the president.
16. False. Monetary policy shifts the LM curve. Fiscal policy shifts the IS curve.
17. False. This is only correct in the aggregate demand model where investment and net exports do not depend on the interest rate.
18. True. Increases in either the money supply or government spending raise income.
19. False. Increases in the money supply lower interest rates, while increases in government spending raise them.
20. True. They both shift the aggregate demand curve to the right.
21. False. Interest rates and, to a lesser extent, output adjust.
22. True. Investment is exogenous in the aggregate demand model and endogenous in the IS-LM model.
23. False. The sensitivity of investment and net exports to interest rates affects the slope of the IS curve, not the LM curve.
24. False. A decrease in the price level causes a movement along the aggregate demand curve, not a shift of the curve.
25. An increase in the interest rate raises the exchange rate, making U.S. goods more expensive compared to foreign goods. This decreases exports and increases imports, decreasing net exports.
26. The price level is called predetermined because, in each period, its value is determined by events that have occurred in previous periods.
27. No. Investment is spending on items such as factories and houses, and has nothing to do with the return on financial assets.
28. The real interest rate equals the nominal interest rate minus the expected rate of inflation.
29. Crowding out decreases the effectiveness of government spending.
30. The demand for money increases with income and the price level, and decreases with the interest rate.
31. Monetary policy changes the supply of money, shifting the LM curve. The IS curve depends on spending balance, which is unaffected by the money supply.
32. Fiscal policy, changes in government spending or taxes, affects spending balance, shifting the IS curve. The LM curve depends on the supply of and demand for money, which are unaffected by spending balance.
33. Since both the IS and LM curves shift to the left, output decreases. You cannot say what happens to the interest rate without knowing the magnitudes of the decreases and the coefficients of the consumption, investment, net export, and money demand equations.
34. Spending balance occurs and the demand for money equals the supply of money.

35. Yes. Changes in the exogenous component of consumption (*a*), investment (*e*), or net exports (*g*) shift the aggregate demand curve by shifting the IS curve.
36. The aggregate demand curve is drawn with P and Y on the axes. A shift of the curve can only be caused by a variable, such as M, that is not on one of the axes. Changes in variables on the axes, P and Y, cause shifts along the curve. For the LM curve, neither P nor M is on the axes, so they can both cause shifts of the curve.

Solutions to Review Problems

3. a. The IS curve is derived from the condition for spending balance.

   $Y = 300 + .8(Y - .2Y) + 200 - 1{,}500R + 200 + 100 - .04Y - 500R$
   $= 800 + .6Y - 2{,}000R$
   $= 2{,}000 - 5{,}000R.$

   b. The LM curve is derived from the condition that the demand for money equal the supply of money with a predetermined price level.

   $550 = .5Y - 2{,}000R$
   $Y = 1{,}100 + 4{,}000R.$

   c. Using the IS and LM curves,

   $2{,}000 - 5{,}000R = 1{,}100 + 4{,}000R$
   $900 = 9{,}000R, R = .10$ (10 percent).

   Substituting back into either the IS or LM curve, $Y = \$1{,}500$.

4. Starting with the LM curve,

   $M/P = .5Y - 2{,}000R,$
   $Y = 2(M/P) + 4{,}000R.$

   Using the condition for spending balance,

   $Y = 300 + .8(Y - .2Y) + 200 - 1{,}500R + G + 100 - .04Y - 500R$
   $4{,}000R = 1{,}200 - .8Y + 2G.$

   Substituting the spending balance condition into the LM curve,

   $Y = 2(M/P) + 1{,}200 - .8Y + 2G$
   $= 1.11(M/P) + 666.7 + 1.11G.$

   An increase in government spending has less effect on output than in the earlier problem because of crowding out.

5. The technique for this problem is the same as for Problem 3.

   a. $Y = 400 + .9(Y - .5Y) + 300 - 2{,}000R + 100 + 100 - .05Y - 1{,}000R$
   $= 900 + .4Y - 3{,}000R$
   $= 1{,}500 - 5{,}000R.$

   b. $180 = .4Y - 1{,}000R$
   $Y = 450 + 2{,}500R.$

THE IS-LM MODEL

c. $R = .14$ (14 percent), $Y = \$800$.

6. The technique for this problem is the same as for Problem 4.
From the LM curve,

$$Y = 2.5(M/P) + 2,500R.$$

From the condition for spending balance,

$$2,500R = 666.67 - .5Y + .83G.$$

Substituting the spending balance condition into the LM curve,

$$Y = 1.67(M/P) + 444.5 + .55G.$$

This illustrates that crowding out can cause an increase in government spending to have a less than proportionate effect on income, a result that is not possible if investment and net exports do not depend on the interest rate.

7. The technique for this problem is the same as for Problem 3.

a. $Y = 400 + .9(Y - .3333Y) + 200 - 1,800R + 200 + 200 - .1Y - 200R$
    $= 1,000 + .5Y - 4,000R$
    $= 2,000 - 4,000R.$

b. $1,104 = .8Y - 3,000R$
    $Y = 1,380 + 3,750R.$

c. $R = .08$ (8 percent), $Y = \$1,680$.

8. The technique for this problem is the same as for Problem 4.
From the LM curve,

$$Y = 1.25(M/P) + 3,750R.$$

From the condition for spending balance,

$$3,750R = 1,500 - .94Y + 1.875G.$$

Substituting the spending balance condition into the LM curve,

$$Y = .64(M/P) + 773.2 + .97G.$$

Government spending is less effective because of crowding out.

CHAPTER 8 The Complete Model

Main Objectives

First, in Chapters 4 and 5, we developed the long-run growth model to understand how potential output evolves over time and to analyze the effects of monetary and fiscal policy over a period of three or more years. Then, in Chapters 6 and 7, we developed the aggregate demand and IS-LM models to understand the workings of the economy over a short-run period of one year or less. In this chapter, we develop the important concept of price adjustment. This concept links the short-run and long-run models to the complete model. You should understand the dynamic effects of monetary and fiscal policies in the complete model and the crucial role that expectations of inflation play in the price-adjustment process.

Key Terms and Concepts

Prices are **sticky**; that is, they are not adjusted quickly by firms in response to demand conditions. In the short-run IS-LM model of Chapter 7, the price level is predetermined and the level of output is determined by aggregate demand. In the long-run growth model of Chapter 5, as shown in Figure 8–1, output is equal to potential GNP and the price level is determined by aggregate demand.

In the short run, output can be above or below its potential level. When output is above potential GNP, unemployment, as we saw in Chapter 3 when we discussed Okun's law, is below the natural rate. When output is below potential GNP, unemployment is above the natural rate. In the long run, output equals potential GNP and unemployment equals the natural rate.

THE COMPLETE MODEL

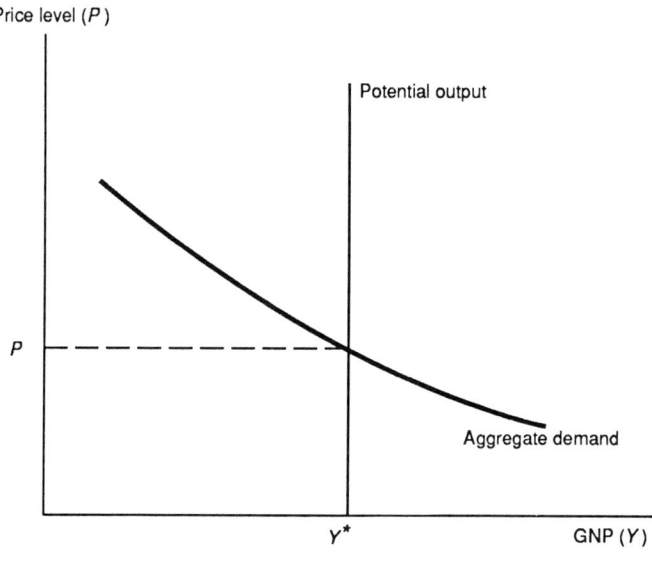

Figure 8–1

The process of **price adjustment** describes the transition from the short to the long run. There are two aspects of price adjustment. First, if firms and workers expect that inflation will occur, they will write contracts and set prices in accord with their expectations. An important factor that determines expected inflation is the rate of inflation that prevailed over the past few years. The process by which past inflation gets translated into expected inflation, and then into actual inflation, is called **inflationary momentum.**

The second aspect of price adjustment is the state of the labor market. Prices rise when output is above potential GNP and unemployment is below the natural rate, and fall when output is below potential GNP and unemployment is above the natural rate. The rate of inflation is the rate of change of the price level, and can be expressed as

$$\pi = (P - P_{-1})/P_{-1}, \qquad (8\text{-}1)$$

where π is the rate of inflation, P is the current price level, and P_{-1} is the last period's price level. When prices are rising, the inflation rate is positive. When prices are falling, the inflation rate is negative.

The **Phillips curve** is an algebraic formulation of price adjustment,

$$\pi = \pi^e + f(Y_{-1} - Y^*)/Y^*, \qquad (8\text{-}2)$$

where π^e is the expected rate of inflation, Y^* is potential GNP, Y_{-1} is last period's GNP, and f is a positive coefficient. It says that inflation equals expected inflation plus a term that is positive if output is greater than potential and negative if output is less than potential. Prices are predetermined because the current price level is determined by last period's output Y_{-1}, not by current output Y. Incorporating expectations of inflation into the Phillips curve makes it possible for inflation to be positive even if output is below potential GNP.

If inflation were fairly constant from year to year, the best forecast of current inflation π would be last period's inflation π_{-1}. The price-adjustment equation would become

$$\pi = \pi_{-1} + f(Y_{-1} - Y^*)/Y^*. \tag{8-3}$$

When inflation is variable, other factors such as previous years' inflation rates and expectations of future money supply growth would also influence expected inflation.

The price-adjustment equation with expected inflation equal to last period's inflation, Equation 8-3, has three important properties. First, the only way to reduce inflation is to have a recession. Output must be below potential GNP for inflation to be less than last period's inflation. Second, the larger the gap between actual and potential GNP, the greater the increase in the inflation rate (or decrease in the inflation rate if the gap is negative). Third, if output is permanently above potential GNP inflation will rise without bound; this is called the **accelerationist** or **natural rate property**.

Aggregate demand and price adjustment can be combined to analyze the short- and long-run effects of monetary and fiscal policy. For the moment, assume that expected inflation is always zero. Suppose that, beginning with output equal to potential GNP, the Fed increases the money supply. In the short run, with predetermined prices, the stimulus to aggregate demand lowers interest rates and raises output above potential as described in Chapter 7. This causes inflation, as can be seen from the price-adjustment equation, 8-2. The inflation causes prices to rise over time, decreasing real money and output. As output falls toward potential, the rate of inflation decreases. In the long run, output returns to potential GNP with zero inflation at the original interest rate and a higher price level. Monetary policy is neutral in the long run. All real variables—GNP, consumption, investment, net exports, and interest rates—return to their original levels. Unlike the real business cycle model, monetary policy is not neutral in the short run. It has a powerful effect on output before prices have time to adjust.

Fiscal policy, such as an increase in government spending, looks very similar to monetary policy. Output rises above potential in the short run. This causes inflation, which increases prices and drives output back to potential in the long run. There are, however, important differences

THE COMPLETE MODEL

between monetary and fiscal policy. Fiscal policy raises interest rates in the short run. As prices rise, real money falls and interest rates keep rising. In the long run, potential output is attained with both higher prices and higher interest rates. *The sum of investment and net exports is decreased by the same amount that government spending is increased.* This is called **complete crowding out**. Even though fiscal policy does not change real output in the long run, it is not neutral because it changes investment, net exports, and interest rates.

Expansionary monetary and fiscal policies are illustrated in Figure 8–2. Both expansionary policies shift the aggregate demand curve to the right. In the short run, output rises along the predetermined price line. Over time, prices rise and output falls along the aggregate demand curve until, in the long run, output returns to potential.

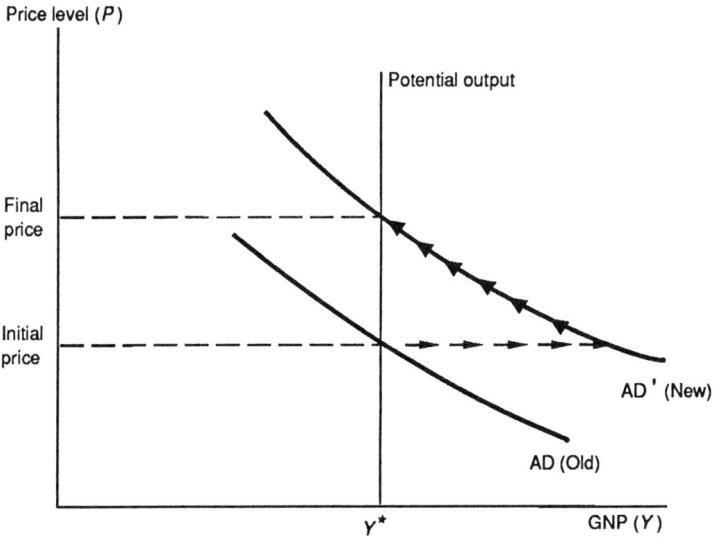

Figure 8–2

The above description of monetary and fiscal policy is incomplete because it ignores the impact of expected inflation. Incorporating expected inflation into the Phillips curve does not affect either the short-run or the long-run results. What it does change is the **dynamics**: the transition between the short and the long run. With expected inflation always equal to zero, past inflation influences current inflation only because, by raising current prices, it affects the difference between actual and potential output. With expected inflation equal to last period's inflation, as in Equation 8–3, past inflation also influences current inflation directly. The major difference for monetary and fiscal policy is that the transition from the short to the long run is no longer smooth.

Inflation increases as output falls toward potential, driving prices above their long-run level. Output falls below potential, causing a recession that finally brings inflation down. Prices fall and output rises as the economy cycles back to the long run. Prices and output are said to **overshoot** their long-run levels. The cyclical movement of prices and output along the aggregate demand curve in response to expansionary policy is shown in Figure 8–3.

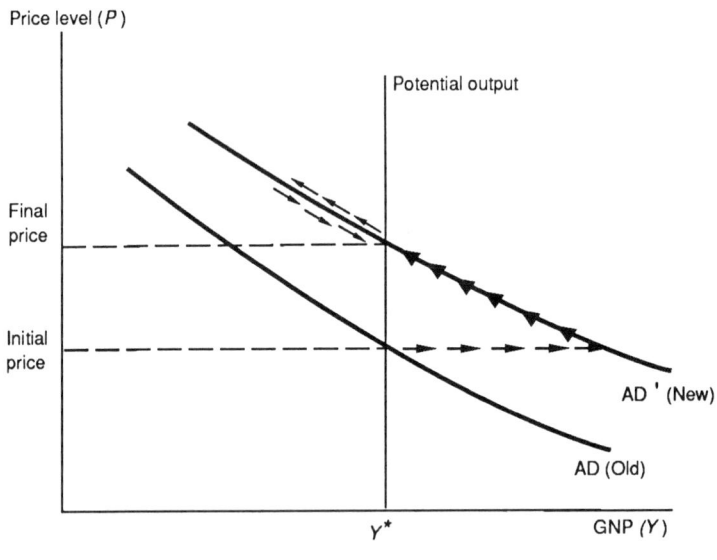

Figure 8–3

Self-Test

Fill in the Blank

1. Prices are called _____ because they are not adjusted quickly by firms in response to demand conditions.

2. The process of _____ describes the transition from the short to the long run.

3. The two aspects of price adjustment are _____ and _____.

4. The rate of inflation is the rate of change of the _____.

5. _____ describes the process by which past inflation causes current inflation.
6. The model that describes how variables change from one year to the next is called _____.
7. The relationship between the rate of inflation and the deviation of real GNP from potential is called the _____ curve.
8. The rate of inflation forecasted by workers and firms is the _____ rate of inflation.
9. The long-run decrease in investment and net exports when government spending increases is called _____.
10. Monetary policy is _____ in the long run.
11. The accelerationist property is also called the _____ property.
12. Prices and output _____ their long-run levels when the process of price adjustment is cyclical.

True-False
13. In the short run, output can be below or above its potential level.
14. In the short run, unemployment can be above or below the natural rate.
15. When output equals potential GNP, inflation is zero.
16. When inflation equals expected inflation, output is equal to last period's GNP.
17. The current price level does not depend on the current level of output.
18. If output is below potential GNP, inflation will be negative.
19. Expected inflation is always equal to last year's inflation.
20. If expected inflation is equal to last year's inflation, it is necessary to have a recession to reduce the rate of inflation.

21. If expected inflation is equal to last year's inflation, output can only be permanently raised above potential by having inflation increase without bound.
22. In the long run fiscal policy completely crowds out investment and net exports.
23. Monetary policy is neutral in both the short and long run.
24. Fiscal policy is neutral in both the short and long run.

Review Questions

25. How is output determined in the short run?
26. How is output determined in the long run?
27. What is the relation between output and unemployment?
28. What is inflationary momentum?
29. What is the accelerationist property?
30. What is the difference between the real business cycle model and the complete model regarding the neutrality of money?
31. Describe the process of price adjustment when firms do not expect prices to rise in the future.
32. How does expected inflation change the process of price adjustment?
33. If there is no expected inflation, describe what happens to GNP and prices when the Fed increases the money supply.
34. How does expected inflation change you answer to Question 33?
35. What happens to GNP and prices when government spending is increased if there is no expected inflation?
36. How does your answer to Question 35 change if there is expected inflation?

Problem Set

Worked Problems

1. Suppose the economy has the aggregate demand curve

$$Y = 500 + 1.25G + .625(M/P)$$

and the price-adjustment schedule

$$\pi = (Y_{-1} - 1{,}250)/1{,}250 + \pi^e.$$

Government spending is $200 billion and the money supply is $800 billion.

a. Assume that expected inflation, π^e, is always zero. Starting from $P_0 = .8$, describe the path of the economy until GNP is within 1 percent of its long-run value.

b. Assume that $\pi^e = \pi_{-1}$. Describe the path of the economy, again starting from $P_0 = .8$ with zero inflation. How does your answer differ from that of Part a?

a. *The initial level of output, Y_0, is found from the aggregate demand curve by setting $P_0 = .8$ and using the given values for government spending and the money supply.*

$$Y_0 = 500 + 1.25\,(200) + .625\,(800)/.8$$
$$= \$1{,}375 \text{ billion}.$$

The inflation rate, π_1, is found from the price-adjustment curve,

$$\pi_1 = (1{,}375 - 1{,}250)/1{,}250 = .1 \ (10 \text{ percent}),$$

and determines the next year's price level:

$$P_1 = .8 + .8(.1) = .88.$$

Y_1 *can now be determined by substituting P_1 into the aggregate demand curve, and so on. The complete answer is presented below.*

Year	π	P	Y
0	.000	.80	$1,375
1	.100	.88	1,318
2	.055	.93	1,289
3	.031	.96	1,271
4	.017	.98	1,262

Output is initially above potential GNP. Prices rise and output falls smoothly until potential GNP is attained with P = 1.

b. *The technique for this part is the same as for Part a except that, when computing inflation, last year's inflation needs to be incorporated. This does not affect π_1, since $\pi_0 = 0$, but $\pi_2 = .055 + \pi_1 = .155$, and so on. This affects the rest of the answer.*

Year	π	P	Y
0	.000	.80	$1,375
1	.100	.88	1,318
2	.155	1.02	1,242
3	.149	1.17	1,177
4	.088	1.27	1,143
5	.002	1.27	1,143
6	−.084	1.16	1,180
7	−.140	1.00	1,250

Output is initially above potential GNP. As above, prices begin to rise and output falls, but now output falls below potential. This causes prices first to stop rising, and then to fall. Output recovers to potential. The numerical answer gives only the first part of the cycle because inflation does not equal zero when output equals potential GNP.

2. Using the same model as in Problem 1, increase government spending by $50 billion starting from potential GNP with the price level $P = 1$.

   a. Calculate the paths of inflation, the price level, and GNP for the first 5 years, in the case where expected inflation is always zero.

   b. Perform the same calculations, this time for 10 years, in the case where expected inflation equals last period's inflation.

   a. Initially, in Year 0, GNP equals potential with $\pi = 0$ and $P = 1$. The increase in government spending first affects output, which can be calculated from the aggregate demand curve with G = $250 billion.

   $$Y_1 = 500 + 1.25(250) + .625(800)/1$$
   $$= \$1,313 \text{ billion.}$$

   The inflation rate, π_2, is found from the price-adjustment curve,

   $$\pi_2 = (1,313 - 1,250)/1,250 = .05 \text{ (5 percent),}$$

   and determines the next year's price level:

   $$P_2 = 1 + 1(.05) = 1.05.$$

   Y_2 can now be determined by substituting P_2 into the aggregate demand curve, and so on. The complete answer is presented in the following table.

THE COMPLETE MODEL

Year	π	P	Y
0	.000	1.00	$1,250
1	.000	1.00	1,313
2	.050	1.05	1,289
3	.031	1.08	1,275
4	.020	1.10	1,266
5	.013	1.11	1,261

The increase in government spending shifts the aggregate demand curve to the right. In the short run, output increases above potential with unchanged prices. Over time, prices rise and output falls smoothly until potential GNP is restored.

b. The technique for this part is the same as for Part a except that, when computing inflation, last year's inflation needs to be incorporated. This does not affect π_2, since $\pi_1 = 0$, but $\pi_3 = .031 + \pi_2 = .081$, and so on. This affects the rest of the answer.

Year	π	P	Y
0	.000	1.00	$1,250
1	.100	1.00	1,313
2	.050	1.05	1,289
3	.081	1.14	1,253
4	.083	1.23	1,217
5	.057	1.30	1,197
6	.015	1.32	1,191
7	−.032	1.28	1,204
8	−.069	1.19	1,232
9	−.083	1.09	1,271
10	−.066	1.02	1,303

Output is initially above potential GNP. As above, prices begin to rise and output falls, but now output falls below potential. This causes prices first to stop rising, and then to fall. Output recovers to potential. The numerical answer gives only part of the cycle because inflation does not equal zero when output equals potential GNP.

Review Problems

3. Suppose the economy has the aggregate demand curve

$$Y = 667 + 1.11G + 1.11(M/P)$$

and the price-adjustment schedule

$$\pi = (Y_{-1} - 1{,}500)/1{,}500 + \pi^e.$$

Government spending is $200 and the money supply is $550.

a. Assume that expected inflation, π^e, is always zero. Starting from $P_0 = 1.4$, describe the path of the economy until GNP is within 1 percent of its long-run value.

b. Assume that $\pi^e = \pi_{-1}$. Describe the path of the economy, again starting from $P_0 = 1.4$, with zero inflation. How does your answer differ from that of Part a?

4. Using the same model as in Problem 3, increase the money supply by $100 starting from potential GNP with the price level $P=1$.

a. Calculate the paths of inflation, the price level, and GNP for the first 5 years, in the case where expected inflation is always zero.

b. Perform the same calculations, this time for 7 years, in the case where $\pi^e = \pi_{-1}$.

5. Suppose the economy has the aggregate demand curve

$$Y = 445 + .55G + 1.67(M/P)$$

and the price-adjustment schedule

$$\pi = .8(Y_{-1} - 800)/800 + \pi^e.$$

Government spending is $100 and the money supply is $180.

a. Assume that expected inflation, π^e, is always zero. Starting from $P_0 = .8$, describe the path of the economy until GNP is within 1 percent of its long-run value.

b. Assume that $\pi^e = .4\pi_{-1}$. Describe the path of the economy, again starting from $P_0 = .8$ with zero inflation. How does your answer differ from that of Part a?

6. Using the same model as in Problem 5 above, decrease government spending by $20 and the money supply by $20 starting from potential GNP with the price level $P = 1$.

a. Calculate the paths of inflation, the price level, and GNP for the first 5 years, in the case where expected inflation is always zero.

b. Perform the same calculation, this time for 7 years, in the case where $\pi^e = .4\pi_{-1}$.

7. Suppose the economy has the aggregate demand curve

$$Y = 734 + 1.21G + .64(M/P)$$

and the price-adjustment schedule

$$\pi = (Y_{-1} - 1{,}680)/1{,}680 + \pi^e.$$

Government spending is $200 and the money supply is $1,100.

a. Assume that expected inflation, π^e, is always zero. Starting from $P_0 = .8$, describe the path of the economy until GNP is within 1 percent of its long-run value.

b. Assume that $\pi^e = \pi_{-1}$. Describe the path of the economy, again starting from $P_0 = .8$ with zero inflation. How does your answer differ from that of Part a?

8. Using the same model as in Problem 7, increase the money supply by 10 percent starting from potential GNP with the price level $P = 1$.

a. Calculate the paths of inflation, the price level, and GNP for the first 5 years, in the case where expected inflation is always zero.

b. Perform the same calculation, this time for 7 years, in the case where expected inflation equals last period's inflation.

Answers to the Self-Test

1. Sticky
2. Price adjustment
3. Expected inflation and the state of the labor market
4. Price level
5. Inflationary momentum
6. Dynamic
7. Phillips
8. Expected
9. Complete crowding out
10. Neutral
11. Natural rate
12. Overshoot
13. True. In the short run, aggregate demand determines output at a predetermined price. It is only over time that price adjustment moves output toward potential GNP.
14. True. In the short run, with sticky prices, unemployment can be above or below its long-run, natural rate.
15. False. When output equals potential GNP, inflation is equal to expected inflation.
16. True. When output equals last period's GNP, the second term of the Phillips curve, Equation 8–2, is zero, leaving inflation equal to expected inflation.

17. True. Current prices are affected by past, but not current, output. This is what is meant by prices being predetermined.
18. False. If expected inflation is high enough, inflation can be positive even if output is below potential GNP.
19. False. Other factors, such as people's expectations of future monetary policy, also influence expected inflation.
20. True. Real GNP must fall below potential GNP, sending the economy into a recession, for current inflation to be reduced below last year's inflation.
21. True. The rate of inflation would have to increase each year to keep inflation above expected inflation and output above potential output.
22. True. In the long run the decrease in investment and net exports exactly equals the increase in government spending, and output is unchanged.
23. False. While monetary policy is neutral in the long run, it is not neutral in the short run.
24. False. Fiscal policy is not neutral in either the short or the long run.
25. In the short run, output is determined by the intersection of the aggregate demand curve and the predetermined price level.
26. In the long run, output is determined by potential GNP.
27. When output is above (below) potential GNP, unemployment is below (above) the natural rate. Unemployment equals the natural rate when output equals potential GNP.
28. Inflationary momentum is the process by which past inflation affects inflationary expectations, which in turn causes current inflation.
29. The accelerationist property is that, if real GNP is kept above potential permanently, inflation will increase without bound.
30. According to the real business cycle model, money is neutral in both the short and long run. In the complete model, while money is neutral in the long run, it is not neutral in the short run.
31. With no expected inflation, prices will rise (inflation will be positive) if output is greater than potential GNP, and will fall (inflation will be negative) if output is less than potential GNP.
32. With expected inflation, if output is greater than potential GNP, inflation will be higher than expected inflation. If output is less than potential GNP, inflation will be lower than expected inflation.
33. An increase in the money supply shifts the aggregate demand curve to the right. In the short run, output increases and the price level is unchanged. Over time, prices rise and output falls. In the long run, output returns to potential at a higher price level. Money is neutral in the long run—consumption, investment, net exports, and interest rates return to their original levels.
34. Since prices are predetermined, expectations of inflation do not change the short-run results. Once prices begin to rise, people expect more inflation, which in turn increases actual inflation. Price adjustment is no longer smooth. Prices and output cycle before the long run is attained. The results for the long run are also unaffected by expectations of inflation.

THE COMPLETE MODEL

35. An increase in government spending also shifts the aggregate demand curve to the right. Output increases with an unchanged price level in the short run. Over time, prices rise and output falls. In the long run, output returns to potential at a higher price level. There is complete crowding out in the long run. The higher interest rate causes investment and net exports to decrease by the same amount that government spending increased.
36. The answer to this question is the same as the answer to Question 34. Expectations of inflation affect the transition from the short to the long run, but they do not change either the short- or the long-run results.

Solutions to Review Problems

3. a.

Year	π	P	Y
0	.000	1.40	$1,325
1	−.117	1.24	1,382
2	−.079	1.14	1,423
3	−.051	1.08	1,453
4	−.031	1.05	1,472

b.

Year	π	P	Y
0	.000	1.40	$1,325
1	−.117	1.24	1,382
2	−.196	1.00	1,500
3	−.196	.80	1,652
4	−.095	.72	1,732
5	.060	.76	1,692
6	.188	.90	1,565
7	.231	1.11	1,439

4. a.

Year	π	P	Y
0	.000	1.00	$1,500
1	.000	1.00	1,611
2	.074	1.07	1,561
3	.041	1.11	1,537
4	.024	1.14	1,524
5	.016	1.16	1,512

b.

Year	π	P	Y
0	.000	1.00	$1,500
1	.000	1.00	1,611
2	.074	1.07	1,561
3	.115	1.19	1,494
4	.111	1.32	1,435
5	.067	1.41	1,401
6	.001	1.41	1,400
7	−.067	1.32	1,437

5. a.

Year	π	P	Y
0	.000	.80	$876
1	.076	.86	849
2	.049	.90	833
3	.033	.93	823
4	.023	.95	816

b.

Year	π	P	Y
0	.000	.80	$876
1	.076	.86	849
2	.079	.93	824
3	.056	.98	806
4	.030	1.01	798
5	.009	1.02	795

6. a.

Year	π	P	Y
0	.000	1.00	$800
1	.000	1.00	756
2	−.044	.96	768
3	−.032	.93	777
4	−.023	.91	783
5	−.017	.89	788

b.

Year	π	P	Y
0	.000	1.00	$800
1	.000	1.00	756
2	−.044	.96	768
3	−.050	.91	782
4	−.038	.88	794
5	−.021	.86	799
6	−.010	.85	803
7	−.001	.85	804

7. a.

Year	π	P	Y
0	.000	.80	$1,856
1	.105	.88	1,773
2	.055	.93	1,734
3	.032	.96	1,709
4	.017	.98	1,697

b.

Year	π	P	Y
0	.000	.80	$1,856
1	.105	.88	1,773
2	.160	1.02	1,666
3	.151	1.17	1,575
4	.089	1.27	1,529
5	−.001	1.27	1,529
6	−.091	1.15	1,586
7	−.056	1.09	1,625

8. a.

Year	π	P	Y
0	.000	1.00	$1,680
1	.000	1.00	1,750
2	.042	1.04	1,719
3	.023	1.06	1,704
4	.014	1.07	1,696
5	.009	1.08	1,693

b.

Year	π	P	Y
0	.000	1.00	$1,680
1	.000	1.00	1,750
2	.042	1.04	1,719
3	.065	1.11	1,675
4	.062	1.18	1,633
5	.034	1.22	1,611
6	−.007	1.21	1,615
7	−.045	1.15	1,646

CHAPTER 9 Macroeconomic Policy: A First Look

Main Objectives

When we considered monetary and fiscal policy in Chapter 8, we saw that neither could be used to increase output permanently above potential GNP. A more realistic goal of macroeconomic policy is to guide the economy as it returns to potential GNP following a disturbance. Another is to reduce inflation if it has become too high, as in the late 1970s. Macroeconomic policy-making often presents difficult choices between policies that eliminate recessions quickly and those that keep inflation low. Chapter 9 introduces the economic policy decisions made by the Fed and by the administration, and how macroeconomists analyze these decisions. Its examination of recent Fed policies to reduce inflation gives you some practice with the macroeconomic analysis developed in Chapters 6–8.

Key Terms and Concepts

Economic shocks or **disturbances** are events other than policy changes that move the economy away from potential GNP. An **aggregate demand disturbance** is one that shifts the aggregate demand curve. Examples of aggregate demand disturbances are changes in investment, net exports, and money demand. A **price disturbance** is an event that shifts the price-adjustment curve. Examples of price disturbances are increases in the price of imported oil and widespread anticipation of inflation by firms that leads them to increase prices.

In the short run, aggregate demand disturbances change output without affecting prices. In the absence of a policy response, the analysis of aggregate demand disturbances is exactly the same as the analysis of monetary and fiscal policy in Chapter 8. For instance, an increase in investment demand shifts the aggregate demand curve to the right, raising output above potential in the short run. Over time, prices rise and output falls until potential GNP is again attained.

Another example is an increase in money demand, which has exactly the same effects as a decrease in the money supply.

Price disturbances affect both output and prices in the short run. Consider a positive price shock, such as an oil price shock, that shifts up the price-adjustment curve. In the short run, the price level rises, dropping output below potential GNP. If there is no policy response, the process of price adjustment will cause prices to fall slowly and output to rise until potential output is eventually restored at the original price level. The economy is in a recession until potential GNP is attained. The path taken by the economy following a price disturbance is illustrated in Figure 9–1.

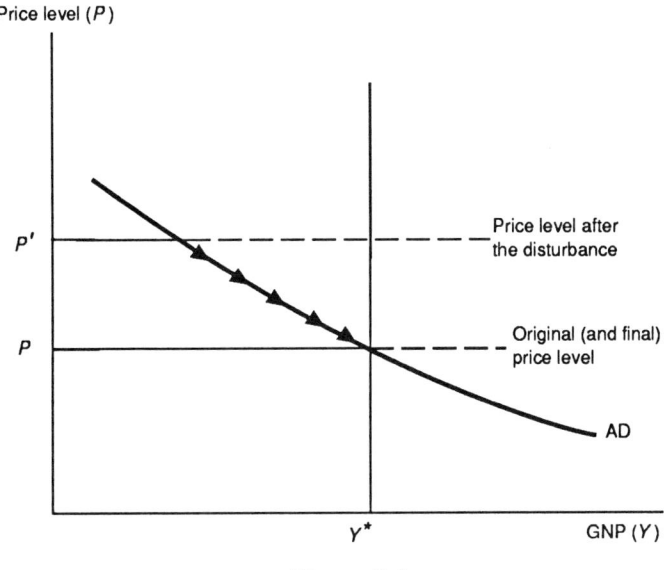

Figure 9–1

Activist or **countercyclical stabilization policy** is monetary or fiscal policy that attempts to counter the effects of *aggregate demand disturbances*. These are considered undesirable because they cause fluctuations in real GNP and in inflation. Suppose that an increase in money demand shifts the aggregate demand curve to the left. With no policy response, there will be a recession until falling prices raise real money sufficiently to restore potential GNP. Instead of allowing the economy to suffer through the recession, the Fed can increase the money supply to meet the additional demand for money. This immediately shifts the aggregate demand curve to the right, restoring potential output. Shifts to investment demand can be similarly counteracted.

Accommodative monetary policy is an increase in the money supply in response to a *price disturbance*. A policy that holds the money supply constant is called **nonaccommodative**. A price disturbance increases the price level and decreases output below potential in the short run. This presents the Fed with several difficult choices. While accommodative policy, as shown in Figure 9–2, returns output quickly to potential, it has the cost of further increasing the price level. Nonaccommodative policy, however, causes a sustained recession until prices fall. A more extreme alternative, decreasing the money supply to fight inflation, deepens the recession.

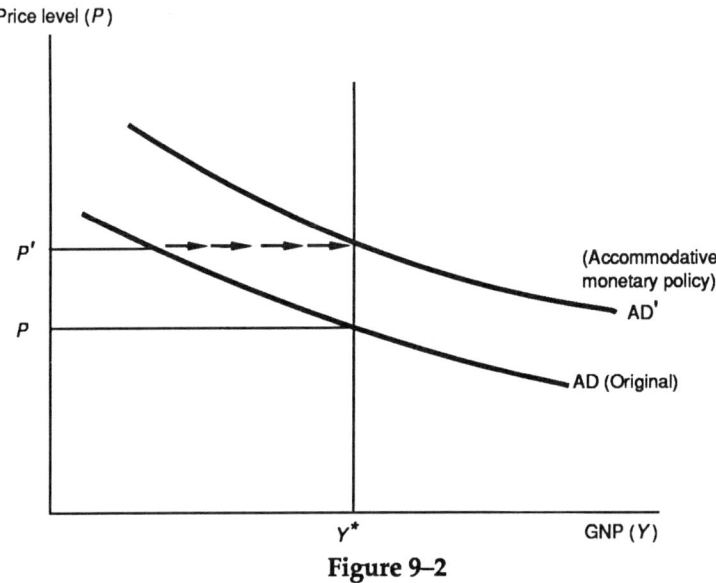

Figure 9–2

In order to give good policy advice, it is important for macroeconomists to understand the causes of fluctuations. For example, if GNP falls because an aggregate demand or price shock has reduced it below potential, there is a case for policy intervention to speed the return to equilibrium. On the other hand, if GNP falls because of a decrease in potential GNP, policy intervention is probably undesirable.

If policy reacts in a systematic manner to economic disturbances, then it is no longer exogenous. A **policy rule** is a description of endogenous economic policy. Because of the experience of the 1980s, where discussions of fiscal policy were dominated by the long-term question of how to reduce the federal budget deficit, we focus our attention on monetary policy rules. An example of such a policy rule is the monetarist proposition to fix the rate of growth of the money supply. Another is accommodative monetary policy, increasing the money supply in response to a price disturbance.

Many economists favor adopting policy rules because their use may have favorable effects through expectations and because a binding rule may prevent attempts to increase output above potential GNP. Policy rules are also important because of **time inconsistency**, the temptation of policy-makers, in order to stimulate the economy, to announce one plan and then enact another. In such situations, policy rules can be advantageous if they commit policy-makers to follow their announced plans.

Disinflation is a reduction in the *rate* of inflation. **Deflation** (a negative rate of inflation) is a reduction in the price level itself. The problem of disinflation is closely related to the problem of how to respond to price shocks. In order to lower inflation, the Fed must decrease the rate of growth of the money supply. From the Phillips curve with expectations of inflation equal to last period's inflation,

$$\pi = \pi_{-1} + f(Y_{-1} - Y^*)/Y^*, \qquad (9-1)$$

we know that it is necessary to have a recession to lower inflation. The Fed has two choices. It can lower the money supply slowly, causing a small recession, but only gradually decreasing inflation and restoring potential output. Alternatively, it can decrease the money supply quickly, creating a large recession, but quickly bringing down inflation and returning the economy to potential output. With a choice between a long-lasting small recession and a shorter large recession, there are no easy answers. Starting in 1979, with inflation over 10 percent, the Fed decreased money supply growth very quickly. This caused the largest recession since the Great Depression but also brought the inflation rate to under 4 percent by 1984.

Expansionary (or **looser**) monetary policy is an increase in the money supply, while expansionary fiscal policy is an increase in government purchases, an increase in transfers, or a decrease in taxes. **Contractionary** (or **tighter**) policy is the reverse. The words *expansionary* and *contractionary* are sometimes used to measure changes against growing trends so that, for example, a decrease in the rate of growth of the money supply from 10 to 5 percent would be called contractionary.

In principle, either monetary or fiscal policy can be used to counteract aggregate demand disturbances. One element of the choice between the two is their differing effects on interest rates. A fiscal expansion raises interest rates, decreasing investment and net exports. A monetary expansion lowers interest rates, raising investment and net exports.

A more basic question is whether monetary and fiscal policy should be used at all to counteract aggregate demand disturbances. These debates usually focus on monetary policy because the Fed can respond more quickly to changing economic conditions.

Monetarists believe that changes in the money supply have such strong effects on real GNP in the short run that monetary policy should not be used to counteract aggregate demand disturbances. Because the impact of monetary policy occurs with a lag and the length of the lag is uncertain, they believe it is impossible to smooth out fluctuations in real GNP the way we have described. Instead, monetary policy alternates between two extremes: too expansionary and too contractionary. The result, monetarists believe, is to increase, rather than to mitigate, fluctuations in real GNP. A second monetarist argument against activist stabilization policy is that, for short-run political reasons, governments are tempted to overstimulate the economy past potential GNP, causing higher and higher rates of inflation.

Economists of the **equilibrium school** take issue with our assumption of price stickiness. They believe prices are flexible and that GNP is always close to its potential value. If so, any systematic attempt to use monetary policy to affect real GNP will be offset by changes in the price level. They also believe that disinflation can be accomplished much more quickly and at much lower cost than we have argued. Both monetarists and economists of the equilibrium school advocate a constant rate of growth of the money supply, but for completely different reasons. Monetarists believe that monetary policy has such powerful effects on real GNP in the short run that it should not be used for stabilization. In the equilibrium model, since systematic monetary policy has no effect on real GNP, even in the short run, its growth should be kept constant in order to stabilize prices.

Self-Test

Fill in the Blank

1. A shock to investment, net exports, or money demand is an

   _____.

2. A price disturbance shifts the _____.

3. Policy that attempts to counter aggregate demand disturbances is called _____ or _____ stabilization policy.

4. Policies that increase the money supply in response to price shocks are called _____ policies.

5. Holding the money supply constant in response to a price shock is called a _____ policy.

6. Disinflation is the problem of _____ the rate of inflation.

7. Deflation is a reduction in the _____.
8. The temptation of policy-makers to announce one plan and then enact another is called _____.
9. An increase in the money supply is _____ monetary policy.
10. An increase in government purchases is _____ fiscal policy.
11. An increase in taxes is _____ fiscal policy.
12. A decrease in the rate of growth of the money supply is called _____.

True-False
13. Aggregate demand disturbances do not affect the price level in the short run.
14. Price shocks do not affect output in the short run.
15. Monetarists believe that monetary policy should be used to counter aggregate demand disturbances.
16. Economists of the equilibrium school believe that monetary policy should be used to counter aggregate demand disturbances.
17. Aggregate demand disturbances do not affect output in the long run.
18. Price shocks do not affect the price level in the long run.
19. An oil price increase is an example of an aggregate demand disturbance.
20. Using appropriate monetary policy, it is possible to reduce inflation without causing a recession.
21. Monetary and fiscal policy can both be used to counteract aggregate demand disturbances.
22. Monetary and fiscal expansions both raise net exports.
23. Lowering the rate of inflation is called deflation.
24. Economists of the equilibrium school believe that it is very costly to reduce the rate of inflation.

Review Questions

25. What is the difference between an aggregate demand disturbance and a price disturbance?
26. Describe several examples of aggregate demand and price disturbances.
27. Describe the effects of a contractionary aggregate demand disturbance, such as a decrease in investment demand, with no change in policy.
28. How can countercyclical stabilization policy be used to counter the effects of a contractionary aggregate demand disturbance?
29. Describe the effects of a positive price shock with no change in policy.
30. How can accommodative monetary policy be used in response to a price shock?
31. Contrast the views of monetarists and economists of the equilibrium school regarding the use of monetary policy.
32. What is a policy rule? What are two examples of such a rule?
33. Why are policy rules advantageous, compared to exogenous policy, in situations involving time inconsistency?
34. What are the choices faced by the Fed if it wishes to reduce the rate of inflation?
35. What happened to inflation and GNP, starting in 1979, after the Fed lowered the rate of growth of the money supply?
36. Why do monetary and fiscal expansions have different effects on investment and net exports?

Problem Set

Worked Problems

1. Suppose the economy has the aggregate demand curve
$$Y = 500 + 1.25G + .625(M/P) + Z_d$$
and the price-adjustment schedule
$$\pi = (Y_{-1} - Y^*)/Y^*,$$

where Z_d is an aggregate demand shock. Potential GNP $Y^* =$ $1,250 billion, government spending $G =$ $200 billion, and the money supply $M =$ $800 billion.

a. Starting at potential output with the price level $P = 1$ and inflation $\pi = 0$, an aggregate demand disturbance $Z_d = -\$100$ billion occurs in the first year. No further shocks occur ($Z_d =$ –$100 billion in all future years). Describe the path of the economy until GNP is within 1 percent of its long-run value.

b. How can the Fed offset the aggregate demand disturbance and keep output equal to potential GNP?

a. *In the first year output decreases by 100 (the amount of the aggregate demand disturbance) to $1,150 billion. The inflation rate π_2 is found from the price-adjustment curve,*

$$\pi_2 = (1{,}150 - 1{,}250)/1{,}250 = -.08 \; (-8 \; percent),$$

and determines the price level:

$$P_2 = 1 + 1(-.08) = .92.$$

Output is found from the aggregate demand curve using the given values for government spending, the money supply, and the aggregate demand disturbance:

$$Y_2 = 500 + 1.25(200) + .625(800)/.92 - 100$$
$$= \$1{,}193 \; billion.$$

The inflation rate π_3 can be computed by substituting Y_2 into the price-adjustment curve, and so on. It takes 5 years to return to within 1 percent of potential GNP:

Year	π	P	Y
0	.000	1.00	$1,250
1	.000	1.00	1,150
2	-.080	.92	1,193
3	-.045	.88	1,219
4	-.025	.86	1,233
5	-.014	.85	1,240

The aggregate demand disturbance lowers output below potential at an unchanged price level. Over time, prices fall and output rises until potential GNP is restored.

b. *In order to offset the shock, the money supply should be increased so that $.625 \, (\Delta M/P) = -Z_d$. The money supply is therefore raised by 160 to $960 billion.*

2. Suppose the economy had the aggregate demand curve
$$Y = 500 + 1.25G + .625(M/P)$$
and the price-adjustment schedule
$$\pi = (Y_{-1} - Y^*)/Y^* + Z_p,$$
where Z_p is a price shock. Potential GNP $Y^* = \$1{,}250$ billion, government spending $G = \$200$ billion, and the money supply $M = \$800$ billion.

a. Starting at potential output with the price level $P = 1$ and inflation $\pi = 0$, a price disturbance of 10 percent occurs in the first year ($Z_p = .1$). No further shocks occur ($Z_p = 0$ in all future years). Describe the path of the economy until GNP is within 1 percent of its long-run value.

b. Suppose that, starting in the first year, the Fed increases the money supply by 5 percent. Compare the new path of prices and output to the original path.

a. The first year's price level is raised from 1 to 1.1 by the 10 percent price disturbance. Output is found from the aggregate demand curve,
$$Y_1 = 500 + 1.25(200) + .625(800)/1.1$$
$$= \$1{,}250 \text{ billion,}$$
which determines the inflation rate π_2, and so on.

Year	π	P	Y
0	.000	1.00	$1,250
1	.100	1.10	1,205
2	−.036	1.06	1,222
3	−.023	1.04	1,233
4	−.014	1.03	1,238

The price disturbance raises prices and lowers output below potential. Over time, prices fall and output rises until potential GNP is restored.

b. The technique for this part is the same as for Part a except that, starting in Year 1, the new money supply is substituted in the aggregate demand curve. The accommodative policy restores output to within 1 percent of potential in 3 years at the cost of a higher price level.

Year	π	P	Y
0	.000	1.00	$1,250
1	.100	1.10	1,227
2	−.018	1.08	1,236
3	−.011	1.07	1,242

Review Problems

3. Suppose the economy has the aggregate demand curve

$$Y = 667 + 1.11G + 1.11(M/P) + Z_d$$

and the price-adjustment schedule

$$\pi = (Y_{-1} - Y^*)/Y^*,$$

where Z_d is an aggregate demand shock. Potential GNP $Y^* = \$1,500$, government spending $G = \$200$, and the money supply $M = \$550$.

a. Starting at potential output with the price level $P = 1$ and inflation $\pi = 0$, an aggregate demand disturbance $Z_d = -\$150$ occurs in the first year. No further shocks occur ($Z_d = -\$150$ in all future years). Describe the path of the economy until GNP is within 1 percent of its long-run value.

b. How can the Fed offset the aggregate demand disturbance and keep output equal to potential GNP?

4. Suppose the economy has the aggregate demand curve

$$Y = 667 + 1.11G + 1.11(M/P)$$

and the price-adjustment schedule

$$\pi = (Y_{-1} - Y^*)/Y^* + Z_p,$$

where Z_p is a price shock. Potential GNP $Y^* = \$1,500$, government spending $G = \$200$, and the money supply $M = \$550$.

a. Starting at potential output with the price level $P = 1$ and inflation $\pi = 0$, a price disturbance of 15 percent occurs in the first year ($Z_p = .15$). No further shocks occur ($Z_p = 0$ in all future years). Describe the path of the economy until GNP is within 1 percent of its long-run value.

b. Suppose that, starting in the first year, the Fed increases the money supply by 4 percent. Compare the new path of prices and output to the original path.

5. Suppose the economy has the aggregate demand curve

$$Y = 445 + .55G + 1.67(M/P) + Z_d$$

and the price-adjustment schedule

$$\pi = (Y_{-1} - Y^*)/Y^*,$$

where Z_d is an aggregate demand shock. Potential GNP $Y^* = \$800$, government spending $G = \$100$, and the money supply $M = \$180$.

a. Starting at potential output with the price level $P = 1$ and inflation $\pi = 0$, an aggregate demand disturbance $Z_d = -\$50$ occurs in the first year. No further shocks occur ($Z_d = -\$50$ in all future years). Describe the path of the economy until GNP is within 1 percent of its long-run value.

b. How can the Fed offset the aggregate demand disturbance and keep output equal to potential GNP?

6. Suppose the economy has the aggregate demand curve

$$Y = 445 + .55G + 1.67(M/P)$$

and the price-adjustment schedule

$$\pi = (Y_{-1} - Y^*)/Y^* + Z_p,$$

where Z_p is a price shock. Potential GNP $Y^* = \$800$, government spending $G = \$100$, and the money supply $M = \$180$.

a. Starting at potential output with the price level $P = 1$ and inflation $\pi = 0$, a price disturbance of 10 percent occurs in the first year ($Z_p = .1$). No further shocks occur ($Z_p = 0$ in all future years). Describe the path of the economy until GNP is within 1 percent of its long-run value.

b. Suppose that, starting in the first year, the Fed increases the money supply by 5 percent. Compare the new path of prices and output to the original path.

7. Suppose the economy has the aggregate demand curve

$$Y = 734 + 1.21G + .64(M/P) + Z_d$$

and the price-adjustment schedule

$$\pi = (Y_{-1} - Y^*)/Y^*,$$

where Z_d is an aggregate demand disturbance. Government spending $G = \$200$, the money supply $M = \$1,100$, and potential output $Y^* = 1,680$.

a. Starting at potential output with the price level $P = 1$ and inflation $\pi = 0$, an aggregate demand disturbance $Z_d = -\$100$ occurs in the first year. No further shocks occur ($Z_d = -\$100$ in all future years). Describe the path of the economy until GNP is within 1 percent of its long-run value.

b. How can the Fed offset the aggregate demand disturbance and keep output equal to potential GNP?

8. Suppose the economy has the aggregate demand curve

$$Y = 734 + 1.21G + .64(M/P)$$

and the price-adjustment schedule

$$\pi = (Y_{-1} - Y^*)/Y^* + Z_p,$$

where Z_p is a price disturbance. Government spending $G = \$200$, the money supply $M = \$1,100$, and potential output $Y^* = 1,680$.

a. Starting at potential output with the price level $P = 1$ and inflation $\pi = 0$, a price disturbance of 20 percent occurs in the first year ($Z_p = .20$). No further shocks occur ($Z_p = 0$ in all future years). Describe the path of the economy until GNP is within 1 percent of its long-run value.

b. Suppose that, starting in the first year, the Fed increases the money supply by 10 percent. Compare the new path of prices and output to the original path.

Answers to the Self-Test

1. Aggregate demand disturbance
2. Price-adjustment curve
3. Activist or countercyclical
4. Accommodative
5. Nonaccommodative
6. Reducing
7. Price level
8. Time inconsistency
9. Expansionary
10. Expansionary
11. Contractionary
12. Contractionary
13. True. Aggregate demand disturbances only affect output in the short run.
14. False. Price shocks affect both output and the price level in the short run.
15. False. Monetarists believe that monetary policy should not be used to counter such disturbances.
16. False. They believe that monetary policy is incapable of countering such disturbances.
17. True. In the long run, output is equal to potential GNP, which is unaffected by aggregate demand disturbances.
18. True. Unless there is a policy response, prices return to their original level in the long run.

19. False. An oil price increase is a price shock.
20. False. Any attempt to reduce inflation must lower output below potential GNP, causing a recession.
21. True. Both monetary and fiscal policy shift the aggregate demand curve.
22. False. While monetary expansions raise net exports, fiscal expansions lower them.
23. False. Disinflation is a reduction in the rate of inflation. Deflation is negative inflation.
24. False. They believe that inflation can be reduced with low cost.
25. Aggregate demand disturbances shift the aggregate demand curve while price disturbances shift the price-adjustment curve.
26. Changes in investment, net exports, and money demand are examples of aggregate demand disturbances while oil price shocks and expectations of inflation are examples of price disturbances.
27. In the short run, output declines at an unchanged price level. Over time, prices fall and output increases until potential GNP is restored.
28. Expansionary fiscal or monetary policy can be used to shift the aggregate demand curve to the right, restoring potential GNP without a prolonged recession.
29. In the short run, prices rise and output falls. Over time, prices fall and output increases until potential GNP is restored.
30. Accommodative monetary policy, increasing the money supply in response to a price shock, shortens the recession at the cost of increasing the price level.
31. Monetarists believe that monetary policy should not be used to counter aggregate demand disturbances because it is too powerful and will be misused. Economists of the equilibrium school believe that it should not be used because it is powerless to affect real GNP.
32. A policy rule is a description of endogenous economic policy. Two examples of policy rules are the monetarist proposition to fix the rate of growth of the money supply and an accommodative monetary policy that increases the money supply in response to a price shock.
33. The advantage of policy rules is that they can commit policy-makers to follow their announced plans.
34. The Fed can decrease the money supply sharply, causing a quick reduction in inflation but a large and short recession, or it can decrease the money supply more gradually, causing a slower reduction in inflation but also a smaller and longer recession.
35. Inflation remained high through 1981. It dropped sharply in 1982, and fell to under 4 percent by 1984. There was a large recession, with GNP 11 percent below potential in 1982, followed by a recovery.
36. Monetary and fiscal expansions have different effects on investment and net exports because they have different effects on interest rates.

MACROECONOMIC POLICY: A FIRST LOOK

Solutions to Review Problems

3. a.

Year	π	P	Y
0	.000	1.00	$1,500
1	.000	1.00	1,350
2	−.100	.90	1,417
3	−.055	.85	1,457
4	−.029	.83	1,479
5	−.014	.82	1,485

b. The money supply should be increased by $135 to $685.

4. a.

Year	π	P	Y
0	.000	1.00	$1,500
1	.015	1.15	1,420
2	−.053	1.09	1,450
3	−.034	1.05	1,469
4	−.021	1.03	1,483

b.

Year	π	P	Y
0	.000	1.00	$1,500
1	.015	1.15	1,441
2	−.039	1.11	1,464
3	−.024	1.08	1,475
4	−.017	1.06	1,487

The accommodative policy mitigates the recession at the cost of a higher price level.

5. a.

Year	π	P	Y
0	.000	1.00	$800
1	.000	1.00	750
2	−.062	.94	771
3	−.037	.91	782
4	−.022	.89	788
5	−.015	.88	793

b. The money supply should be increased by $30 to $210.

6. a.

Year	π	P	Y
0	.000	1.00	$800
1	.010	1.10	773
2	−.033	1.06	783
3	−.022	1.04	790
4	−.013	1.03	793

b.

Year	π	P	Y
0	.000	1.00	$800
1	.010	1.10	787
2	−.016	1.08	792

The accommodative policy mitigates the recession at the cost of a higher price level.

7. a.

Year	π	P	Y
0	.000	1.00	$1,680
1	.000	1.00	1,580
2	−.060	.94	1,625
3	−.033	.91	1,650
4	−.018	.89	1,663

b. The money supply should be increased by $156 to $1,256.

8. a.

Year	π	P	Y
0	.000	1.00	$1,680
1	.200	1.20	1,563
2	−.070	1.12	1,607
3	−.044	1.07	1,633
4	−.028	1.04	1,653
5	−.016	1.02	1,664

b.

Year	π	P	Y
0	.000	1.00	$1,680
1	.200	1.20	1,621
2	−.035	1.16	1,644
3	−.021	1.14	1,658
4	−.013	1.12	1,664

The accommodative policy mitigates the recession at the cost of a higher price level.

PART II

The Micro Foundations of Aggregate Demand

CHAPTER 10 Consumption Demand

Main Objectives

A basic principle of microeconomics is that people set their consumption plans in order to maximize their satisfaction, or utility. The simple consumption function discussed in Chapter 6, which says that people consume a constant fraction of their current disposable income, is an incomplete description of consumer behavior. Chapter 10 develops a more complete description by examining the empirical evidence regarding consumption and by relating consumption not only to current income, but to expectations of future income and to interest rates as well. You should learn the more sophisticated consumption model. Also, you should understand the implications of this model for the IS-LM analysis developed in Chapter 7 and for the analysis of price adjustment developed in Chapter 8. Indeed, a habit you should begin in this chapter is always to consider the impact of any new details on the model developed in Chapters 6, 7, and 8.

Key Terms and Concepts

Consumption is spending by households. Macroeconomists break consumption into three broad categories: durable goods, or those that are consumed over a number of years, like automobiles; nondurable goods, or those that are consumed during the year that they are purchased, like laundry detergent; and services, or professional attention, such as a visit to the barber or the doctor.

The central relationship between consumption and GNP is that, over the long run, **consumption expenditures** and GNP grow at about the same rate, but, over short-run business cycles, consumption expenditures fluctuate less than GNP. These fluctuations would be even smaller if we measured true consumption rather than consumption expenditures, so that consumer durables would be counted as providing consumption over the years that they are used rather than being considered as fully consumed during the period in which they are purchased.

One reason that consumption fluctuates less than GNP in the short run is because consumption depends on personal disposable income, which itself fluctuates less than GNP. Depreciation, taxes, and retained earnings by corporations are all part of GNP but not part of disposable income, while transfers from the government such as unemployment insurance and social security are part of disposable income but not part of GNP. Disposable income does not fall as much as GNP during recessions because tax collections decline while transfers increase. Tax collections and transfers are called **automatic stabilizers** because of their built-in stabilizing effect on disposable income.

The **Keynesian consumption function** discussed in Chapter 6 relates consumption to current disposable income,

$$C = a + bY_d, \tag{10-1}$$

where b, the marginal propensity to consume, has been measured at about .91 for the United States.

While this equation fits the data fairly well, there are aspects of consumption that it cannot explain. One of these is that, on average, fluctuations in consumption are not only smaller than fluctuations in GNP, they are smaller than fluctuations in disposable income: While the long-run marginal propensity to consume is equal to .92, the short-run marginal propensity to consume is equal to .72. If consumption actually followed the simple Keynesian consumption function, the short- and long-run marginal propensities to consume would be equal.

Two theories of consumption were developed during the 1950s in response to the defects in the simple Keynesian consumption function. The **permanent-income theory**, developed by Milton Friedman, postulates that consumption depends not on current income, but on a measure of a family's average long-run, or permanent, income:

$$C = b_p Y_p, \tag{10-2}$$

where Y_p is permanent income and b_p is a coefficient. Empirical tests by Friedman, using a weighted average of current and past incomes as a proxy for permanent income, demonstrated that his formulation fit the data better than the simple Keynesian consumption function.

The **life-cycle theory**, developed by Franco Modigliani, is based on a family planning consumption over its entire lifetime and incorporates assets into the Keynesian consumption function:

$$C = b_1 Y_d + b_2 A, \tag{10-3}$$

where A is assets held by the family and b_1 and b_2 are coefficients. Empirical work by Albert Ando of the University of Pennsylvania and

Franco Modigliani found that, as predicted by the life-cycle theory, holdings of assets influence consumption.

The text highlights the similar feature of the permanent-income and life-cycle theories: Each is a **forward-looking theory of consumption**. The most important aspect of forward-looking theories is that expected future, as well as current, income influences consumption. Families face an **intertemporal budget constraint**: They cannot have significantly negative assets. This constraint limits their consumption, but within it they can choose a wide range of consumption plans.

Without further assumptions, the forward-looking theory allows for such a wide range of consumption plans that it cannot be tested. Therefore, economists qualify it by assuming that most people prefer to keep their consumption fairly steady from year to year, rather than have their consumption fluctuate with their yearly income. Other factors come into play in determining which smooth consumption path a family will choose. For instance, the **bequest motive**, which describes parents' preferences for assets at the end of their lifetimes, must also be known in order to determine whether the family will choose a high or a low smooth consumption path.

The most important proposition of the forward-looking theory of consumption is the difference between the **marginal propensity to consume out of a temporary change in income** and the **marginal propensity to consume out of a permanent change in income**. Consider a tax cut that raises disposable income. If the tax cut is permanent, the increase in disposable income is also permanent and consumption will increase by the marginal propensity to consume times the change in income. If the tax cut is temporary, disposable income will return to its original level once the tax cut ends. A family's lifetime disposable income will increase much less than if the tax cut were permanent, which will cause consumption to increase much less than under a permanent cut.

Another feature of the forward-looking theory of consumption involves **anticipated changes in income**. Suppose a permanent tax cut was announced one year in advance. With the announcement, people would know that their lifetime disposable income had increased and would immediately raise their consumption. The increase in consumption would occur before the tax cut actually took place.

The forward-looking theory of consumption has been extensively tested over the last thirty-five years. The most compelling evidence in favor of the forward-looking theory as opposed to the simple Keynesian theory is that the short-run marginal propensity to consume is smaller than the long-run marginal propensity to consume. Additional evidence comes from examining two temporary changes in policy: the tax surcharge of 1968 and the tax rebate and social security bonus of 1975. In both cases, the response of consumption to the change in disposable income was small.

Recent empirical work on the forward-looking theory, using rational expectations to measure future income prospects, raises some interesting questions. This research indicates that consumption is more responsive to temporary changes in income than the forward-looking theory predicts, although clearly not as responsive as in the simple Keynesian theory. Other research involving individual family histories, using panel or longitudinal surveys, produces the same result. One explanation for these results is that some consumers are **liquidity constrained**—they cannot borrow as easily as the forward-looking model suggests.

Real interest rates also influence consumption. If the real interest rate is positive, as it generally is, people have an incentive to defer spending. On the other hand, consumption today is preferred to consumption in the future, and this is measured by the **rate of time preference**. If the real interest rate is greater than the rate of time preference, people will shift some of their consumption toward the future. These effects, like all relative price changes, are theoretically ambiguous. Higher real interest rates also raise income, which would tend to increase consumption. Indeed, the effects of real interest rates on consumption have not been strongly confirmed empirically.

Personal saving is personal disposable income minus consumption. A recurring puzzle which has received a great deal of attention is why the **personal saving rate**, personal saving as a percentage of personal disposable income, is higher in Japan than in the United States. One factor is that, in high-growth countries such as Japan, young people tend to have higher incomes than old people did when they were young. According to the forward-looking theory, since young people tend to save and old people tend to dissave, this raises the overall saving rate. Another explanation is that high land and housing prices in Japan require families to save more for a down payment. Other factors, such as differences in the tax and social security systems between the two countries, may also favor saving in Japan.

The issues raised in this chapter have conflicting effects on the slope of the IS curve. Forward-looking consumers have a smaller marginal propensity to consume out of disposable income than is predicted by the Keynesian consumption function, making the multiplier smaller and the IS curve steeper than it seemed in Chapter 7. On the other hand, higher real interest rates decrease consumption, making GNP more sensitive to the interest rate and the IS curve flatter than in Chapter 7. Which effect dominates is an empirical question.

The forward-looking theory of consumption also has implications for shifts in the IS curve due to tax changes. If a tax cut is permanent, the IS curve will shift much more than if it is temporary. Expectations of future tax cuts will also shift the IS curve.

Self-Test

Fill in the Blank

1. Over short-run business cycles, consumption expenditures fluctuate _____ than GNP.
2. Changes in taxes and transfers that cause disposable income to fluctuate less than GNP are called _____.
3. The short-run marginal propensity to consume is _____ than the long-run marginal propensity to consume.
4. The forward-looking theory of consumption combines the _____ and _____ theories.
5. The _____ limits the amount of consumption by a family over a period of years.
6. The forward-looking theory of consumption assumes that most people prefer to keep a _____ consumption path.
7. The forward-looking theory of consumption predicts that the effects of tax changes will differ depending on whether they are _____ or _____.
8. Consumers are _____ if they cannot borrow as easily as the forward-looking model suggests.
9. The _____ is the relative price between present and future consumption.
10. The _____ measures the preference for consumption today over consumption in the future.
11. Forward-looking consumers have a _____ marginal propensity to consume than is predicted by the Keynesian consumption function.

12. According to the forward-looking theory, anticipated tax changes shift the _____.

True-False

13. Consumption fluctuates less than consumption expenditures.
14. The relation between consumption expenditures and GNP is the same over short-run business cycles as it is over the long run.
15. Automatic stabilizers decrease fluctuations in disposable income.
16. According to the simple Keynesian consumption function, the short-run marginal propensity to consume is equal to the long-run marginal propensity to consume.
17. The intertemporal budget constraint means that, in any single year, a family cannot consume more than its disposable income.
18. People choose a smooth consumption path because of the bequest motive.
19. The simple Keynesian consumption function predicts that consumption will respond equally to temporary and permanent tax cuts.
20. The forward-looking theory of consumption predicts that consumption will respond equally to temporary and permanent tax cuts.
21. According to the forward-looking theory the announcement of a tax cut one year in the future will increase consumption immediately.
22. If consumers are liquidity constrained, consumption would respond more to temporary changes in income than the forward-looking theory predicts.
23. If consumption is negatively related to the real interest rate, the IS curve is flatter.
24. According to the forward-looking theory, the IS curve is steeper than it seemed in Chapter 7.

Review Questions

25. What is the difference between consumption and consumption expenditures?
26. What is the most important reason that consumption fluctuates less than GNP?

27. What is the major piece of evidence against the simple Keynesian consumption function?

28. What is the basic difference between the forward-looking theory of consumption and the simple Keynesian consumption function?

29. What does the forward-looking theory assume about people's preferences for steady versus erratic consumption?

30. Describe the early empirical evidence on the permanent-income and the life-cycle theories.

31. Why did the 1968 tax surcharge and the 1975 tax rebate provide support for the forward-looking theory?

32. What is the recent empirical evidence that points out defects in the forward-looking theory?

33. Why does consumption depend on the real interest rate?

34. Why does the forward-looking theory of consumption affect the slope of the IS curve?

35. Why do temporary tax changes cause smaller shifts of the IS curve than permanent tax changes?

36. Why do expectations of future tax cuts shift the IS curve?

37. How does the forward-looking theory help explain why saving is higher in Japan than in the United States?

Problem Set

Worked Problems

1. Suppose that consumption is of the form

$$C = 500 + .8Y_p,$$

where Y_p is permanent disposable income. Suppose also that consumers estimate their permanent disposable income by a simple average of disposable income in the current and past years:

$$Y_p = .5(Y_d + Y_{d-1}),$$

where Y_d is current disposable income.

a. Suppose that disposable income Y_d is equal to $5,000 billion in Years 1 and 2. What is consumption in Year 2?

b. What are the short- and long-run marginal propensities to consume?

c. Suppose that disposable income increases to $6,000 billion in Year 3 and then remains at $6,000 billion in all future years. What is consumption in Years 3 and 4 and all remaining years? Explain why consumption responds the way it does to an increase in income.

a. Permanent income in Year 2 = .5(5,000 + 5,000) = $5,000 billion. Consumption in Year 2 = 500 + .8(5,000) = $4,500 billion.

b. The short-run marginal propensity to consume = (.8)(.5) = .4. The long-run marginal propensity to consume = .8.

c. Permanent income in Year 3 = .5(6,000 + 5,000) = $5,500 billion. Consumption in Year 3 = 500 + .8(5,500) = $4,900 billion. Permanent income in Year 4 and all remaining years = .5(6,000 + 6,000) = $6,000 billion. Consumption in Year 4 and all remaining years = 500 + .8(6,000) = $5,300 billion. Consumption responds less in Year 3 than in Year 4 and thereafter because the short-run marginal propensity to consume is smaller than the long-run marginal propensity to consume.

2. Suppose that consumption is given by

$$C = 100 + .9Y_d - 1{,}000R$$

rather than by the consumption function in Problem 1 of Chapter 7. Add this consumption function to the other three equations of the IS-LM model:

$$\begin{aligned} Y &= C + I + G + X & \text{(Income identity)} \\ I &= 200 - 500R & \text{(Investment)} \\ X &= 100 - .12Y - 500R & \text{(Net exports)} \\ M &= (.8Y - 2{,}000R)P & \text{(Money demand)} \end{aligned}$$

with government spending $G = \$200$ billion, the tax rate $t = .2$, the nominal money supply $M = \$800$ billion, and the predetermined price level $P = 1$.

a. What is the IS curve? Compare it with the IS curve in Problem 1 of Chapter 7.

b. Derive the aggregate demand curve and calculate the effect of increases in government spending or real money on GNP. Compare your answer with Problem 2 of Chapter 7.

a. As in Chapter 7, the IS curve is derived by substituting consumption, investment, net exports, and government spending into the income identity:

$$Y = 1{,}500 - 5{,}000R.$$

It is flatter than the IS curve in Chapter 7, Y = 1,500 − 2,500R, because consumption depends negatively on the interest rate.

b. *The aggregate demand curve is calculated as in Chapter 7. From the LM curve,*

$$Y = 1.25(M/P) + 2{,}500R.$$

From the condition for spending balance,

$$2{,}500R = 500 - .5Y + 1.25G.$$

Substituting the spending balance condition into the LM curve, we derive the aggregate demand curve:

$$Y = .83(M/P) + 333 + .83G.$$

Because the IS curve is flatter, increases in government spending have less effect on GNP than in Chapter 7, while increases in real money have more effect.

Review Problems

3. Suppose that consumption is of the form

$$C = 200 + .9Y_p,$$

where Y_p is permanent disposable income. Suppose also that consumers estimate their permanent disposable income by a weighted average of disposable income in the current and past years:

$$Y_p = .7Y_d + .3Y_{d-1},$$

where Y_d is current disposable income.

a. Suppose that disposable income Y_d is equal to $6,000 in Years 1 and 2. What is consumption in Year 2?

b. Suppose that disposable income increases to $7,000 in Year 3 and then remains at $7,000 in all future years. What is consumption in Years 3 and 4 and all remaining years?

c. What are the short- and long-run marginal propensities to consume? How do they explain your answer to Part b?

4. Suppose that consumption is of the form

$$C = 300 + .9Y_p,$$

where Y_p is permanent disposable income. Suppose also that consumers estimate their permanent disposable income by a weighted average of disposable income in the current and past two years:

$$Y_p = .6Y_d + .3Y_{d-1} + .1Y_{d-2},$$

where Y_d is current disposable income.

a. Suppose that disposable income Y_d is equal to $8,000 in Years 1, 2, and 3. What is consumption in Year 3?

b. Suppose that disposable income increases to $9,000 in Year 4 and then remains at $9,000 in all future years. What is consumption in Years 4, 5, and 6 and all remaining years?

c. What are the short- and long-run marginal propensities to consume?

5. Suppose that consumption is given by

$$C = 300 + .8Y_d - 1{,}000R$$

rather than by the consumption function in Problem 3 of Chapter 7. Completing the IS-LM model,

$Y = C + I + G + X$	(Income identity)
$I = 200 - 1{,}500R$	(Investment)
$X = 100 - .04Y - 500R$	(Net exports)
$M = (.5Y - 2{,}000R)P$	(Money demand)

with government spending $G = \$200$, the tax rate $t = .2$, the nominal money supply $M = \$550$, and the predetermined price level $P = 1$.

a. What is the IS curve? Compare it with the IS curve from Problem 3 of Chapter 7.

b. Derive the aggregate demand curve and calculate the effect of increases in government spending or real money on GNP. Compare your answer with Problem 4 of Chapter 7.

6. Suppose that consumption is given by

$$C = 400 + .9Y_d - 1{,}500R$$

rather than by the consumption function in Problem 5 of Chapter 7. Completing the IS-LM model,

$Y = C + I + G + X$	(Income identity)
$I = 300 - 2{,}000R$	(Investment)
$X = 100 - .05Y - 1{,}000R$	(Net exports)
$M = (.4Y - 1{,}000R)P$	(Money demand)

with government spending $G = \$100$, the tax rate $t = .5$, the nominal money supply $M = \$180$, and the predetermined price level $P = 1$.

CONSUMPTION DEMAND

a. What is the IS curve? Compare it with the IS curve in Problem 5 of Chapter 7.

b. Derive the aggregate demand curve and calculate the effect of increases in government spending or real money on GNP. Compare your answer with Problem 6 of Chapter 7.

7. Suppose that consumption is given by

$$C = 400 + .9Y_d - 1{,}750R$$

rather than by the consumption function in Problem 7 of Chapter 7. Completing the IS-LM model,

$$Y = C + I + G + X \quad \text{(Income identity)}$$
$$I = 200 - 1{,}800R \quad \text{(Investment)}$$
$$X = 200 - .1Y - 200R \quad \text{(Net exports)}$$
$$M = (.8Y - 3{,}000R)P \quad \text{(Money demand)}$$

with government spending $G = \$200$ billion, the tax rate $t = .3333$, the nominal money supply $M = \$1{,}104$ billion, and the predetermined price level $P = 1$.

a. What is the IS curve? Compare it with the IS curve in Problem 7 of Chapter 7.

b. Derive the aggregate demand curve and calculate the effect of increases in government spending or real money on GNP. Compare your answer with Problem 8 of Chapter 7.

Answers to the Self-Test

1. Less
2. Automatic stabilizers
3. Smaller
4. Permanent-income and life-cycle
5. Intertemporal budget constraint
6. Steady
7. Temporary or permanent
8. Liquidity constrained
9. Real interest rate
10. Rate of time preference
11. Smaller
12. IS curve
13. True. Consumption expenditures count consumer durables, such as automobiles, when they are purchased rather than over the time they are used.

14. False. Over the long run, consumption expenditures and GNP grow at about the same rate, but, over short-run business cycles, consumption expenditures fluctuate less than GNP.
15. True. Automatic stabilizers such as taxes, which fall during recessions, and transfers, which rise, are the reason that disposable income fluctuates less than GNP.
16. True. The simple Keynesian consumption function is that consumption depends on current disposable income, which equates the short- and long-run marginal propensities to consume.
17. False. The intertemporal budget constraint limits consumption over a period of many years, not for any single year.
18. False. People choose a smooth consumption path because they prefer steady to erratic consumption. The bequest motive determines which smooth path they choose.
19. True. They both raise current disposable income by the same amount.
20. False. A temporary tax cut causes only a small increase in lifetime disposable income, and so causes only a small increase in consumption.
21. True. The announcement of a future tax cut increases lifetime disposable income and, to maintain a smooth consumption path, consumption increases immediately.
22. True. Liquidity-constrained consumers are not able to borrow sufficiently to smooth consumption as much as the forward-looking theory predicts.
23. True. A negative relation between consumption and the real interest rate makes GNP more sensitive to the interest rate and the IS curve flatter.
24. False. The forward-looking theory incorporates two conflicting factors, making the total effect ambiguous.
25. The distinction applies only to consumer durables. Consumption expenditure occurs when the good, such as a car, is purchased. Consumption occurs as the car is used up.
26. The most important reason that consumption fluctuates less than GNP is that consumption depends on disposable income, which itself fluctuates less than GNP.
27. The short-run marginal propensity to consume is less than the long-run marginal propensity to consume.
28. The simple Keynesian consumption function depends only on current disposable income, while the forward-looking theory depends on both current and expected disposable income.
29. It assumes that people prefer steady rather than erratic consumption.
30. Milton Friedman found that the permanent-income formulation of the consumption function fit the data better than the simple Keynesian formulation. Albert Ando and Franco Modigliani found that, as predicted by the life-cycle theory, assets as well as disposable income influence consumption.
31. Both the 1968 tax surcharge and the 1975 tax rebate were temporary. As predicted by the forward-looking theory, neither had much effect on consumption.
32. Recent empirical evidence assuming rational expectations finds that consumption is more sensitive to temporary changes in income than

CONSUMPTION DEMAND

would be predicted by the forward-looking theory. Studies using individual family histories find the same result.

33. The real interest rate, as the relative price between present and future consumption, influences the choice of whether to consume more today or more tomorrow.
34. According to the forward-looking theory, the multiplier is smaller than in Chapter 7, making the IS curve steeper, but consumption depends on real interest rates, making the IS curve flatter.
35. Temporary tax changes have less effect on consumption than permanent tax changes, causing smaller shifts of the IS curve.
36. Expectations of future tax cuts increase consumption, shifting the IS curve.
37. Japan is growing faster than the United States. In high-growth countries, young people (who tend to save) have higher incomes than old people (who tend to dissave) did when they were young. This raises the overall saving rate.

Solutions to Review Problems

3. a. Permanent income in Year 2 = .7(6,000) + .3(6,000) = $6,000.
      Consumption in Year 2 = 200 + .9(6,000) = $5,600.
   b. Permanent income in Year 3 = .7(7,000) + .3(6,000) = $6,700.
      Consumption in Year 3 = 200 + .9(6,700) = $6,230. Permanent income in Year 4 and all remaining years = $7,000. Consumption in Year 4 and all remaining years = 200 + .9(7,000) = $6,500.
   c. The short-run marginal propensity to consume = (.9)(.7) = .63. The long-run marginal propensity to consume = .9. In Part b, consumption in Year 3 increases by $630, the short-run marginal propensity to consume, .63, times the change in disposable income, $1,000. Consumption in Year 4 and thereafter increases by $900, the long-run marginal propensity to consume, .9, times the change in income.
4. a. Consumption in Year 3 = $7,500.
   b. Consumption in Year 4 = $8,040, in Year 5 = $8,310, and in Year 6 and in all subsequent years = $8,400.
   c. The short-run marginal propensity to consume = .54. The long-run marginal propensity to consume = .9.
5. a. The IS curve is $Y = 2,000 - 7,500R$. It is flatter than the IS curve in Chapter 7.
   b. The aggregate demand curve is $Y = 1.3(M/P) + 523 + .87G$. Because the IS curve is flatter, increases in government spending have less effect on GNP than in Chapter 7, while increases in real money have more effect.
6. a. The IS curve is $Y = 1,500 - 7,500R$. It is flatter than the IS curve in Chapter 7.

b. The aggregate demand curve is $Y = 1.88(M/P) + 334 + .42G$. Because the IS curve is flatter, increases in government spending have less effect on GNP than in Chapter 7, while increases in real money have more effect.

7. a. The IS curve is $Y = 2{,}000 - 7{,}500R$. It is flatter than the IS curve in Chapter 7.
   b. The aggregate demand curve is $Y = .83(M/P) + 533 + .67G$. Because the IS curve is flatter, increases in government spending have less effect on GNP than in Chapter 7, while increases in real money have more effect.

CHAPTER 11 Investment Demand

Main Objectives

Investment is the most volatile component of aggregate demand. Chapter 11 expands the simple investment demand function of Chapter 7 by examining the microeconomic underpinnings of investment behavior. You should learn how investment, influenced by the forward-looking behavior of firms, depends in a systematic way on output as well as on interest rates. You should also be able to explain the effects of investment models in the IS-LM framework.

Key Terms and Concepts

Investment is the flow of newly produced capital goods. It consists of three subcategories: **nonresidential fixed investment**, or business purchases of new plants and equipment; **residential fixed investment**, or construction of new houses and apartments; and **inventory investment**, or increases in stocks of goods produced but not yet sold.

The **desired capital stock** is the amount of factories, equipment, and supplies that firms desire. It is determined by equating the marginal cost and the marginal benefit of employing more capital. Firms need to be forward looking in order to determine the marginal benefit.

The **rental price of capital** is the cost of using capital for one year. It depends on the real price of new equipment, the real interest rate, and the rate of depreciation:

$$R^K = (R + d)P^K, \qquad (11\text{-}1)$$

where R^K is the rental price of capital, R is the interest rate, d is the rate of depreciation, and P^K is the price of new equipment.

Since the rental price of capital is the cost of using capital, the desired capital stock declines if the rental price of capital rises. The desired capital stock increases if planned output rises because it is generally advantageous to use more of both capital and labor to produce additional output. It also increases if the wage rises because a higher wage lowers the cost of capital relative to labor. Algebraically,

$$K^* = k(W/R^K)Y, \qquad (1\text{-}2)$$

where K^* is the desired capital stock, W is the wage, R^K is the rental price of capital, Y is output, and k is a coefficient.

The **investment function** shows the amount of investment a firm will undertake during the year. If there is no depreciation, investment equals the change in the actual capital stock, $K - K_{-1}$. If there are no lags in the investment process so that firms can attain their desired capital stock within one year, investment can be written as the difference between the desired capital stock and last year's capital stock,

$$I = K^* - K_{-1} = k(W/R^K)Y - K_{-1}, \qquad (11\text{-}3)$$

where I is investment. The investment function shows that investment depends positively on the wage rate and output, and negatively on the rental price of capital. Since the rental price of capital rises with the real interest rate, investment depends negatively on the interest rate.

The **accelerator** describes the relation between investment and output. If the desired capital stock is attained within one year, this year's capital stock, K, depends on this year's output, Y, and so last year's capital stock, K_{-1}, depends on last year's output, Y_{-1}. Then the level of investment, I, which is the change in the capital stock, ΔK, depends on the change in output, ΔY. When output accelerates—when its change gets bigger—investment increases.

A large part of investment serves to replace, rather than add to, the capital stock. The **rate of depreciation** is the fraction of the capital stock that wears out each year. If a constant fraction d of the existing capital stock wears out each year, the net investment function, Equation 11-3, can be changed into a gross investment function by adding d times K_{-1} to the right-hand side of the equation.

While net investment, the change in the capital stock, depends on the change in output, replacement investment is related to the level of the capital stock and depends on the level of output. Thus investment depends on both the level and the change in output.

Lags in the investment function prevent the capital stock from being adjusted to its desired level immediately. For many investment projects, such as building a new factory, there is a lag of several years between the decision to invest and the completion of the project. These lags can be modeled by modifying the investment function,

$$I = s(K^* - K_{-1}), \qquad (11\text{-}4)$$

where s is the fraction of the difference between the desired and actual capital stock that can be changed within one year. Studies indicate that the value of s is between one-tenth and one-third.

The Tax Reform Act of 1986 had substantial effects on investment. While the reduction in the corporate tax rate lowered the rental price of capital, the elimination of the investment tax credit and reduction of the accelerated depreciation of capital for tax purposes raised it. The total effect was to raise the rental price of capital by about 10 percent, thereby reducing investment. More positively, by eliminating tax-based incentives, the Tax Reform Act caused investment to be allocated more efficiently.

As with consumption, the effect of tax changes on investment depends on whether the changes are temporary or permanent. **Anticipated tax changes** can have perverse effects: For instance, expectations of an increase in the investment tax credit one year from now will decrease current investment as firms wait for the tax credit to come into effect before starting investment projects. Expectations of the elimination of the investment tax credit can explain why investment rose at the end of 1985, just before the credit was eliminated, and then fell in early 1986.

Residential investment can be analyzed in much the same way as business investment. One difference is that the annual rate of depreciation for business equipment is about 10 percent while the rate of depreciation for houses is about 2 percent. Consequently, the real interest rate is a much larger fraction of the rental price of housing than it is of the rental price of business capital, and residential investment is much more sensitive to fluctuations in interest rates than is business investment. Monetary policy, through its effect on interest rates, has a very large effect on residential construction.

Inventory investment can also be analyzed like business investment. The **pipeline function** describes inventories that are an intrinsic part of the production process, such as automobile parts held by a car manufacturer. The **buffer-stock function** describes finished goods that are ready for sale, such as automobiles held by a car dealer. About two-thirds of inventories are held for the pipeline function, with the other third for the buffer-stock function.

Investment depends positively on real GNP and negatively on the real interest rate. In terms of the IS-LM framework, the dependence of investment on GNP increases the multiplier, raising the intercept of the IS curve and making it flatter. Because of lags in the investment process, the response of investment to changes in interest rates is small in the very short run and increases over time. This makes the IS curve close to vertical in the very short run, but flatter over longer periods.

Self-Test

Fill in the Blank

1. The three categories of investment spending are _____, _____, and _____.
2. Fluctuations in investment are _____ than fluctuations in real GNP.
3. The cost of capital to a firm is measured by the _____ of capital.
4. Firms invest if their actual capital stock differs from their _____ capital stock.
5. The desired capital stock depends on the _____, _____, and _____.
6. If there is no depreciation, investment is the change in the _____.
7. Investment depends _____ on the wage rate, _____ on the rental price of capital, and _____ on output.
8. The _____ shows the amount of investment a firm will undertake during the year.
9. The _____ is the fraction of the capital stock that wears out each year.
10. _____ in the investment function prevent the capital stock from being adjusted to its desired level immediately.
11. The accelerator describes the effect of the _____ of output on the _____ of investment.
12. The two functions of inventories are the _____ and _____ functions.

INVESTMENT DEMAND

True-False

13. Investment is the least volatile component of aggregate demand.
14. The rental price of capital increases if the rate of depreciation rises.
15. The desired capital stock increases when output rises.
16. Investment is high when wages are high.
17. When the price of new equipment rises investment is high.
18. The actual capital stock is always equal to the desired capital stock.
19. Gross investment is equal to the change in the capital stock.
20. The accelerator describes the effect of the level of output on the change of investment.
21. The Tax Reform Act of 1986 has caused investment to be allocated less efficiently.
22. Anticipated and unanticipated tax credits have the same effects on investment.
23. Monetary policy has more effect on residential investment than on business fixed investment.
24. Inventory investment tends to be closely related to changes in production.

Review Questions

25. Why do firms need to be forward looking when they determine their desired capital stock?
26. How is the rental price of capital determined?
27. What are the determinants of the desired capital stock?
28. Why does investment depend negatively on the real interest rate?
29. Why does the level of investment depend on the change of output?
30. Why does the level of investment depend on the level of output?
31. Why are there lags in the investment process?
32. Describe how the tax system influences investment.
33. Why is residential investment very sensitive to fluctuations in the interest rate?

34. What is the relation between the interest sensitivity of investment and the slope of the IS curve?
35. Why do lags in the investment process make the IS curve steeper in the very short run?
36. How did the Tax Reform Act of 1986 affect investment?
37. How can the increase in investment during the fourth quarter of 1985 be explained by the Tax Reform Act of 1986?

Problem Set

Worked Problems

1. Suppose that the demand for investment is given by

$$I = .5(K^* - K_{-1}),$$

where K^* is the desired stock of capital given by

$$K^* = .025(Y/R),$$

where Y is output and R is the interest rate. Assume that there is no depreciation.

   a. Calculate the desired capital stock in Year 1 if output is $1,000 billion and the interest rate is .1 (10 percent).

   b. What is the level of investment in Year 1 if the capital stock in Year 0 was $150 billion?

   c. Assuming that output and the interest rate are constant, what is investment in Years 2 and 3 and all subsequent years?

   a. The desired capital stock $K^* = .025(1,000)/.1 = \$250$ billion.

   b. Investment $I_1 = .5(250 - 150) = \$50$ billion.

   c. The capital stock K_1 increases by I_1 to $200 billion. Since the desired capital stock K^* is unchanged,

   $$I_2 = .5(250 - 200) = \$25 \text{ billion.}$$

   Similarly,

   $$I_3 = .5(250 - 225) = \$12.5 \text{ billion.}$$

   Investment will decrease by one-half each year and will eventually approach zero.

INVESTMENT DEMAND

2. Suppose that investment is given by

$$I = 200 - 500R + .2Y$$

rather than by the investment function in Problem 1 of Chapter 7. Add this investment function to the other equations of the IS-LM model:

$$Y = C + I + G + X \quad \text{(Income identity)}$$
$$C = 100 + .9Y_d \quad \text{(Consumption)}$$
$$X = 100 - .12Y - 500R \quad \text{(Net exports)}$$
$$M = (.8Y - 2{,}000R)P \quad \text{(Money demand)}$$

with government spending $G = \$200$ billion, the tax rate $t = .2$, the nominal money supply $M = \$800$ billion, and the predetermined price level $P = 1$.

a. What is the IS curve? Compare it with the IS curve in Problem 1 of Chapter 7.

b. Derive the aggregate demand curve and calculate the effect of increases in government spending or real money on GNP. Compare your answer with Problem 2 of Chapter 7.

a. As in Chapter 7, the IS curve is derived by substituting consumption, investment, net exports, and government spending into the income identity:

$$Y = 3{,}000 - 5{,}000R.$$

Because investment depends positively on income, the multiplier is greater than in the sample problem of Chapter 7. This makes the IS curve flatter with a larger intercept.

b. The aggregate demand curve is calculated as in Chapter 7. From the LM curve,

$$Y = 1.25(M/P) + 2{,}500R.$$

From the condition for spending balance,

$$2{,}500R = 1{,}000 - .5Y + 2.5G.$$

Substituting the condition for spending balance into the LM curve, we derive the aggregate demand curve,

$$Y = .83(M/P) + 667 + 1.67G.$$

Because of the larger multiplier, increases both in government spending and in real money have more effect on GNP than in the model used in Chapter 7.

Review Problems

3. Suppose that the demand for investment is given by

$$I = .2(K^* - K_{-1}),$$

where K^* is the desired stock of capital given by

$$K^* = .01(Y/R),$$

where Y is output and R is the interest rate. Assume that there is no depreciation.

   a. Calculate the desired capital stock in Year 1 if output is $2,000 and the interest rate is .05 (5 percent).

   b. What is the level of investment in Year 1 if the capital stock in Year 0 was $200?

   c. Assuming that output and the interest rate are constant, what is investment in Years 2 and 3 and all subsequent years?

4. Answer Problem 3 if the interest rate is .10 (10 percent).

5. Suppose that investment is given by

$$I = 200 - 1{,}500R + .2Y$$

rather than by the investment function in Problem 3 of Chapter 7. Complete the IS-LM model:

   $Y = C + I + G + X$ (Income identity)
   $C = 300 + .8Y_d$ (Consumption)
   $X = 100 - .04Y - 500R$ (Net exports)
   $M = (.5Y - 2{,}000R)P$ (Money demand)

   with government spending $G = \$200$, the tax rate $t = .2$, the nominal money supply $M = \$550$, and the predetermined price level $P = 1$.

   a. What is the IS curve? Compare it with the IS curve in Problem 3 of Chapter 7.

   b. Derive the aggregate demand curve and calculate the effect of increases in government spending or real money on GNP. Compare your answer with Problem 4 of Chapter 7.

6. Suppose that investment is given by

$$I = 300 - 2{,}000R + .1Y$$

INVESTMENT DEMAND

rather than by the investment function in Problem 5 of Chapter 7. Completing the IS-LM model:

$Y = C + I + G + X$ (Income identity)
$C = 400 + .9Y_d$ (Consumption)
$X = 100 - .05Y - 1,000R$ (Net exports)
$M = (.4Y - 1,000R)P$ (Money demand)

with government spending $G = \$100$, the tax rate $t = .5$, the nominal money supply $M = \$180$, and the predetermined price level $P = 1$.

a. What is the IS curve? Compare it with the IS curve in Problem 5 of Chapter 7.

b. Derive the aggregate demand curve and calculate the effect of increases in government spending or real money on GNP. Compare your answer with Problem 6 of Chapter 7.

7. Suppose that investment is given by

$$I = 200 - 1,800R + .1Y$$

rather than by the investment function in Problem 7 of Chapter 7. Completing the IS-LM model:

$Y = C + I + G + X$ (Income identity)
$C = 400 + .9Y_d$ (Consumption)
$X = 200 - .1Y - 200R$ (Net exports)
$M = (.8Y - 3,000R)P$ (Money demand)

with government spending $G = \$200$, the tax rate $t = .3333$, the nominal money supply $M = \$1,104$, and the predetermined price level $P = 1$.

a. What is the IS curve? Compare it with the IS curve in Problem 7 of Chapter 7.

b. Derive the aggregate demand curve and calculate the effect of increases in government spending or real money on GNP. Compare your answer with Problem 8 of Chapter 7.

Answers to the Self-Test

1. Nonresidential fixed investment, residential fixed investment, and inventory investment
2. Greater
3. Rental price
4. Desired
5. Wage rate, level of output, and rental price of capital
6. Actual capital stock

7. Positively, negatively, and positively
8. Investment function
9. Rate of depreciation
10. Lags
11. Change of output on the level of investment
12. Pipeline and buffer stock
13. False. Investment is the most volatile component of aggregate demand.
14. True. Higher depreciation raises the rental cost of capital, which increases the rental price.
15. True. With higher output, firms want to use more capital in production.
16. True. High wages cause firms to substitute toward capital, which raises the desired capital stock and investment.
17. False. An increase in the price of new equipment raises the rental price of capital, which lowers the desired capital stock and investment.
18. False. Lags in the investment process can cause the actual and desired capital stock to differ.
19. False. Net investment is equal to the change in the capital stock. Gross investment also includes investment to replace depreciated capital.
20. False. The accelerator describes the effect of the change of output on the level of investment.
21. False. By eliminating tax-based incentives, the Tax Reform Act of 1986 caused investment to be allocated more efficiently.
22. False. An unanticipated tax credit raises investment immediately. An anticipated tax credit first decreases investment while firms wait for the credit to occur.
23. True. Residential investment is more sensitive to interest rates than business fixed investment.
24. True. Most inventory investment is for the pipeline function, which closely follows changes in production.
25. Firms determine their desired capital stock by equating the marginal benefits of capital to the rental cost of capital. They need to be forward looking in order to determine the marginal benefits.
26. The rental price of capital is the price of new equipment multiplied by the sum of the real interest rate plus the rate of depreciation.
27. The determinants of the desired capital stock are the wage rate, the level of output, and the rental price of capital.
28. A higher real interest rate raises the rental price of capital, lowering the desired capital stock and investment.
29. In a world without depreciation, the level of investment is the change in the capital stock. Since the level of the capital stock depends on the level of output, the change in the capital stock depends on the change in output.
30. Replacement investment, the fraction of investment that serves to replace the depreciated capital stock, depends on the level of the capital stock and thus on the level of output.
31. Much investment spending, such as building new factories, takes time and cannot be completed within one year.
32. Taxation of capital decreases investment. Tax incentives for investment, such as the investment tax credit, stimulate investment.

INVESTMENT DEMAND

33. Because the rate of depreciation of houses is low, the interest rate is a large fraction of the rental price of housing and residential investment is very sensitive to fluctuations in the interest rate.
34. The greater the interest sensitivity of investment, the flatter the IS curve.
35. Lags in the investment process make investment very insensitive to interest rates in the very short run, making the IS curve steeper in the very short run than it is otherwise.
36. The Tax Reform Act of 1986 raised the rental price of capital, lowering investment.
37. Expectations that, as part of the Tax Reform Act, the investment tax credit would be eliminated beginning in 1986 raised investment in the fourth quarter of 1985.

Solutions to Review Problems

3. a. The desired capital stock $K^* = .01(2,000)/.05 = \$400$.
   b. Investment $I_1 = .2(400 - 200) = \$40$.
   c. The capital stock K_1 increases by 40 to 240. Since the desired capital stock K^* is unchanged,

   $$I_2 = .2(400 - 240) = \$32$$
   $$I_3 = .2(400 - 272) = \$25.6.$$

   Investment will decrease by one-fifth each year and will eventually approach zero.

4. a. The desired capital stock $K^* = .01(2,000)/.1 = \$200$.
   b. Investment $I_1 = .2(400 - 400) = 0$ since the actual capital stock equals the desired capital stock.
   c. Investment equals zero in all subsequent years.

5. a. The IS curve is $Y = 4,000 - 10,000R$. It is flatter with a larger intercept than the IS curve in Chapter 7.
   b. The aggregate demand curve is $Y = 1.43(M/P) + 857 + 1.43G$. Because the multiplier is larger, increases in both government spending and real money have more effect on GNP than in Chapter 7.

6. a. The IS curve is $Y = 1,800 - 6,000R$. It is flatter with a larger intercept than the IS curve in Chapter 7.
   b. The aggregate demand curve is $Y = 1.76(M/P) = 470 + .58G$. Because the multiplier is larger, increases in both government spending and real money have more effect on GNP than in Chapter 7.

7. a. The IS curve is $Y = 2,500 - 5,000R$. It is flatter with a larger intercept than the IS curve in Chapter 7.
   b. The aggregate demand curve is $Y = .71(M/P) + 857 + 1.07G$. Because the multiplier is larger, increases in both government spending and real money have more effect on GNP than in Chapter 7.

CHAPTER 12   Foreign Trade and the Exchange Rate

Main Objectives

During the 1980s, issues involving foreign trade and the exchange rate played a central role in the performance of the U.S. economy. The unprecedented trade deficit and roller-coaster ride of the dollar led to proposals for protectionism and exchange-rate stabilization. Chapter 12 discusses the causes of trade imbalances and exchange-rate fluctuations, considers the effects of these foreign influences on the U.S. economy, and analyzes whether proposals for protectionism and exchange-rate stabilization will do more harm than good.

Key Terms and Concepts

Exports are sales of goods and services to the rest of the world. **Imports** are purchases of goods and services from the rest of the world. **Net exports** are exports minus imports. There is a **trade surplus** when exports are greater than imports and a **trade deficit** when imports are greater than exports. A trade deficit must be financed by borrowing from abroad. This borrowing is called a **capital inflow**.

The **exchange rate** is the price of one currency in terms of another. For the United States, it is the amount of foreign currency that can be bought with one dollar, for example 2 West German marks. If more foreign currency can be bought with one dollar, say 3 marks, then we say that the dollar rises or **appreciates** with respect to that currency. If less foreign currency can be bought with one dollar, then the dollar falls or **depreciates**.

Currencies are traded in the foreign exchange market, which is a worldwide network of banks rather than a single organized market. For a variety of reasons, the major industrialized countries fixed exchange rates prior to 1971. Today's international monetary system is called a **floating or flexible exchange-rate system** because there is a free market in foreign exchange. The **trade-weighted exchange rate** is an average of several different exchange rates, each weighted by the amount of trade with the United States. It measures the exchange rate between the United States and the rest of the world.

The **real exchange rate** is a measure of the relative price of goods produced in the United States compared to the price of goods produced in the rest of the world (ROW),

$$\text{Real exchange rate} = EP/P_w, \qquad (12\text{-}1)$$

where E is the trade-weighted exchange rate, P is the U.S. price level, and P_w is the ROW price level. The exchange rate E is sometimes called the **nominal exchange rate**. In the short run, both the U.S. and ROW price levels are predetermined and the real exchange rate, EP/P_w, varies with the exchange rate (E). In the long run, prices are flexible and the real exchange rate is constant. **Purchasing power parity** is a theory proposing that the real exchange rate is constant. It does not hold for the short run, but does for the long run.

The **net export function** relates net exports to real income and the real exchange rate,

$$X = g - mY - n(EP/P_w), \qquad (12\text{-}2)$$

where g is a constant and m and n are coefficients. Net exports depend negatively on real income because, as domestic income rises, our imports increase. The coefficient m is called the **marginal propensity to import**. Net exports depend negatively on the real exchange rate because a higher real exchange rate makes our goods more expensive relative to foreign goods. This increases our imports and decreases our exports.

When the U.S. interest rate rises in comparison to other interest rates, U.S. assets become more attractive and the dollar appreciates. The positive relation between the real exchange rate and the U.S. interest rate can be expressed as

$$EP/P_w = q + vR, \qquad (12\text{-}3)$$

where q is a constant and v is a coefficient. Combining the equation for the real exchange rate with the net export function enables us to derive the open-economy IS curve, which was discussed in Chapter 7.

The **open-economy IS curve** differs from what the IS curve would be in a closed economy in two ways. First, net exports depend negatively on income, which makes the open-economy multiplier, $1/[1 - b(1 - t) + m]$, smaller than the closed-economy multiplier and the IS curve steeper. This reduction in the size of the multiplier is called **leakage**. Second, as can be seen by combining Equations 12–2 and 12–3, net exports depend negatively on the interest rate. This makes the IS curve flatter. The LM curve is the same as for a closed economy.

Expansionary monetary policy lowers interest rates, causes the exchange rate to depreciate, and increases output above potential in the short run. Over time, prices rise and output falls toward potential. In the long run, the real exchange rate returns to parity and the nominal exchange rate depreciates by the increase in the price level. Monetary policy is neutral in the long run.

Expansionary fiscal policy increases interest rates, causes the exchange rate to appreciate, increases the trade deficit (or reduces the trade surplus), and raises output above potential in the short run. The government budget deficit is partially financed by the capital inflow from abroad. Over time, prices rise and output falls toward potential. In the long run, the interest rate and real exchange rate are permanently higher.

Changes in the exchange rate have an immediate impact on the price level for a small country by changing the price of imports. The situation is quite different for the United States. Importers tend to keep the dollar price of their goods stable through swings in the exchange rate. For the large U.S. economy, movements in the exchange rate do not create price shocks.

Protectionist policies include **tariffs** on imports, **quotas** on the quantity of imports, and outright **bans** on some imports. They help domestic producers by lessening foreign competition but hurt consumers by raising prices on imported goods. The effects on prices are sticky for tariffs, but immediate for quotas. Protection stimulates net exports and shifts the IS curve outward, raising interest rates and the exchange rate. Protectionist policies also invite retaliation by our trading partners, which would undo any benefits and reduce the welfare of all involved nations.

The Fed can **stabilize** the exchange rate by using monetary policy to keep the interest rate constant, which would make the LM curve perfectly flat. In that case, monetary policy could not be used for other goals, such as preventing fluctuations in unemployment or prices. With a flat LM curve, fiscal policy becomes more powerful but spending disturbances, such as investment shocks, that shift the IS curve cause large movements in GNP.

The theory of **interest-rate parity** proposes that the interest-rate differential between dollar bonds and bonds denominated in foreign currency $(R - R_w)$ is equal to the expected rate of depreciation of the dollar. **Covered interest-rate parity** predicts that the interest-rate differential is equal to the percentage difference between the forward or future and current exchange rates. Covered interest-rate parity holds almost exactly, while interest-rate parity holds only approximately.

Self-Test

Fill in the Blank

1. Net exports are _____ minus _____.
2. Exchange rates are _____ when they are determined by market forces.
3. When the United States runs a trade deficit, the amount we borrow from abroad is the _____.
4. The nominal exchange rate adjusted for changes in purchasing power between the United States and the ROW is the _____.
5. The theory that the real exchange rate is constant is called _____.
6. The net export function says that net exports depend negatively on _____ and _____.
7. The coefficient that describes how much imports rise when income rises is the _____.
8. The difference between United States and ROW interest rates is called the _____.
9. Interest-rate parity suggests that the interest-rate differential is equal to the _____.
10. The reduction in the size of the multiplier because net exports depend negatively on income is called _____.
11. Protectionist measures include _____, _____, and _____ on imports.
12. The Fed can limit exchange-rate fluctuations by using monetary policy to _____ the exchange rate.

True-False

13. Appreciation of the dollar occurs when the exchange rate rises.
14. Since the exchange rate is flexible, the United States is powerless to affect it.
15. The theory of purchasing power parity says that the nominal exchange rate is constant.
16. Movements in nominal and real exchange rates are unrelated.
17. When domestic income rises, net exports fall.
18. When the real exchange rate appreciates, net exports fall.
19. The exchange rate and interest rate are negatively correlated.
20. The open-economy LM curve is steeper than what the LM curve would be in a closed economy.
21. For an open economy, monetary policy is not neutral in the long run because increases in the money supply depreciate the exchange rate.
22. Changes in the exchange rate have an immediate impact on the U.S. price level.
23. Protectionist measures appreciate the exchange rate.
24. The Fed can stabilize the exchange rate and allow interest rates to fluctuate.

Review Questions

25. Why is the open-economy multiplier smaller than the closed-economy multiplier?
26. Compare the slope of the open-economy IS curve to what the IS curve would be in a closed economy.
27. What are the short- and long-run effects of a decrease in government spending?
28. What are the short- and long-run effects of a decrease in the money supply?
29. What is the relation between the government budget deficit and capital inflow from abroad?
30. Why does the exchange rate appreciate when the interest rate rises?
31. Briefly describe today's international monetary system.

32. Why do changes in the exchange rate have different impacts on the price level of the United States than they do for a small country?

33. Why do protectionist measures help domestic producers but hurt consumers?

34. Why does exchange-rate stabilization increase fluctuations of GNP in response to spending disturbances?

35. Why can't monetary policy be used both to stabilize the exchange rate and to stabilize prices?

36. Explain the difference between interest-rate parity and covered interest-rate parity.

Problem Set

Worked Problems

1. Consider the following macroeconomic model:

Y	$= C + I + G + X$	(Income identity)
C	$= 100 + .8Y_d$	(Consumption)
I	$= 300 - 1{,}000R$	(Investment)
X	$= 195 - .1Y - 100(EP/P_w)$	(Net exports)
EP/P_w	$= .75 + 5R$	(Real exchange rate)
M	$= (.8Y - 2{,}000R)P$	(Money demand)

    with government spending $G = \$200$ billion, the tax rate $t = .25$, and the money supply $M = \$800$ billion. The U.S. price level P is predetermined at 1 and the ROW price level P_w is always equal to 1.

    a. What are the IS curve, the LM curve, and values of Y, R, and E predicted by this model?

    b. Derive the aggregate demand curve. Calculate the effect of an increase in government spending of $50 billion on Y, R, and E.

    a. *The IS curve is derived by substituting the values for C, I, G, and X into the income identity:*

    $$Y = 1{,}440 - 3{,}000R.$$

    The LM curve is derived by equating money supply and demand:

    $$Y = 1{,}000 + 2{,}500R.$$

    Values for Y and R are found from the IS and LM curves:

$Y = \$1,200$ billion, $R = .08$ (8 percent).

With $P = P_W = 1$, $E = EP/P_W = .75 + 5(.08) = 1.15$.

b. *The aggregate demand curve is calculated as in Chapter 7. From the LM curve,*

$$Y = 1.25(M/P) + 2,500R.$$

From the condition for spending balance,

$$2,500R = 867 - .83Y + 1.67G.$$

Substituting the spending balance condition into the LM curve, we derive the aggregate demand curve:

$$Y = .68(M/P) + 474 + .91G.$$

If G increases by $50 billion to $250 billion,

$$Y = 474 + .68(800) + .91(250) = \$1,246 \text{ billion}.$$

The interest rate can be calculated from the LM curve:

$$R = [Y - 1.25(M/P)]/2,500$$
$$= [1,246 - 1.25(800)]/2,500 = .098 \text{ (9.8 percent)}.$$

With $P = P_W = 1$, $E = 1.24$.

2. Assume that prices in Problem 1 adjust according to the price-adjustment equation

$$\pi = .5(Y_{-1} - Y^*)/Y^*,$$

where π is the rate of inflation and potential output Y^* is equal to $1,200 billion. As in Problem 1, increase government spending by $50 billion starting from potential GNP. Calculate the paths of inflation, the price level, output, the interest rate, and the real and nominal exchange rates for 4 years. Describe the economy after prices have fully adjusted.

The technique for calculating π, P, and Y is described in Problem 2 of Chapter 8. Once Y is determined, R can be found from either the IS or LM curve. Knowing R, the real exchange rate can be calculated. The nominal exchange rate E (with $P_W = 1$) is equal to the real exchange rate divided by P.

Year	π	P	Y	R	EP/P_W	E
0	.000	1.00	$1,200	.080	1.15	1.15
1	.000	1.00	1,246	.098	1.24	1.24
2	.019	1.02	1,235	.102	1.26	1.24
3	.015	1.04	1,224	.103	1.27	1.23
4	.012	1.04	1,224	.105	1.28	1.23

FOREIGN TRADE AND THE EXCHANGE RATE

Once prices adjust fully, output will return to its original level. The real interest rate and the real exchange rate will both be higher. The nominal exchange rate will also appreciate, but not as much as the real exchange rate.

Review Problems

3. Consider the following macroeconomic model:

Y	$= C + I + G + X$	(Income identity)
C	$= 300 + .75 Y_d$	(Consumption)
I	$= 300 - 2{,}000R$	(Investment)
X	$= 500 - .2Y - 200(EP/P_w)$	(Net exports)
EP/P_w	$= .5 + 5R$	(Real exchange rate)
M	$= (.5Y - 2{,}000R)P$	(Money demand)

   with government spending $G = \$200$, the tax rate $t = .2$, and the money supply $M = \$550$. The U.S. price level P is predetermined at 1 and the ROW price level P_w is always equal to 1.

   a. What are the IS curve, the LM curve, and values of Y, R, and E predicted by this model?

   b. Derive the aggregate demand curve. Calculate the effect of an increase in the money supply of $100 on Y, R, and E.

4. Assume that prices in Problem 3 adjust according to the price-adjustment equation

   $$\pi = (Y_{-1} - Y^*)/Y^*,$$

   where π is the rate of inflation and potential output Y^* is equal to $1,500. As in Problem 3, increase the money supply by $100 starting from potential GNP. Calculate the paths of inflation, the price level, output, the interest rate, and the real and nominal exchange rates for 4 years. Describe the economy after prices have fully adjusted.

5. Consider the following macroeconomic model:

Y	$= C + I + G + X$	(Income identity)
C	$= 400 + .8Y_d$	(Consumption)
I	$= 400 - 3{,}000R$	(Investment)
X	$= 114 - .2Y - 40(EP/P_w)$	(Net exports)
EP/P_w	$= .75 + 5R$	(Real exchange rate)
M	$= (.4Y - 1{,}000R)P$	(Money demand)

   with government spending $G = \$100$, the tax rate $t = .5$, and the money supply $M = \$180$. The U.S. price level P is predetermined at 1 and the ROW price level P_w is always equal to 1.

a. What are the IS curve, the LM curve, and values of Y, R, and E predicted by this model?

b. Derive the aggregate demand curve and calculate the effect of increases in government spending and the money supply of $20 on Y, R, and E.

6. Assume that prices in Problem 5 adjust according to the price-adjustment equation

$$\pi = (Y_{-1} - Y^*)/Y^*,$$

where π is the rate of inflation and potential output Y^* is equal to $750. As in Problem 5, increase the money supply and government spending by $20 starting from potential GNP. Calculate the paths of inflation, the price level, output, the interest rate, and the real and nominal exchange rates for 4 years. Describe the economy after prices have fully adjusted.

Answers to the Self-Test

1. Exports minus imports
2. Floating or flexible
3. Capital inflow
4. Real exchange rate
5. Purchasing power parity
6. Real income and the real exchange rate
7. Marginal propensity to import
8. Interest-rate differential
9. Expected rate of depreciation
10. Leakage
11. Tariffs, quotas, and bans
12. Stabilize
13. True. When the exchange rate rises, one dollar can buy more foreign currency.
14. False. U.S. monetary and fiscal policies have powerful effects on the exchange rate.
15. False. Purchasing power parity says that the real exchange rate is constant, not that the nominal exchange rate is constant.
16. False. Nominal and real exchange rates move closely together in the short run.
17. True. Higher domestic income increases imports, causing net exports to fall.
18. True. Real exchange rate appreciation increases the relative price of domestic goods, causing net exports to fall.

19. False. They move together, or are positively correlated.
20. False. The closed- and open-economy LM curves are identical.
21. False. It is the real, not the nominal, exchange rate that matters for the neutrality of money. Increases in the money supply do not change the long-run real exchange rate.
22. False. Importers tend to keep the dollar price of their goods stable in the short run.
23. True. Protection shifts the IS curve outward, raising interest rates and appreciating the exchange rate.
24. False. In order to stabilize the exchange rate, the Fed holds interest rates constant.
25. The open-economy multiplier is smaller than the closed-economy multiplier because imports are negatively related to income.
26. We do not know which IS curve is steeper. The open-economy IS curve is steeper because the multiplier is smaller, but it is flatter because net exports depend negatively on the interest rate.
27. In the short run, a decrease in government spending lowers interest rates, depreciates the exchange rate, causes a trade surplus, and lowers output. In the long run, prices fall, output returns to potential, and the real exchange rate and interest rate are lower.
28. In the short run, a decrease in the money supply raises interest rates, appreciates the exchange rate, and lowers output. In the long run, prices fall, output returns to potential, the nominal interest rate appreciates by the amount that prices fall, and the real exchange rate is unchanged.
29. The government budget deficit is partially financed by borrowing abroad, causing a capital inflow.
30. When the interest rate rises, domestic assets become more attractive and the exchange rate appreciates.
31. Today's international monetary system is a floating or flexible exchange-rate system.
32. Exchange-rate changes immediately affect the price level for a small country by changing the price of imports. The United States is insulated from these price changes in the short run because importers keep the dollar price of their goods stable.
33. Protectionist measures help domestic producers by reducing foreign competition but hurt consumers by raising the prices of imports.
34. The Fed stabilizes the exchange rate by keeping the interest rate constant. This makes the LM curve flat, increasing fluctuations of GNP when spending disturbances shift the IS curve.
35. Both price and exchange-rate stabilization require the Fed to set the money supply, and it can only be set at one level at a time.
36. Interest-rate parity means that the interest-rate differential equals the expected rate of depreciation. Covered interest-rate parity means that the interest-rate differential equals the difference between the forward and current exchange rates.

Solutions to Review Problems

3. a. The IS curve is $Y = 2,000 - 5,000R$. The LM curve is $Y = 1,100 + 4,000R$. $Y = 1,500$, $R = .10$, and $E = 1.0$.
   b. The aggregate demand curve is $Y = 1.11(M/P) + 741 + .74G$. If M increases by $100 to $650, $Y = $1,611$, $R = .078$, and $E = .89$.

4.

Year	π	P	Y	R	EP/P_W	E
0	.000	1.00	$1,500	.100	1.00	1.00
1	.000	1.00	1,611	.078	.89	.89
2	.074	1.07	1,563	.087	.94	.88
3	.042	1.11	1,536	.091	.97	.86
4	.024	1.14	1,524	.096	.98	.86

Once prices fully adjust, output will return to its original level. The nominal exchange rate will depreciate by the same percentage that prices increase. The real interest rate and the real exchange rate will both be unchanged.

5. a. The IS curve is $Y = 1,230 - 4,000R$. The LM curve is $Y = 450 + 2,500R$. $Y = 750$, $R = .12$, and $E = 1.35$.
   b. The aggregate demand curve is $Y = 1.54(M/P) + 425 + .48G$. If M and G increase by $20, $Y = 791, $R = .116$, and $E = 1.33$.

6.

Year	π	P	Y	R	EP/P_W	E
0	.000	1.00	$750	.120	1.35	1.35
1	.000	1.00	791	.116	1.33	1.33
2	.054	1.05	775	.120	1.35	1.29
3	.034	1.09	767	.123	1.37	1.26
4	.022	1.11	759	.123	1.37	1.23

Once prices fully adjust, output will return to its original level. The real interest rate and the real exchange rate will both be slightly higher because of the increase in government spending. The nominal exchange rate will depreciate because it is more affected by the increase in the money supply than by the increase in government spending.

CHAPTER 13 The Government's Budget Deficit and Aggregate Demand

Main Objectives

The record-setting U.S. government budget deficit of the 1980s focused attention on the government's influence on the economy. We have already glimpsed the government's influence on aggregate demand: It purchases goods and services, it makes transfer payments such as social security and unemployment compensation, and it taxes personal and business income. Until now, we have treated the government as exogenous—not explained by our model. Chapter 13 looks closely at each of these influences and ties them into the model. You should learn how the government reacts to economic fluctuations and how these reactions influence economic policy. You should also understand the relation between deficits, consumption, and interest rates.

Key Terms and Concepts

The **government budget** is a summary of the government's yearly spending plans. It consists of both **outlays**, purchases of goods and services and transfer payments, and **receipts**, taxes and other revenue. The government budget includes both the federal budget and state and local government budgets.

Automatic stabilizers are government transfer programs that respond to the state of the economy. These include social security, unemployment insurance, food stamps, welfare, and Medicaid. In a recession, with low income and high unemployment, transfer payments from these programs automatically increase.

Tax receipts also rise and fall with economic fluctuations. The **elasticity of real tax receipts** with respect to real GNP is greater than 1. For every 1 percent change in real GNP, tax receipts change by more than 1 percent. The most important reason the elasticity is greater than 1 is that the income tax system is progressive—tax rates rise and fall with income. **Discretionary** changes in tax rates during recessions, such as the tax cuts of the early 1960s and early 1980s, also contribute to the high elasticity of real tax receipts.

The **budget deficit** is the difference between outlays and receipts. It is equal to government **purchases** plus **transfers** plus **interest on the government debt** minus **taxes**. The **structural** or **full-employment deficit** is the one that would occur, given the current fiscal policies, if the economy were at full employment. The **cyclical deficit** is the difference between the actual deficit and the structural deficit. It measures the impact of the current state of the economy on the deficit.

The relation between the deficit and interest rates is one of the most important issues regarding the government's role in affecting aggregate demand. Over the past 35 years, the empirical evidence suggests that the relation between deficits and high real interest rates is relatively weak. The period 1982–89 seems to be an exception, as both real interest rates and the budget deficit reached all-time highs.

Government debt at the start of next year equals debt at the start of this year plus this year's deficit (or minus the surplus). This relationship is called the **intertemporal government budget constraint**:

$$D_{t+1} = D_t + G_t + F_t + RD_t - T_t, \qquad (13\text{–}1)$$

where D is government debt, G is purchases, F is transfers, R is the interest rate (so RD is interest payments on the debt), and T is taxes. The government budget is balanced when the stock of government debt is not growing.

With high federal budget deficits throughout the 1980s, the economic significance of the national debt has become a topic of great concern. According to standard analysis, deficit spending raises consumption, causing interest rates to rise and investment to fall. Debt displaces productive capital in portfolios, creating a **burden of the national debt**.

An alternative analysis, however, combines the forward-looking theory of consumption with the intertemporal government budget constraint to argue that there is no burden of the debt. When the government lowers taxes in order to raise disposable income, it must borrow. Eventually, this borrowing must be paid back through tax increases. If families are rational and very forward looking, they will anticipate these tax increases and not change their consumption.

If consumption does not change, there is no reason for interest rates or investment to change. The proposition that government budget deficits will not affect consumption, and therefore do not affect interest rates, is called **Ricardian equivalence**, after the nineteenth-century British economist David Ricardo. Even if these tax increases will not occur until

GOVERNMENT BUDGET DEFICIT AND AGGREGATE DEMAND

the next generation, it has been argued by Robert Barro of Harvard University that consumption will not increase because the family should be viewed as a dynasty in which future generations are as important as the current generation. While these ideas are by no means universally accepted, there is no strong consensus among macroeconomists regarding the magnitude of the burden of the debt.

Another problem in evaluating the significance of the debt is that it is not even clear how the deficit should be measured. Some economists argue that traditional techniques, which treat all government purchases as consumption, overstate the magnitude of the deficit. A different issue is that, while the debt is usually stated in nominal terms, it can also be measured in real terms. The **real deficit** is the change in the real debt.

Fiscal policy shifts the IS curve directly through government purchases, and indirectly through the effect of taxes and transfers on consumption. The experience of the last 35 years is that government purchases rarely offset fluctuations in aggregate demand, leading to the conclusion that government purchases should be thought of as a disturbance, rather than as an instrument to control aggregate demand. The magnitude of the effect of tax cuts, both because of uncertainty about whether the cut will be permanent or temporary and because of the possibility that people increase saving in anticipation of future tax increases, is highly uncertain.

Government reaction functions are descriptions of the systematic response of fiscal policy to economic fluctuations. They are examples of **policy rules**, discussed in Chapter 9. For instance, we have seen that transfer payments rise and fall in relation to the departures of output from potential GNP. An algebraic government reaction function for transfer payments might be

$$F = 350 - .25(Y - Y^*), \tag{13-2}$$

where F is transfer payments, Y is GNP, and Y^* is potential GNP. Transfer payments are automatic stabilizers because, when income rises above potential, transfer payments automatically fall. This reduces the multiplier and makes the IS curve steeper.

Self-Test

Fill in the Blank

1. Federal government purchases of goods and services and transfers are called _____ .

2. Most federal government purchases of goods and services are for _____.

3. The largest single purchase item for state and local governments is _____.

4. Government transfer programs that respond to the state of the economy are _____.

5. The elasticity of changes in real tax receipts with respect to changes in real GNP is _____ 1.

6. The government budget deficit is the difference between government _____ and _____.

7. The _____ or _____ deficit is the deficit that would occur if the economy were at potential GNP.

8. The _____ deficit is the difference between the actual deficit and the structural deficit.

9. The relation between the deficit and the accumulation of debt is the _____.

10. The change in the real debt is the _____.

11. The proposition that government budget deficits do not affect consumption is called _____.

12. _____ are descriptions of the systematic response of fiscal policy to economic fluctuations.

True-False

13. Most federal government outlays are purchases of goods and services.

14. The federal and state and local governments raise revenue from similar sources.

15. Like the federal government, state and local governments usually run deficits.

16. Programs to increase federal purchases of goods and services have been a major force toward ending recessions.
17. Automatic stabilizers help mitigate recessions.
18. Tax receipts fluctuate more than real GNP.
19. There has been a strong empirical relation between deficits and high real interest rates during the past 35 years.
20. During the past few years, it seems that the relation between deficits and high real interest rates has gotten stronger.
21. The intertemporal budget constraint says that the government budget must be balanced each year.
22. Automatic stabilizers make the IS curve steeper.
23. If tax cuts do not affect consumption, they will not affect interest rates.
24. Ricardian equivalence is the only explanation for tax cuts not affecting consumption.

Review Questions

25. What are the government transfer programs that constitute automatic stabilizers?
26. How can deficit spending create a burden of the national debt?
27. Aside from automatic stabilizers, how are taxes lowered during recessions?
28. Why do deficits increase during recessions?
29. What is the difference between structural and cyclical deficits?
30. What is the intertemporal government budget constraint?
31. If families are very forward looking, why might a tax cut not affect consumption at all?
32. How can fiscal policy shift the IS curve?
33. Why are transfer payments automatic stabilizers?
34. How do automatic stabilizers affect the slope of the IS curve?
35. What is Ricardian equivalence?
36. Why should government purchases be thought of as disturbances to aggregate demand?

Problem Set

Worked Problems

1. Suppose that federal government purchases $G = \$500$ billion, taxes $T = .4Y$, and transfers $F = .2Y$, with the price level $P = 1$. The federal debt D is $\$1,000$ billion with the interest rate $R = .1$ (10 percent).

   a. If real output $Y = \$2,000$ billion, what is the deficit?

   b. Calculate the structural deficit if potential output $Y^* = \$2,500$ billion.

   c. What is the cyclical deficit in Part b?

   a. The deficit $= G + F + RD - T$
   $= G + .2Y + .1(1,000) - .4Y$
   $= 500 + 400 + 100 - 800$
   $= \$200$ billion.

   b. The structural deficit $= G + .2Y^* + .1(1,000) - .4Y^*$
   $= 500 + 500 + 100 - 1,000$
   $= \$100$ billion.

   c. The cyclical deficit $=$ Actual deficit $-$ Structural deficit
   $= 200 - 100 = \$100$ billion.

2. Suppose that transfer payments are given by

   $F = 180 - .2(Y - Y^*)$

   with potential output $Y^* = \$1,600$ billion. Add this reaction function to the IS-LM model given by Problem 1 of Chapter 7:

$Y = C + I + G + X$	(Income identity)
$C = 100 + .9Y_d$	(Consumption)
$I = 200 - 500R$	(Investment)
$X = 100 - .12Y - 500R$	(Net exports)
$M = (.8Y - 200R)P$	(Money demand)

   with government spending $G = \$200$ billion, the tax rate $t = .2$, the nominal money supply $M = \$800$ billion, and the predetermined price level $P = 1$.

   a. What is the IS curve? Compare it with the IS curve in Problem 1 of Chapter 7.

   b. Derive the aggregate demand curve and calculate the effect of increases in government spending or real money on GNP. Compare your answer with Problem 2 of Chapter 7.

GOVERNMENT BUDGET DEFICIT AND AGGREGATE DEMAND

a. As in Chapter 7, the IS curve is derived by substituting consumption, investment, net exports, and government spending into the income identity. It is important to remember that disposable income Y_d = income Y + transfers F − taxes T.

$$Y = 100 + .9[Y + 180 - .2(Y - 1{,}600) - .2Y] + 200 - 500R$$
$$+ 200 + 100 - .12Y - 500R$$
$$= 1{,}050 + .42Y - 1{,}000R$$
$$= 1{,}810 - 1{,}724R.$$

It is steeper than the IS curve in Chapter 7 because the multiplier is smaller.

b. The aggregate demand curve is calculated as in Chapter 7. From the LM curve,

$$Y = 1.25(M/P) + 2{,}500R.$$

From the condition for spending balance,

$$2{,}500R = 2{,}125 - 1.45Y + 2.5G.$$

Substituting the spending balance condition into the LM curve, we derive the aggregate demand curve,

$$Y = .51(M/P) + 867 + 1.02G.$$

Both monetary and fiscal policies are less effective than in Chapter 7 because the automatic stabilizers decrease the multiplier.

Review Problems

3. Suppose that federal government purchases $G = \$200$, taxes $T = .3Y$, and transfers $F = .1Y$, with the price level $P = 1$. The federal debt D is $750 with the interest rate $R = .08$ (8 percent).

   a. If real output $Y = \$1{,}000$, what is the deficit?

   b. Calculate the structural deficit if potential output $Y^* = \$1{,}300$.

   c. What is the cyclical deficit in Part b?

4. Suppose that federal government purchases $G = \$400$, taxes $T = .4Y$, and transfers $F = .1Y$, with the price level $P = 1$. The federal debt D is $1,000 with the interest rate $R = .12$ (12 percent).

   a. If real output $Y = \$1{,}500$ billion, what is the deficit?

   b. Calculate the structural deficit if potential output $Y^* = \$2{,}000$.

   c. What is the cyclical deficit in Part b?

5. Suppose that transfer payments are given by
$$F = 200 - .2(Y - Y^*)$$
with potential output $Y^* = \$1,000$. Add this reaction function to the IS-LM model given by Problem 3 of Chapter 7:

$$
\begin{aligned}
Y &= C + I + G + X & \text{(Income identity)} \\
C &= 300 + .8Y_d & \text{(Consumption)} \\
I &= 200 - 1{,}500R & \text{(Investment)} \\
X &= 100 - .04Y - 500R & \text{(Net exports)} \\
M &= (.5Y - 2{,}000R)P & \text{(Money demand)}
\end{aligned}
$$

with government spending $G = \$200$, the tax rate $t = .2$, the nominal money supply $M = \$550$, and the predetermined price level $P = 1$.

a. What is the IS curve? Compare it with the IS curve in Problem 3 of Chapter 7.

b. Derive the aggregate demand curve and calculate the effect of increases in government spending or real money on GNP. Compare your answer with Problem 4 of Chapter 7.

6. Suppose that transfer payments are given by
$$F = 120 - .1(Y - Y^*)$$
with potential output $Y^* = \$800$. Add this reaction function to the IS-LM model given by Problem 5 of Chapter 7:

$$
\begin{aligned}
Y &= C + I + G + X & \text{(Income identity)} \\
C &= 400 + .9Y_d & \text{(Consumption)} \\
I &= 300 - 2{,}000R & \text{(Investment)} \\
X &= 100 - .05Y - 1{,}000R & \text{(Net exports)} \\
M &= (.4Y - 1{,}000R)P & \text{(Money demand)}
\end{aligned}
$$

with government spending $G = \$100$, the tax rate $t = .5$, the nominal money supply $M = \$180$, and the predetermined price level $P = 1$.

a. What is the IS curve? Compare it with the IS curve in Problem 5 of Chapter 7.

b. Derive the aggregate demand curve and calculate the effect of increases in government spending or real money on GNP. Compare your answer with Problem 6 of Chapter 7.

7. Suppose that transfer payments are given by
$$F = 300 - .3333(Y - Y^*)$$
with potential output $Y^* = \$2,100$. Add this reaction function to the IS-LM model given by Problem 7 of Chapter 7:

$$Y = C + I + G + X \quad \text{(Income identity)}$$
$$C = 400 + .9Y_d \quad \text{(Consumption)}$$
$$I = 200 - 1{,}800R \quad \text{(Investment)}$$
$$X = 200 - .1Y - 200R \quad \text{(Net exports)}$$
$$M = (.8Y - 3{,}000R)P \quad \text{(Money demand)}$$

with government spending $G = \$200$, the tax rate $t = .3333$, the nominal money supply $M = \$1{,}104$, and the predetermined price level $P = 1$.

a. What is the IS curve? Compare it with the IS curve in Problem 7 of Chapter 7.

b. Derive the aggregate demand curve and calculate the effect of increases in government spending or real money on GNP. Compare your answer with Problem 8 of Chapter 7.

Answers to the Self-Test

1. Outlays
2. National defense
3. Education
4. Automatic stabilizers
5. Greater than
6. Outlays and receipts
7. Structural or full-employment
8. Cyclical
9. Intertemporal budget constraint
10. Real deficit
11. Ricardian equivalence
12. Government reaction functions
13. False. Transfer payments exceed government purchases.
14. False. The federal government raises almost all of its revenue from income and social security taxes. About 40 percent of state and local government receipts comes from property and sales taxes.
15. False. State and local governments usually run surpluses.
16. False. Because these spending programs have been small with long lags, they have not significantly contributed toward ending recessions.
17. True. By quickly raising disposable income, automatic stabilizers increase aggregate demand and help mitigate recessions.
18. True. Tax receipts fluctuate more than real income because tax rates rise with income.
19. False. The empirical relation between deficits and real interest rates is weak.
20. True. Both real interest rates and the budget deficit reached all-time highs during the 1982–89 period.

21. False. The intertemporal budget constraint describes the evolution of government debt over time. It does not require that the budget be balanced in any single year.
22. True. Automatic stabilizers lower the marginal propensity to consume, lower the multiplier, and make the IS curve steeper.
23. True. If consumption is unaffected, the IS curve will not shift and interest rates will not change.
24. False. Consumers may not react to tax cuts because of uncertainty regarding whether they are temporary or permanent.
25. Automatic stabilizers are social security, unemployment insurance, food stamps, welfare, and Medicaid.
26. If deficit spending lowers investment, debt replaces productive capital in portfolios, creating a burden of the national debt.
27. Discretionary changes in taxes, such as the 1964 and 1981 tax cuts, have lowered taxes during recessions.
28. Government outlays rise during recessions because of automatic stabilizers and receipts fall because of the progressive tax system, causing budget deficits.
29. The structural deficit is the deficit that would occur at potential GNP. The cyclical deficit is the difference between the actual deficit and the structural deficit.
30. The intertemporal budget constraint says that the change in the government debt is equal to the deficit.
31. Very forward-looking families, using the government intertemporal budget constraint, will anticipate future tax increases and not change their consumption.
32. Government purchases shift the IS curve directly and policies on taxes and transfers shift the IS curve through the consumption function.
33. Transfer payments are automatic stabilizers because they fall when income rises above potential.
34. Automatic stabilizers operating through taxes and transfers reduce the marginal propensity to consume, reduce the multiplier, and make the IS curve steeper.
35. Ricardian equivalence is the proposition that government budget deficits will not affect consumption.
36. Government purchases should be thought of as disturbances to aggregate demand because, historically, they have rarely been timed to offset fluctuations in aggregate demand.

Solutions to Review Problems

3. a. The deficit = 200 + 100 + 60 − 300 = $60.
   b. The structural deficit = 200 + 130 + 60 − 390 = 0.
   c. The cyclical deficit = $60.
4. a. The deficit = $70.
   b. The structural deficit = −$80 (surplus of $80).
   c. The cyclical deficit = $150.

5. a. The IS curve is $Y = 2{,}000 - 3{,}571R$. It is steeper than the IS curve in Chapter 7.
   b. The aggregate demand curve is $Y = .99(M/P) + 911 + .99G$. Both monetary and fiscal policy are less effective than in Chapter 7 because the multiplier is smaller.
6. a. The IS curve is $Y = 1{,}565 - 4{,}348R$. It is steeper than the IS curve in Chapter 7.
   b. The aggregate demand curve is $Y = 1.59(M/P) + 519 + .53G$. Both monetary and fiscal policy are less effective than in Chapter 7 because the multiplier is smaller.
7. a. The IS curve is $Y = 2{,}375 - 2{,}500R$. It is steeper than the IS curve in Chapter 7.
   b. The aggregate demand curve is $Y = .5(M/P) + 1{,}275 + .75G$. Both monetary and fiscal policy are less effective than in Chapter 7 because the multiplier is smaller.

CHAPTER 14 The Monetary System

Main Objectives

In the basic model presented in Chapters 7 and 8, we saw how changes in the money supply and shocks to money demand play a central role in economic fluctuations. Now in Chapter 14 we examine these factors more closely, and focus on the Federal Reserve System, a powerful force in macroeconomic policy-making. We look at the selection of policy rules available to the Fed, and see how the Fed's choice among these rules influences the effectiveness of both monetary and fiscal policy. After reading the chapter, you should know what the Fed can and cannot do.

Key Terms and Concepts

The **monetary system** specifies how people pay each other when they conduct transactions (the means of payment) and the meaning of the prices put on goods (the unit of account). Although these are conceptually two separate functions, the dollar performs both in the United States.

The **money supply** consists of **currency**, the government's paper money and coins, plus **deposits** that individuals and firms hold at banks. The **monetary base** is currency plus **reserves** that banks hold at the Fed. The monetary base is also called **high-powered money**.

The Fed changes the money supply through **open-market operations**, purchases or sales of government bonds from the public with money. The money supply is increased by an open-market purchase and decreased by an open-market sale. The Fed directly controls the monetary base. The money supply is also influenced by the **reserve ratio** (r), the percentage of checking deposits that banks are required to hold on reserve at the Fed, and the **currency deposit ratio** (c), the amount of currency people hold as a ratio of their checking deposits.

The relation between the monetary base (M_B) and the money supply (M) is given by

$$M = mM_B, \qquad (14\text{--}1)$$

where $m = (1 + c)/(r + c)$ is the **monetary base multiplier**. Because the reserve ratio r is less than 1, the monetary base multiplier, which measures how much the money supply changes as a result of an open-market operation, is greater than 1.

Banks, in their intermediation role, receive deposits from and make loans to the private sector. **Required reserves** are the amount, currently 12 percent, of their deposits that banks have to hold. **Excess reserves** are banks' actual reserves minus required reserves. The Fed can lend reserves to banks, and this lending, by increasing the amount of reserves held by banks, increases the monetary base just as an open-market operation does. The **discount rate** is the interest rate on these borrowings.

The **Federal Open Market Committee (FOMC)** makes decisions about monetary policy. It gives specific instructions to the trading desk at the New York Fed about how to conduct week-by-week policy. These instructions usually tell the trading desk to buy and sell government securities to keep the interest rate at values consistent with targets for real GNP growth, inflation, and the rate of growth of monetary aggregates such as M_2. For example, the FOMC will raise the interest rate if inflation threatens to rise and lower the interest rate if lower than normal GNP growth threatens a recession.

The **government budget identity** says that government spending (G) plus transfers (F) plus interest on the government debt (RD) minus taxes (T) equals the change in the monetary base (ΔM_B) plus the change in bonds (ΔB):

$$G + F + RD - T = \Delta M_B + \Delta B. \qquad (14\text{--}2)$$

We can use the government budget identity to be more precise in our definitions of monetary and fiscal policy. Fiscal policy is bond-financed changes in government spending, transfers, and taxes. Suppose government spending is increased. The monetary base and money supply remain unchanged ($\Delta M_B = 0$) while $\Delta G = \Delta B$. Monetary policy is an increase in the monetary base matched by a decrease in government bonds ($\Delta M_B = -\Delta B$). The government budget deficit, $G + F - T$, remains unchanged.

The demand for money, as we saw in Chapter 7, depends positively on income and negatively on interest rates. One classification of the demand for money, originated by Keynes, distinguishes among three motives: the **transactions motive**, or the desire to hold money to facilitate day-to-day transactions; the **precautionary motive**, or the desire to hold money in case of unexpected expense; and the **speculative motive**, or the desire to hold money because of an expected decrease in the future price of bonds. **Liquidity preference** summarizes the fact that money, as the most liquid of all assets, can be sold readily if the need arises.

The transactions demand for money can be analyzed by using inventory theory. The **square-root rule** says that the value of average money holdings M that minimizes the total costs of holding money is given by

$$M = \sqrt{kW/2R_o}, \qquad (14\text{--}3)$$

where k is the cost of making each transaction, W is income for the period, and R_o is the opportunity cost of holding money rather than another asset.

The demand for money as a store of wealth encompasses the precautionary and speculative demands. Money is riskless but pays relatively low interest, while bonds are risky but have a higher expected return. In general, people who are averse to risk hold a diversified portfolio and balance their wealth between money and bonds.

An additional motive for holding checking account balances is to pay for banking services. Service charges on most checking accounts can be eliminated by keeping a high enough balance. When you do this, the return on your wealth is paid in services rather than in cash.

Combing all of the motives for holding money, the **demand for currency** depends negatively on the interest rate and positively on income and the price level. The **demand for checking deposits** depends negatively on the difference between the market interest rate and the rate on checking deposits, and positively on income and the price level.

The **velocity** of money is defined as the ratio of nominal GNP to the money stock. It is a measure of the number of final goods transactions performed by the money stock during the year. Velocity is inversely related to money demand.

We have seen how the Fed, using open-market operations, can change the level of the monetary base. In conducting monetary policy, the Fed must choose among a set of targets:

Target the Money Supply (M_1). The Fed sets the monetary base to keep the money supply at a specified level. This produces the upward-sloping LM curve discussed in Chapter 7. Expansionary fiscal policy, as we have seen earlier, increases income and increases interest rates. If banks held only required reserves and the currency deposit ratio did not depend on the interest rate, so that the monetary base multiplier was constant, the money supply could be targeted exactly. Since the monetary base multiplier is not constant, the money supply can be targeted only approximately.

Target the Interest Rate. The Fed varies the monetary base, by conducting daily open-market operations, to keep the interest rate constant. The LM curve is a horizontal line at the prescribed interest

THE MONETARY SYSTEM

rate. Expansionary fiscal policy raises income without raising interest rates in the short run. There is no crowding out. Monetary policy that keeps interest rates constant when fiscal policy changes is called accommodative.

Target the Level of GNP. The Fed increases or decreases the monetary base to keep GNP constant. The LM curve is a vertical line at the prescribed level of GNP. Expansionary fiscal policy raises the interest rate without changing GNP. There is complete crowding out. Because GNP is observed with a lag, targeting GNP is more difficult to implement than targeting the money supply or the interest rate.

Shocks to the IS and LM curves also influence the Fed's choice among policy rules. Suppose, for example, that investment demand is erratic, causing the IS curve to shift a lot. Then the best policy for the Fed is to keep the LM curve steep through money supply or GNP targets. This mitigates the effect on GNP of the fluctuating IS curve. If, on the other hand, erratic money demand causes the LM curve to shift repeatedly, the best policy for the Fed is to keep the LM curve flat through interest-rate targets. By changing the money supply in response to fluctuating money demand, the effect on GNP can be minimized. One reason that the Fed has placed more emphasis in recent years on interest-rate targets than on money-supply targets is that shocks to the LM curve have become more serious.

Lags in the effect of monetary policy greatly complicate the Fed's choices among various policies. These lags are the lag in the investment process and the lag in the response of net exports to dollar depreciation. At first, monetary expansion decreases interest rates without much effect on GNP. The peak effect on GNP takes about one to two years, after investment and net exports respond to the lower interest rates.

Coordination of monetary and fiscal policy can bring any desired combination of changes in GNP and the interest rate in the short run. For example, expansionary monetary and fiscal policy can raise GNP and keep the interest rate constant, while expansionary fiscal and contractionary monetary policy could raise the interest rate and keep GNP constant. The choice of the proper mix of monetary and fiscal policy is also influenced by concern about the international value of the dollar and the current account.

Self-Test

Fill in the Blank

1. A monetary system specifies the _____ and the _____.

2. Banks accept deposits and make loans in their _____ role.
3. The amount of reserves that banks hold above their required reserves is called _____ reserves.
4. The interest rate on borrowing by banks from the Fed is the _____ rate.
5. The _____ makes decisions about monetary policy.
6. According to Keynes, the three motives in people's demands for money are the _____, _____, and _____ motives.
7. A financial asset, such as money, is _____ if it can be sold readily.
8. The ratio of nominal GNP to the money stock is called _____.
9. The money supply is equal to the monetary base times the _____.
10. A monetary policy that keeps interest rates constant when fiscal policy changes is said to _____ the new policy.
11. The monetary base is _____ plus _____.
12. The monetary base is also called _____.

True-False
13. Required reserves account for most banks' holding of reserves.
14. Money is the most liquid of all assets.
15. The opportunity cost of holding currency is the market interest rate.
16. The opportunity cost of holding checking deposits is the market interest rate.
17. If the Fed targets the interest rate, the LM curve will be horizontal.

THE MONETARY SYSTEM

173

18. If the Fed targets GNP, the LM curve will be horizontal.
19. If the Fed targets the interest rate, fiscal policy will be very effective.
20. If the Fed targets the interest rate, shocks to investment will produce large fluctuations in GNP.
21. The peak effect of monetary policy on GNP occurs very quickly.
22. In the short run, GNP cannot be increased without changing the interest rate.
23. The monetary base multiplier is constant.
24. The velocity of money is constant.

Review Questions

25. According to the square-root rule, what are the determinants of people's average money balances?
26. Why, according to Keynes's speculative motive, does the demand for money decrease with the interest rate?
27. What determines the demand for currency?
28. What determines the demand for checking deposits?
29. Describe the three policy rules available to the Fed.
30. Why has the Fed placed more emphasis on interest-rate targets than on money-supply targets in recent years?
31. How does the policy rule adopted by the Fed influence the effectiveness of fiscal policy?
32. If the Fed wishes to minimize the effects of shocks on GNP, what policy rule should it follow?
33. What are the two lags in the effect of monetary policy?
34. Why does concern about the international value of the dollar make decisions regarding the fiscal and monetary policy mix more difficult?
35. What is the government budget identity?
36. How do monetary and fiscal policy differ in their effects on the monetary base?

Problem Set

Worked Problems

1. a. According to the square-root rule, what is the average money balance M if income $W = \$1{,}000$ billion, the cost of making a transaction $k = 4$, and the opportunity cost of holding money $R_o = .05$ (5 percent)?

   b. What happens to the average money balance M if income increases to $\$2{,}000$ billion?

   a. The square-root rule says that the average money balance

   $$M = \sqrt{kW/2R_o}$$
   $$= \sqrt{4(1{,}000)/2(.05)}$$
   $$= \sqrt{40{,}000}$$
   $$= \$200 \text{ billion.}$$

   b. The average money balance

   $$= \sqrt{4(2{,}000)/2(.05)}$$
   $$= \sqrt{80{,}000}$$
   $$= \$283 \text{ billion.}$$

   The average money balance is higher because the demand for money increases when income rises.

2. Suppose that the money supply is given by

   $$M = 800 - .2(Y - Y^*)$$

   with potential output $Y^* = \$1{,}250$ billion. Add this monetary policy rule to the equations in Problem 1 of Chapter 7:

$Y = C + I + G + X$	(Income identity)
$C = 100 + .9Y_d$	(Consumption)
$I = 200 - 500R$	(Investment)
$X = 100 - .12Y - 500R$	(Net exports)
$M = (.8Y - 2{,}000R)P$	(Money demand)

   with government spending $G = \$200$ billion, the tax rate $t = .2$, and the predetermined price level $P = 1$.

a. What is the LM curve? Compare it with the LM curve in Problem 1 of Chapter 7.

b. Derive the aggregate demand curve and calculate the effect of an increase in government spending on GNP. Compare your answer with Problem 2 of Chapter 7.

a. *The LM curve is derived by equating the supply of money with the demand for money:*

$$800 - .2(Y - 1{,}250) = .8Y - 2{,}000R$$
$$Y = 1{,}050 + 2{,}000R.$$

It is steeper than the LM curve of Chapter 7 because of the Fed's "leaning against the wind" policy of decreasing the money supply when output rises above potential.

b. *The LM curve is*

$$Y = 1{,}050 + 2{,}000R.$$

From the condition for spending balance,

$$2{,}000R = 800 - .8Y + 2G.$$

Substituting the spending balance condition into the LM curve, we derive the aggregate demand curve:

$$Y = 1{,}028 + 1.11G.$$

An increase in government spending has less effect on GNP than in Chapter 7 because the LM curve is steeper.

Review Problems

3. a. According to the square-root rule, what is the average money balance M if income $W = \$6{,}000$, the cost of making a transaction $k = 3$, and the opportunity cost of holding money $R_o = .1$ (10 percent)?

   b. What happens to the average money balance M if the opportunity cost of holding money R_o increases to .15?

4. a. According to the square-root rule, what is the average money balance M if income $W = \$2{,}000$, the cost of making a transaction $k = 5$, and the opportunity cost of holding money $R_o = .08$ (8 percent)?

   b. What happens to the average money balance M if the cost of making a transaction k rises to 6?

5. Suppose that the money supply is given by

$$M = 550 - .3(Y - Y^*)$$

with potential output $Y^* = \$1,500$. Add this monetary policy rule to the equations in Problem 3 of Chapter 7:

$$\begin{aligned}
Y &= C + I + G + X & \text{(Income identity)} \\
C &= 300 + .8Y_d & \text{(Consumption)} \\
I &= 200 - 1,500R & \text{(Investment)} \\
X &= 100 - .04Y - 500R & \text{(Net exports)} \\
M &= (.5Y - 2,000R)P & \text{(Money demand)}
\end{aligned}$$

with government spending $G = \$200$, the tax rate $t = .2$, and the predetermined price level $P = 1$.

a. What is the LM curve? Compare it with the LM curve in Problem 3 of Chapter 7.

b. Derive the aggregate demand curve and calculate the effect of an increase in government spending on GNP. Compare your answer with Problem 4 of Chapter 7.

6. Suppose that the money supply is given by

$$M = 180 - .6(Y - Y^*)$$

with potential output $Y^* = \$800$. Add this monetary policy rule to the equations in Problem 5 of Chapter 7:

$$\begin{aligned}
Y &= C + I + G + X & \text{(Income identity)} \\
C &= 400 + .9Y_d & \text{(Consumption)} \\
I &= 300 - 2,000R & \text{(Investment)} \\
X &= 100 - .05Y - 1,000R & \text{(Net exports)} \\
M &= (.4Y - 1,000R)P & \text{(Money demand)}
\end{aligned}$$

with government spending $G = \$100$, the tax rate $t = .5$, and the predetermined price level $P = 1$.

a. What is the LM curve? Compare it with the LM curve in Problem 5 of Chapter 7.

b. Derive the aggregate demand curve and calculate the effect of an increase in government spending on GNP. Compare your answer with Problem 6 of Chapter 7.

7. Suppose that the money supply is given by

$$M = 1,104 - .2(Y - Y^*)$$

with potential output $Y^* = \$1,680$. Add this monetary policy rule to the equations in Problem 7 of Chapter 7:

$$Y = C + I + G + X \quad \text{(Income identity)}$$
$$C = 400 + .9Y_d \quad \text{(Consumption)}$$
$$I = 200 - 1{,}800R \quad \text{(Investment)}$$
$$X = 200 - .1Y - 200R \quad \text{(Net exports)}$$
$$M = (.8Y - 3{,}000R)P \quad \text{(Money demand)}$$

with government spending $G = \$200$, the tax rate $t = .3333$, and the predetermined price level $P = 1$.

a. What is the LM curve? Compare it with the LM curve in Problem 7 of Chapter 7.

b. Derive the aggregate demand curve and calculate the effect of an increase in government spending on GNP. Compare your answer with Problem 8 of Chapter 7.

Answers to the Self-Test

1. Means of payment and unit of account
2. Intermediation
3. Excess
4. Discount
5. Federal Open Market Committee
6. Transactions, precautionary, and speculative
7. Liquid
8. Velocity
9. Monetary base multiplier
10. Accommodate
11. Currency plus reserves
12. High-powered money
13. True. Excess reserves are small.
14. True. It can be sold most readily.
15. True. The market interest rate is the forgone return on currency.
16. False. The opportunity cost of holding checking deposits is the market interest rate minus the interest rate paid on checking deposits minus the avoided service charges.
17. True. A constant interest rate is a horizontal LM curve.
18. False. If the Fed targets GNP, the LM curve will be vertical.
19. True. There would be no crowding out.
20. True. Because the LM curve would be horizontal, shocks to investment would produce large fluctuations in GNP.
21. False. The peak effect of monetary policy on GNP occurs in between one and two years.
22. False. Coordinated expansionary fiscal and monetary policy can increase GNP in the short run without changing the interest rate.
23. False. The monetary base multiplier depends on the reserve ratio and the currency deposit ratio, neither of which is constant.
24. False. Velocity changes when the demand for money changes.

25. The average money balance depends positively on income and the cost of making transactions, and negatively on the opportunity cost of holding money.
26. When interest rates were high people would expect them to fall and bond prices to rise in the future, and would therefore want to hold more bonds and less money.
27. The demand for currency depends negatively on the interest rate and positively on income and the price level.
28. The demand for checking deposits depends negatively on the difference between the market interest rate and the rate on checking deposits, and positively on income and the price level.
29. The Fed can target the level of the money supply, the interest rate, or GNP.
30. Shocks to the LM curve have increased in recent years, making interest-rate targeting, which keeps the LM curve relatively flat, the best policy for reducing fluctuations in GNP.
31. The policy rule adopted by the Fed determines the slope of the LM curve, which influences the effectiveness of fiscal policy.
32. If the IS curve is erratic, say, because of shifts in investment demand, the Fed should maintain a steep LM curve. If the LM curve is erratic, say, because of shifts in money demand, the Fed should maintain a flat LM curve.
33. The two lags in the effect of monetary policy are the response of investment to changes in the interest rate and the response of net exports to changes in the exchange rate.
34. The government can use two instruments, fiscal and monetary policy, to attain two goals, the level of GNP and the interest rate. Concern about the exchange rate adds another goal without adding another instrument, making it likely that all three goals cannot be attained.
35. The government budget identity is that government spending plus transfers plus interest on the government debt minus taxes equals the change in the monetary base plus the change in bonds.
36. Monetary policy increases the monetary base, while fiscal policy leaves it unchanged.

Solutions to Review Problems

3. a. The average money balance $M = \$300$.
   b. $M = \$245$. The demand for money falls when the opportunity cost of holding money rises.
4. a. The average money balance $M = \$250$.
   b. $M = \$274$. The demand for money falls when the cost of making a transaction rises.
5. a. The LM curve is $Y = 1{,}250 + 2{,}500R$. It is steeper than the LM curve in Chapter 7.

THE MONETARY SYSTEM

    b. The aggregate demand curve is $Y = 1{,}333 + .83G$. Because the LM curve is steeper, increases in government spending have less effect on GNP than in Chapter 7.

6. a. The LM curve is $Y = 660 + 1{,}000R$. It is steeper than the LM curve in Chapter 7.
   b. The aggregate demand curve is $Y = 733 + .28G$. Because the LM curve is steeper, increases in government spending have less effect on GNP than in Chapter 7.
7. a. The LM curve is $Y = 1{,}440 + 3{,}000R$. It is steeper than the LM curve in Chapter 7.
   b. The aggregate demand curve is $Y = 1{,}509 + .86G$. Because the LM curve is steeper, increases in government spending have less effect on GNP than in Chapter 7.

PART III

The Micro Foundations of Output Determination and Price Adjustment

CHAPTER 15   The Labor Market and Flexible-Price Theories of Fluctuations

Main Objectives

In Chapters 4 and 5, we developed the long-run growth model to understand the evolution of potential GNP and then, starting in Chapter 6, incorporated sticky prices to explain departures of GNP from potential. In this chapter, we develop the analysis of labor supply and labor demand in more detail. We use this analysis to consider three flexible-price models which attempt to explain economic fluctuations: the real business cycle model, the model with an effect of real interest rates on labor supply, and the misperceptions model. You should understand how these three models operate and be able to evaluate how well they are able to explain fluctuations.

Key Terms and Concepts

The **labor supply schedule for an individual worker** depicts the relation between the real wage and the amount of time that the individual is willing to work. In the aggregate, it shows the relation between employment and the real wage. For each level of employment, the real wage can be interpreted as the value to workers of time spent in alternative activities.

In the long run, as discussed in Chapter 4, there can be substantial variation in the real wage without much effect on the supply of labor. The substitution effect (a higher real wage raises the opportunity cost of leisure) increases labor supply but the income effect (a higher real wage makes workers better off and increases consumption of almost all goods, including leisure time) lowers labor supply. These two effects cancel each other out, making the **long-run labor supply schedule** approximately vertical.

In the short run, however, there can be substantial fluctuations of employment without much change in the real wage. One reason for this is the existence of important alternative activities. During recessions, unemployed workers may prefer to invest in education or home improvement rather than take low-paying jobs. Fixed costs of going to work may also help explain why, as long as the length of the working day does not change, people are willing to work more or fewer days at the same real wage. **Sectoral shifts**, differences in economic conditions among different regions and industries, accompany recessions and make job search a valuable activity. For these reasons, the **short-run labor supply schedule** may be quite flat.

According to standard economic analysis, the **demand for labor schedule** slopes downward due to the diminishing marginal product of labor. In the short run, however, the schedule may be close to horizontal for three reasons: Firms with **unused capacity** (idle plants or work stations), **unused shifts** (such as evenings or weekends), or **complementarities** (situations where higher levels of activity raise productivity) are not likely to exhibit diminishing returns. In the absence of diminishing returns, the real wage that firms are willing to pay does not decrease as employment increases.

We can now illustrate the **real business cycle model** that we studied in Chapter 5. In Figure 15–1, we show how shocks to productivity, which shift the labor demand schedule, cause large changes in employment and output if the labor supply schedule is flat. While these factors are clearly important, we regard it as implausible that exogenous shocks to productivity are large enough and that the labor supply schedule is flat enough to generate fluctuations of the size observed in the economy.

THE LABOR MARKET AND FLEXIBLE-PRICE THEORIES 185

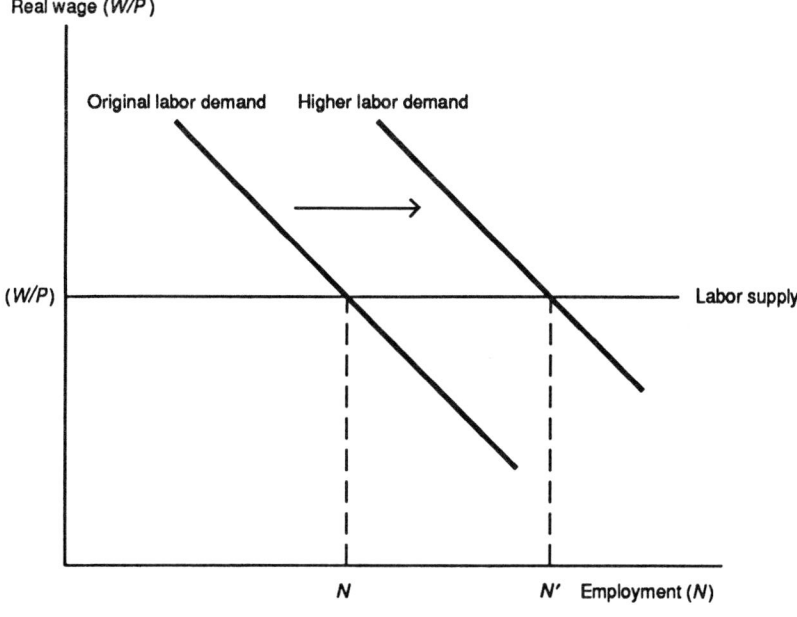

Figure 15–1

The predictions of the real business cycle model change when we incorporate the **effects of real interest rates on labor supply.** Higher real interest rates increase labor supply by making it more attractive to work now and consume later. In Figure 15–2, a higher real interest rate causes the labor supply schedule to shift to the right, increasing employment and output.

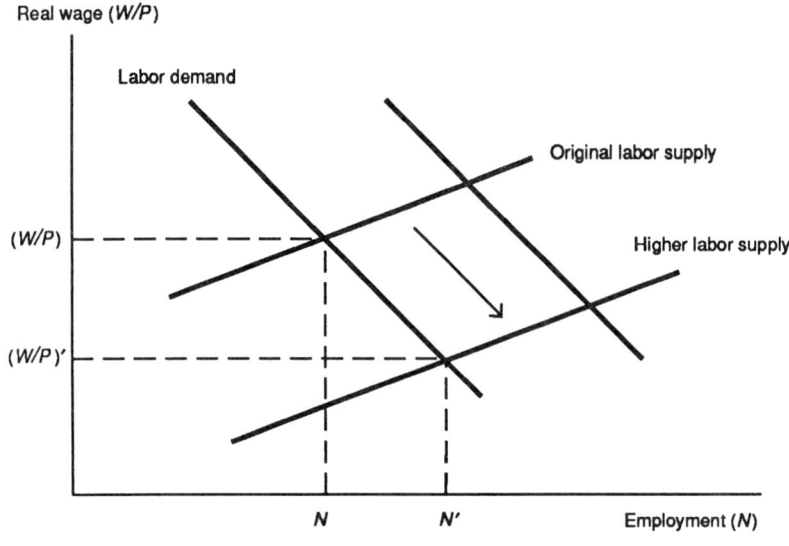

Figure 15-2

According to this model, expansionary fiscal policy (higher government spending or tax cuts) increases the real interest rate, raising employment and output. These predictions for fiscal policy are similar to those of the sticky-price model. Monetary policy, on the other hand, is neutral in the short run, a prediction which is very different than the sticky-price model. Many economists are skeptical both that real interest rates exert the strong effects on labor supply necessary to drive the model and that the theory can account for the magnitude of observed fluctuations in employment and output.

The **misperceptions model** combines flexible prices with incomplete information regarding the real interest rate to explain fluctuations. Unlike other flexible-price models, which incorporate monetary neutrality, monetary expansion may create misperceptions about the real interest rate, raising labor supply, employment, and output in the short run.

Incomplete information is the key to the misperceptions model. Workers, who care about the real interest rate, do not know either the economywide price level or the nominal interest rate, but know their own nominal wage. This, however, is not sufficient information for them to make a correct labor supply decision. If the nominal wage rises because the Fed has increased the money supply, prices will also rise and there is no reason to work harder. On the other hand, if the nominal wage rises because of unusually good conditions in the local labor market, this is an increase in the real interest rate which should increase labor supply

The **Lucas supply curve**, named for Robert Lucas of the University of Chicago, who did the original research on the misperceptions model, is an algebraic representation of these ideas:

$$Y = h(P - P_{-1}) + Y^*. \qquad (15\text{-}1)$$

The Lucas supply curve says says that output Y is greater than potential output Y^* if the price level P is greater than the last period's price level P_{-1}.

When the nominal wage and price levels rise, workers, who do not know whether the cause of this particular change is monetary expansion or good local conditions, increase their labor supply. The coefficient h represents the proportion, in general, of wage changes that come from local markets, which determines how much workers respond to the higher nominal wage.

A more general formulation of the Lucas supply curve is

$$Y = h(P - P^e) + Y^*, \qquad (15\text{-}2)$$

where P^e, the best inference by workers of the purely monetary effect on the price level, is the expected price level. Under this interpretation, output is above potential GNP when prices are above the expected price level.

The **monetary policy ineffectiveness theorem**, due to Thomas Sargent of Stanford University and Neil Wallace of the University of Minnesota, is a striking result obtained by combining the misperceptions model with rational expectations. In the misperceptions model, monetary expansions affect output by creating a wedge between actual and expected prices. If expectations are rational and workers have essentially the same information about the economy as the Fed, systematic monetary policy, which includes all policy rules based on observed conditions, will be anticipated and raise expected as well as actual prices. In the absence of surprises, output is unaffected.

The misperceptions model, which was very influential in the 1970s, does not seem, from the perspective of the 1990s, to offer a convincing explanation of economic fluctuations. First, the central assumption of the model, that workers do not know the money supply, is not at all realistic. Second, while early empirical work seemed supportive, more recent work casts doubt on how well the theory works in practice. Third, recent evidence indicates that a variety of forces—financial shocks, technological shocks, and changes in preferences—are at least as important as monetary shocks in explaining fluctuations in real GNP.

Self-Test

Fill in the Blank

1. For an individual worker the _____ depicts the relation between the real wage and the amount of time that the individual is willing to work.
2. The long-run labor supply schedule is close to _____.
3. The _____ labor supply schedule may be quite flat.
4. The demand for labor schedule slopes downward due to the _____ marginal product of labor.
5. In the short run, the labor demand schedule may be _____.
6. Higher real interest rates _____ labor supply.
7. The _____ model combines flexible prices with incomplete information.
8. In the misperceptions model, workers observe only the _____.
9. The positive relationship between prices and output in the misperceptions model is called the _____.
10. According to the Lucas supply curve, output can exceed potential only if the price level is greater than the _____ price level.
11. According to the _____, systematic monetary policy cannot affect output.
12. The monetary policy ineffectiveness theorem is obtained by combining the misperceptions model with _____.

True-False

13. The long-run labor supply schedule is close to vertical.

THE LABOR MARKET AND FLEXIBLE-PRICE THEORIES 189

14. The short-run labor supply schedule is close to vertical.
15. The demand for labor schedule is close to vertical.
16. Real business cycle theories emphasize monetary factors to explain economic fluctuations.
17. Evidence that the short-run labor supply schedule is flat supports the proposition that the real business cycle model is able to explain economic fluctuations.
18. The misperceptions model differs from the real business cycle model by incorporating sticky prices.
19. In the misperceptions model, fluctuations of output can only be caused by shifts of labor supply and demand.
20. According to the misperceptions model, workers do not know the general price level.
21. The Lucas supply curve says that output will exceed potential GNP only if there is a price surprise.
22. Changes in the money supply have no effect on real GNP in the real business cycle model.
23. Changes in the money supply have no effect on real GNP in the misperceptions model.
24. According to the monetary policy ineffectiveness theorem, monetary policy rules have no effect on real GNP.

Review Questions

25. Why is the long-run labor supply schedule close to vertical?
26. What are the three reasons why the short-run labor supply schedule may be quite flat?
27. What are the three reasons why the short-run demand for labor schedule may be quite flat?
28. Why do real interest rates affect labor supply?
29. What is the impact of incorporating the effects of real interest rates on labor supply on the predictions for fiscal policy in the real business cycle model?
30. What is the impact of incorporating the effects of real interest rates on labor supply on the predictions for monetary policy in the real business cycle model?
31. What is the key assumption that drives the misperceptions model?

32. Why do unanticipated changes in the money supply have real effects in the misperceptions model?

33. In the misperceptions model, why can't the Fed construct a policy rule that has real effects by surprising people?

34. Why are many economists skeptical that the real business cycle model can explain observed economic fluctuations?

35. Why are many economists skeptical that the model which incorporates the effects of real interest rates on labor supply can explain observed economic fluctuations?

36. Why are many economists skeptical that the misperceptions model can explain observed economic fluctuations?

Problem Set

Worked Problems

1. Consider the following flexible-price model:

    $Y^* = C + I + G + X$ (Income identity)
    $C = 100 + .9Y_d$ (Consumption)
    $I = 200 - 500R$ (Investment)
    $X = 100 - .12Y^* - 500R$ (Net exports)
    $M = (.8Y^* - 2{,}000R)P$ (Money demand)

    with potential output $Y^* = \$1{,}250$ billion, government spending $G = \$200$ billion, the tax rate $t = .2$, and the nominal money supply $M = \$800$ billion.

    a. What is the interest rate R?

    b. What is the price level P?

    c. If government spending G increases to $300 billion, what happens to the interest rate and to the price level?

    a. With output always equal to potential GNP, we solve for the interest rate by using the same technique that we used to find the IS curve in Chapter 7:

    $Y^* = C + I + G + X$
    $1{,}250 = 100 + .9[1{,}250 - .2(1{,}250)] +$
    $\qquad 200 - 500R + 200 + 100 - .12(1{,}250) - 500R$
    $1{,}250 = 1{,}350 - 1{,}000R$
    $R = .1$ (10 percent).

b. *The price level is determined by substituting the interest rate, money supply, and potential output into the money demand curve:*

$$M = (.8Y^* - 2{,}000R)P$$
$$800 = [.8(1{,}250) - 2{,}000(.1)]P$$
$$800 = 800P$$
$$P = 1.$$

c. *The interest rate is determined as in Part a.*

$$1{,}250 = 100 + .9[1{,}250 - .2(1{,}250)] + 300 - 1{,}000R + 300$$
$$R = .2 \text{ (20 percent)}.$$

The price level is determined as in Part b.

$$800 = [.8(1{,}250) - 2{,}000(.2)]P$$
$$P = 1.33.$$

The increase in government spending raises both the interest rate and the price level.

2. Suppose that the Lucas supply curve is

$$Y = 475(P - P^e) + Y^*$$

and the aggregate demand curve is

$$Y = 750 + .625(M/P)$$

with the money supply $M = \$800$ billion and potential output $Y^* = \$1{,}250$ billion.

a. What is the price level P if output Y is equal to potential output Y^* with no expected changes in policy?

b. Suppose that the Fed announces that it will increase the money supply to $880 billion and then enacts that policy. What are the new levels of output and the price level?

c. Suppose that the increase in the money supply is unanticipated. What are the new levels of output and the price level?

a. *From the aggregate demand curve with output equal to potential output:*

$$1{,}250 = 750 + .625(800)/P$$
$$P = 1.$$

b. Since the increase in the money supply is anticipated, people expect the new higher price level. With no price surprises, $Y = Y^* = \$1{,}250$ billion. The price level can be calculated from the aggregate demand curve:

$$1{,}250 = 750 + .625(880)/P$$
$$P = 1.1.$$

The price level rises in proportion to the anticipated increase in the money supply. Output is unchanged.

c. Because the increase in the money supply is unanticipated, the expected price does not adjust. From the Lucas supply curve,

$$Y = 475(P - 1) + 1{,}250.$$

From the aggregate demand curve,

$$Y = 750 + .625(880)/P.$$

Solving for P:

$$475(P - 1) + 1{,}250 = 750 + 550/P$$
$$475P^2 + 25P - 550 = 0.$$

Using the quadratic formula:

$$P = \frac{(-25) \pm \sqrt{(25)^2 - 4(475)(-550)}}{2(475)}.$$

The only economically sensible solution is for the price level to be positive:

$$P = 1.05.$$

Solving for Y using the Lucas supply curve:

$$Y = 475(1.05 - 1) + 1{,}250$$
$$= \$1{,}273.75 \text{ billion}.$$

The unanticipated increase in the money supply increases prices less than proportionately and raises output above potential.

Review Problems

3. Consider the following flexible-price model:

$$Y^* = C + I + G + X \quad \text{(Income identity)}$$
$$C = 300 + .8Y_d \quad \text{(Consumption)}$$
$$I = 200 - 1{,}500R \quad \text{(Investment)}$$
$$X = 100 - .04Y^* - 500R \quad \text{(Net exports)}$$
$$M = (.5Y^* - 2{,}000R)P \quad \text{(Money demand)}$$

with potential output $Y^* = \$1{,}750$, government spending $G = \$200$, the tax rate $t = .2$, and the nominal money supply $M = \$550$.

a. What is the interest rate R?

b. What is the price level P?

c. If government spending G increases to $300, what happens to the interest rate and to the price level?

4. Consider the following flexible-price model:

$$Y^* = C + I + G + X \quad \text{(Income identity)}$$
$$C = 400 + .9Y_d \quad \text{(Consumption)}$$
$$I = 300 - 2{,}000R \quad \text{(Investment)}$$
$$X = 100 - .05Y^* - 1{,}000R \quad \text{(Net exports)}$$
$$M = (.4Y^* - 1{,}000R)P \quad \text{(Money demand)}$$

with potential output $Y^* = \$1{,}000$, government spending $G = \$100$, the tax rate $t = .5$, and the nominal money supply $M = \$180$.

a. What is the interest rate R?

b. What is the price level P?

c. If the nominal money supply M increases by 50 percent to $270, what happens to the interest rate and to the price level?

5. Consider the following flexible-price model:

$$Y^* = C + I + G + X \quad \text{(Income identity)}$$
$$C = 470 + .9Y_d \quad \text{(Consumption)}$$
$$I = 600 - 3{,}000R \quad \text{(Investment)}$$
$$X = 400 - .09Y^* - 1{,}000R \quad \text{(Net exports)}$$
$$M = (.8Y^* - 7{,}000R)P \quad \text{(Money demand)}$$

with potential output $Y^* = \$5{,}000$, government spending $G = \$700$, the tax rate $t = .2$, and the money supply $M = \$2{,}580$.

a. What is the interest rate R?

b. What is the price level P?

c. If government spending G falls to $620, what happens to the interest rate and to the price level?

d. If, in addition, the money supply M falls by 1/3 to $1,720, what happens to R and P?

6. Suppose that the Lucas supply curve is

$$Y = 43.3(P - P^e) + Y^*$$

and the aggregate demand curve is

$$Y = 700 + 1.5(M/P)$$

with the money supply $M = \$400$ and potential output $Y^* = \$1,000$.

a. What is the price level P if output Y is equal to potential output Y^* with no expected changes in policy?

b. Suppose that the Fed announces that it will increase the money supply to $480 and then enacts that policy. What are the new levels of output and the price level?

c. Suppose that the increase in the money supply is unanticipated. What are the new levels of output and the price level?

7. Suppose that the Lucas supply curve is

$$Y = 560(P - P^e) + Y^*$$

and the aggregate demand curve is

$$Y = 1,000 + 1.25(M/P)$$

with the money supply $M = \$400$ and potential output $Y^* = \$1,500$.

a. What is the price level P if output Y is equal to potential output Y^* with no expected changes in policy?

b. Suppose that the Fed announces that it will decrease the money supply to $320 and then enacts that policy. What are the new levels of output and the price level?

c. Suppose that the decrease in the money supply is unanticipated. What are the new levels of output and the price level?

8. Suppose that the Lucas supply curve is

$$Y = 556(P - P^e) + Y^*$$

and the aggregate demand curve is

$$Y = 1,582 + .90(M/P)$$

with the money supply $M = \$1,275$ and potential output $Y^* = \$2,500$.

a. What is the price level P if output Y is equal to potential output Y^* with no expected changes in policy?

b. Suppose that the Fed announces that it will decrease the money supply to $1,020 and then enacts that policy. What are the new levels of output and the price level?

c. Suppose that the decrease in the money supply is unanticipated. What are the new levels of output and the price level?

Answers to the Self-Test

1. Labor supply schedule
2. Vertical
3. Short-run
4. Diminishing
5. Close to horizontal
6. Increase
7. Misperceptions
8. Nominal wage
9. Lucas supply curve
10. Expected
11. Monetary policy ineffectiveness theorem
12. Rational expectations
13. True. In the long run, changes in the real wage have little effect on labor supply.
14. False. The short-run labor supply schedule is quite flat.
15. False. The demand for labor schedule either slopes downward or is close to horizontal.
16. False. Real business cycle theories emphasize shifts in the labor demand schedule.
17. True. With a flat short-run labor supply schedule, shifts in the labor demand schedule have greater effects on employment and output.
18. False. Prices are flexible in both models.
19. False. Unanticipated changes in the money supply will also cause fluctuations.
20. True. They estimate the general price based on the knowledge of their own nominal wage.
21. True. Output can exceed potential only if actual prices are greater than expected prices.
22. True. Money is neutral in the real business cycle model.
23. False. Unanticipated changes in the money supply affect real GNP.
24. True. Monetary policy based on a rule, being systematic, will be anticipated and have no real effects.
25. The long-run labor supply schedule is close to vertical because the income and substitution effects cancel each other out.

26. The existence of important alternative activities, fixed costs of going to work, and sectoral shifts all contribute to a flat short-run labor supply schedule.
27. The short-run demand for labor schedule may be quite flat because of unused capacity, unused shifts, and complementarities in production by firms.
28. Higher real interest rates increase labor supply by making it more attractive to work now and consume later.
29. When real interest rates affect labor supply, fiscal policy can affect output in the real business cycle model.
30. None. Monetary policy is still neutral.
31. The key assumption that drives the misperceptions model is incomplete information about the real interest rate.
32. Unanticipated changes in the money supply create price surprises, causing workers to supply more labor.
33. Any policy rule, being systematic and based on observed events, will become known to people. Monetary policy based on such a rule cannot be a surprise.
34. In order to explain observed economic fluctuations, the real business cycle model requires large exogenous shocks to productivity and a very flat labor supply schedule. Both of these are regarded as implausible by many economists.
35. Many economists are skeptical that the effects of real interest rates on labor supply are strong enough for this model to be able to explain observed fluctuations.
36. Skepticism regarding the misperceptions model stems from the unrealistic assumption that workers do not know the money supply, from lack of empirical support, and from doubt that monetary shocks are a central factor in explaining fluctuations.

Solutions to Review Problems

3. a. The interest rate $R = .05$.
   b. The price level $P = .71$.
   c. If government spending increases to $300, R increases to .1 and P rises to .81.
4. a. The interest rate $R = 1$.
   b. The price level $P = .6$.
   c. If the nominal money supply increases by 50 percent to $270, the interest rate is unchanged and the price level rises by 50 percent to .9.
5. a. The interest rate $R = .08$.
   b. The price level $P = .75$.
   c. If government spending falls to $620, R falls to .06 and P falls to .72.
   d. If, in addition, the money supply falls to $1,720, R is unchanged and P falls to .48.
6. a. The price level $P = 2$.
   b. The price level $P = 2.4$. Output is unchanged.
   c. The price level $P = 2.3$. Output $Y = $1,013$.

7. a. The price level $P = 1$.
   b. The price level $P = .8$. Output is unchanged.
   c. The price level $P = .9$. Output Y is $1,444.
8. a. The price level $P = 1.25$.
   b. The price level $P = 1$. Output is unchanged.
   c. The price level $P = 1.1$ Output $Y = $2,417$.

CHAPTER 16   The Firm and the Labor Market with Price and Wage Rigidities

Main Objectives

We saw in Chapter 15 that, although the real business cycle and misperceptions models are in principle able to account for economic fluctuations, many economists are skeptical that the high levels of unemployment present during recessions can be explained by these flexible-price models. Chapter 16 turns to the **wage-price rigidity model**, where the level of employment departs from the intersection of supply and demand during recessions and booms. You should understand the concepts of real and nominal wage and price rigidity, how wages are set in the U.S. economy, and the policy implications of the wage-price rigidity model with staggered wage setting and price determination.

Key Terms and Concepts

Real wage rigidity describes the situation where real wages are sticky—they do not rise enough during a boom or fall enough during a recession to reflect the actual value of workers' time. The major puzzle is to understand why, during recessions, there are unemployed workers who are willing to work at real wages below the prevailing real wage but cannot find jobs. One explanation is that, when demand disturbances are sector specific, it may be optimal for firms to lay off workers rather than reduce wages.

If real wages are rigid, the labor supply curve will be relatively flat. If the labor demand schedule is also relatively flat, the profit earned by firms is insensitive to the level of employment. In that case, firms may have little incentive to choose precisely the level of employment, at the intersection of the labor supply and demand curves, that generates the most profit.

Relative price rigidity is another implication of flat labor supply and demand schedules. According to microeconomic theory, prices P are related to the firm's marginal cost of production MC in the following manner:

$$P = \frac{e}{e-1} MC, \qquad (16\text{--}1)$$

where e is the firm's elasticity of demand and $e/(e-1)$, the **markup ratio**, is at least equal to 1. If the firm has any market power, so that e is less than infinity, the markup ratio is greater than 1.

When demand rises, prices will increase only if either the elasticity of demand rises, which there is no reason to expect in general, or marginal cost increases. If the labor supply and demand curves are both flat, the marginal cost schedule will also be flat. Changes in demand will not affect marginal cost or the firm's price. Changes in wages or other costs of production, however, affect marginal cost and therefore prices.

Nominal price rigidity, or **sticky prices**, is the insensitivity of prices to shifts in demand. We have discussed above several reasons why a firm's prices, or relative prices, are rigid. If these prices are set in terms of the domestic currency, dollars for the United States, nominal prices will be sticky. In high-inflation countries, where prices may be set in terms of commodity units or even a foreign country's currency, nominal prices will not be sticky. Nominal prices can also be sticky because of **menu costs**, the actual costs of changing prices printed in catalogs and price sheets.

Sticky nominal wages are another cause of sticky nominal prices. According to Equation 16–1, prices are a fixed markup over marginal cost, which depends on wages and other inputs to production. If wages are sticky in nominal terms, so will be prices. We shall see below that wage stickiness is an important characteristic of the U.S. economy.

Wage determination in the United States differs between the union and the non-union sectors. Most wage contracts negotiated under major collective-bargaining agreements last three years. In about half of these contracts, the nominal wage is set in advance for all three years. In the other half, the wage is partially indexed to inflation. The indexing provisions are usually less than 100 percent. Wage setting in the union sector is not synchronized. At any one time, only a small fraction of workers are signing contracts. The others either have recently signed contracts or will sign contracts in the near future. Wage contracts are said to be **staggered** because the period in which one contract is in force overlaps the period in which other contracts are in force.

There are three major factors that influence the outcome of wage bargaining in the union sector. The first factor is the state of the labor market. If unemployment is high, labor will be in a relatively weak bargaining position and wage settlements ought to be low. Conversely, wage settlements ought to be high if unemployment is low. The second factor is the wage paid to comparable workers in other industries. Because of the staggering of wage contracts, this includes both the wage settlements of workers who have recently signed contracts and the expected wage settlements of workers who will be signing their contracts in the near future. The third factor is the expected rate of inflation. If inflation is expected to be high, workers will ask for larger wage increases. Firms will be willing to pay them because their own prices are expected to rise.

In the non-union sector, it is typical for wages to be adjusted once each year. Like union contracts, these adjustments are not synchronized. The same factors that influence wage bargaining in the union sector—the state of the labor market, the wage paid to comparable workers, and expected inflation—also influence wage bargaining in the non-union sector.

Whether we consider the union or the non-union sector, it is clear that a worker and employer do not negotiate new wages on a daily, or even a weekly, basis in response to changes in labor demand. This is where the rigidity of the wage rate begins. The **adjustment cost**, which is the cost of renegotiating a contract, makes long-term wage contracts desirable.

Indexing provisions in wage contracts could insure workers against unexpected inflation. The primary reason that indexing is not more widespread, and why it is not 100 percent when it occurs, is that indexing to the cost of living can be harmful if there are import price or technology shocks. With such disturbances, the real wage must eventually decline so that it equals the marginal product of labor. With 100 percent indexation, the real wage cannot adjust. This can be harmful to both workers and firms because, if the real wage cannot decrease to equal the marginal product of labor, firms will reduce employment. If prices rise because of expansionary monetary policy, these problems do not occur. It is not possible, however, to tell in advance what might cause prices to rise. Indexing also adds complexity to wage negotiations and uncertainty about the wage that the workers will actually receive, both of which may be considered undesirable.

A simple algebraic model of staggered wage setting and price determination can be used to express these ideas. Suppose all wage contracts last 2 years, that all wage adjustment occurs at the beginning of the contract, and there is no indexation. Let the subscript "–1" represent the previous period and "+1" represent expectations of the next period. The average wage is given by

$$W = \frac{1}{2}(X + X_{-1}), \qquad (16\text{-}2)$$

where this period's wage W is the simple average of last period's contract wage X_{-1} and this period's contract wage X. The contract wage X is set each period according to

$$X = \frac{1}{2}(W + W_{+1}) - \frac{c}{2}[(U - U^*) + (U_{+1} - U^*)], \qquad (16\text{-}3)$$

where U is the unemployment rate, U^* is the natural rate of unemployment, and c is a coefficient describing the response of wages to unemployment. The contract wage depends on the expected average wage and expected labor market conditions over the life of the contract. Using Equations 16–2 and 16–3, we can solve for the contract wage X to get

$$X = \frac{1}{2}(X_{-1} + X_{+1}) - c[(U - U^*) + (U_{+1} - U^*)]. \qquad (16\text{-}4)$$

The contract wage depends on the past and expected future contract wages as well as on labor market conditions. Wage determination has a backward-looking component X_{-1} and a forward-looking component X_{+1}.

The problem of disinflation can be examined using the wage-price rigidity model with staggered wage setting. If the Fed decreases the rate of growth of the money supply, the contract wage will not fully adjust immediately because it is partly dependent on the past contract wage and current labor market conditions. There will be a recession until enough time has elapsed so that all contracts come up for renewal. The Fed can mitigate, but not eliminate, the recession by announcing the money supply reduction in advance and by **gradualism**, reducing the growth rate slowly rather than reducing the growth rate immediately.

The issue of the effectiveness of monetary policy when expectations are rational is closely related to the problem of disinflation. With staggered wage contracts, even anticipated monetary policy can increase output over potential until all contracts come up for renewal. Since these effects may last for several years, the staggered wage contract model has the potential to explain the observed persistence in economic fluctuations.

The long-run trade-off between inflation and unemployment is the same in the wage-price rigidity model as in the real business cycle and misperceptions models. There is no trade-off between inflation and unemployment in the long run. Regardless of the rate of inflation, as long as it is steady and anticipated the unemployment rate is always equal to the natural rate.

Self-Test

Fill in the Blank

1. In the _____ model, the level of employment departs from the intersection of labor supply and demand.
2. _____ occurs when real wages are sticky.
3. Relative price rigidity is an implication of _____ labor supply and demand schedules.
4. The _____ describes the relation between a firm's price and marginal cost.
5. _____, or _____, is the insensitivity of prices to shifts in demand.
6. _____ are the actual costs of changing prices printed in catalogs.
7. Most wage contracts negotiated under major collective-bargaining agreements last _____.
8. In the non-union sector, wages are typically set for _____.
9. Wage contracts are said to be _____ because the period in which one contract is in force overlaps the period in which other contracts are in force.
10. In an _____ contract, wages automatically adjust if there is inflation.
11. Wages are set for long periods of time because of _____.
12. When the Fed lowers inflation by slowly reducing the rate of growth of the money supply, it is called _____.

True-False

13. In the wage-price rigidity model, the level of employment is determined at the intersection of the labor supply and demand schedules.

14. If real wages are rigid, the labor supply schedule will be relatively flat.
15. If the labor supply and demand schedules are both flat, changes in demand will not have much effect on prices.
16. If the labor supply and demand curves are both flat, changes in wages will not have much effect on prices.
17. Most of the workers in the United States are unionized.
18. Most major union contracts are 100 percent indexed.
19. Most indexed contracts are contingent on the state of the economy.
20. Wage setting in Japan is staggered much as it is in the United States.
21. The real wage in the United States does not fluctuate much during business cycles.
22. Staggered wage setting makes it more difficult for the Fed to bring down inflation.
23. The staggered wage-setting and misperceptions models have the same implications regarding the effectiveness of monetary policy when expectations are rational.
24. The staggered wage-setting and misperceptions models have the same implications regarding the long-run trade-off between inflation and unemployment.

Review Questions

25. What is the major puzzle that economists try to understand regarding real wage rigidity?
26. What is an explanation for real wage rigidity?
27. If the labor supply and labor demand schedules are both relatively flat, what is the relation between profit earned by firms and the level of employment?
28. How is the markup ratio related to the firm's elasticity of demand?
29. What are three major causes of nominal price rigidity?

30. Why are high-inflation countries not characterized by nominal price rigidity?
31. What are the three major factors that influence the outcome of wage bargaining?
32. What are the major similarities and differences between wage setting in the union and the non-union sectors?
33. Why are wages in union contracts generally predetermined for three years?
34. Why is indexing not more widespread?
35. Why is wage determination both backward and forward looking?
36. According to the staggered wage-setting model, how should the Fed conduct disinflation policy in order to mitigate the resultant recession?

Problem Set

Worked Problems

1. Suppose the marginal product of labor is $20 - .25H$ and the marginal rate of substitution between income and leisure is $1.5H - 50$, where H is the number of hours worked. In the absence of wage and price rigidities, what are the number of hours worked and the real wage?

    The number of hours worked will adjust so that the marginal product of labor and the marginal rate of substitution equal the real wage. In this example, the number of hours worked = 40 and the real wage = $10.

2. Suppose that the contract wage is given by

    $$X = \frac{1}{2}(X_{-1} + X_{+1}) - 2[(U - .06) + (U_{+1} - .06)],$$

    where last period's contract wage $X_{-1} = 1$ and the unemployment rate $U = .06$ (6 percent).

    a. If neither the contract wage nor the unemployment rate is expected to change next period, what is the contract wage X?

    b. What is the effect on X if next period's unemployment rate is expected to be .08 (8 percent)?

a. The contract wage $X = \frac{1}{2}(1 + 1) = 1$.

b. The contract wage $X = \frac{1}{2}(1 + 1) - 2(.08 - .06) = .96$. It decreases because the expected employment rate increases.

Review Problems

3. Suppose that the marginal product of labor is $23 - .3H$ and the marginal rate of substitution between income and leisure is $.8H - 32$, where H is the number of hours worked. In the absence of wage and price rigidities, what are the number of hours worked and the real wage?

4. Suppose that the marginal product of labor is $32 - .4H$ and the marginal rate of substitution between income and leisure is $1.5H - 25$, where H is the number of hours worked. In the absence of wage and price rigidities, what are the number of hours worked and the real wage?

5. Suppose that the contract wage is given by

$$X = \frac{1}{2}(X_{-1} + X_{+1}) - 2[(U - .06) + (U_{+1} - .06)],$$

where last period's contract wage $X_{-1} = 1$ and the unemployment rate $U = .09$ (9 percent).

a. If neither the contract wage nor the unemployment rate is expected to change next period, what is the contract wage X?

b. What is the effect on X if next period's contract wage is expected to be .9?

6. Suppose that the contract wage is given by

$$X = \frac{1}{2}(X_{-1} + X_{+1}) - 1.5[(U - .06) + (U_{+1} - .06)],$$

where last period's contract wage $X_{-1} = 1$ and the unemployment rate $U = .04$ (4 percent).

a. If neither the contract wage nor the unemployment rate is expected to change next period, what is the contract wage X?

b. What is the effect on X if next period's unemployment rate is expected to be .06 and next period's contract wage is expected to be 1.06?

Answers to the Self-Test

1. Wage-price rigidity
2. Real wage rigidity
3. Flat
4. Markup ratio
5. Nominal price rigidity, or sticky prices
6. Menu costs
7. Three years
8. One year
9. Staggered
10. Indexed
11. Adjustment costs
12. Gradualism
13. False. Employment departs from the intersection of supply and demand during recessions and booms.
14. True. Real wage rigidity means that employment can vary without much change in the real wage.
15. True. With flat labor supply and demand schedules, changes in demand have little effect on marginal cost or the firm's price.
16. False. Changes in wages affect marginal cost and therefore prices.
17. False. Only about 20 percent of the workers in the United States are unionized.
18. False. While about 50 percent of major union contracts are indexed, most of these contracts have less than 100 percent indexation.
19. False. Those contracts that are indexed are contingent on the cost of living.
20. False. Wage setting in Japan is more synchronized than in the United States.
21. True. There is no noticeable cyclical movement of the real wage.
22. True. Staggered wage setting makes it impossible to bring down inflation without causing a recession.
23. False. Monetary policy is more effective in the staggered wage-setting model.
24. True. There is no long-run trade-off in either model.
25. The major puzzle is to understand why, during recessions, there are unemployed workers who are willing to work at real wages below the prevailing real wage but cannot find jobs.
26. Sector-specific demand disturbances, which may make it optimal for firms to lay off workers rather than reduce wages, provide an explanation for real wage rigidity.
27. With flat labor supply and demand schedules, the profit earned by firms is insensitive to the level of employment.
28. Under perfect competition, the firm's elasticity of demand is infinite and the markup ratio is equal to 1. With any market power, the elasticity is finite and the markup ratio is grater than 1.
29. The three major causes of nominal price rigidity are relative price rigidity, sticky nominal wages, and menu costs.

THE FIRM AND THE LABOR MARKET

30. Nominal price rigidity occurs when prices are set in terms of domestic currency. In high-inflation countries, this may not be the case.
31. Wage bargaining is influenced by the state of the labor market, the wage paid to comparable workers in other industries, and the expected rate of inflation.
32. Wage setting in the non-union sector is governed by the same factors as in the union sector. The major difference is that, while most union contracts last for three years, wages in the non-union sector are typically adjusted once each year.
33. Wages in the union sector are generally predetermined for three years because of adjustment costs.
34. Indexing is not more widespread because it can be harmful if prices rise because of import price or technology shocks.
35. Because wage setting is staggered, previous wage decisions and expectations of future wage settlements both enter into the wage-determination process.
36. The Fed should bring down inflation by announcing the money supply reduction in advance and by reducing the growth rate gradually.

Solutions to Review Problems

3. The number of hours worked = 50. The real wage = $8.
4. The number of hours worked = 30. The real wage = $20.
5. a. The contract wage $X = .88$.
   b. The contract wage X decreases to .83 because the expected contract wage falls.
6. a. The contract wage $X = 1.06$.
   b. The contract wage is unchanged. It increases because the expected contract wage rises and decreases because the expected unemployment rate rises.

CHAPTER 17 Aggregate Dynamics and Price Adjustment

Main Objectives

Chapter 17 is like Chapter 9 in that it integrates the analysis from all the previous chapters and tests its ability to analyze the major issues. Our model now incorporates wage-price rigidities and rational expectations. With this chapter, you should understand how the model can be used to analyze the dynamic response of inflation and output to various disturbances and how the empirical tests of the model using data from several countries provide evidence in support of the theory. You should also be able to explain how changes in policy or the economic environment affect the coefficients of the models of price adjustment and of expected inflation.

Key Terms and Concepts

The **Phillips curve**, introduced in Chapter 8, is our basic model of price adjustment:

$$\pi = f(Y_{-1} - Y^*)/Y^* + \pi^e + Z, \qquad (17\text{--}1)$$

where π is inflation, π^e is expected inflation, Y^* is potential output, Y_{-1} is last period's output, Z is a price shock that reflects changes in the price of raw materials, and f is a coefficient. Inflation depends on **market conditions** (represented by the output gap), expected inflation, and price shocks. Equation 17–1 has a number of important properties.

1. Prices are set as a **markup** over the costs of production. The first two terms in Equation 17–1 reflect the influence of the rate of change in wages. The last term reflects changes in the price of raw materials.

2. Wages respond with a **lag** to unemployment. Since wage contracts are staggered, the average wage cannot fully respond immediately to departures from the natural rate of unemployment. The first term of Equation 17–1 also incorporates Okun's law to relate deviations of output from potential to departures of unemployment from the natural rate.

3. **Wages respond to expected inflation.** When workers expect higher inflation, they incorporate these expectations into their wage negotiations. One reason that workers might expect higher inflation is if workers in other industries have recently signed three-year contracts with large raises for the second and third years.

4. **There is no long-run trade-off between inflation and output.** In the long run, the average effect of supply shocks will be zero and, regardless of the level of inflation, actual and expected inflation will be equal. Thus the market conditions term must be zero and so output must equal potential GNP. We have earlier called the lack of a long-run trade-off the natural rate property or the accelerationist property.

The coefficients of the price-adjustment model respond to changes in economic conditions. The indexing of labor contracts means that wages are affected by current as well as by lagged inflation. This can create a **wage-price spiral** as higher prices and wages reinforce each other, driving each other higher. Indexing makes nominal wages more responsive to market conditions, raising the value of f, and to price shocks, raising the value of Z. If the average length of the business cycle decreases, inflation will be less responsive to departures of output from potential and f will be smaller.

Modeling **expected inflation** is one of the most difficult issues in understanding the price-adjustment process. One factor to consider is forward-looking forecasts. Wage negotiations are influenced by people's expectations of future wage setting. Another factor is staggered contracts and backward-looking wage behavior. Wage negotiations are influenced by contracts signed in the recent past because they have an effect on future inflation. Both factors need to be included in any realistic model of expected inflation.

Another difficulty in modeling expected inflation is that the model itself will change when economic conditions are altered. The **Lucas critique** is the criticism, made forcefully by Robert Lucas in the early 1970s, of macroeconomic models, such as those of expected inflation, that do not change when policy rules are altered.

It is also important to consider whether or not people believe the changes in the policy rules. For example, when the Fed announces a change in monetary policy that puts more weight on controlling inflation, the model of expected inflation will change if people believe the announcement. If the announcement is not believed, the model will not change until an actual change in inflation convinces people that the new policy is real.

A simple algebraic model that relates expected inflation to actual inflation in the previous two years is

$$\pi^e = .4\pi_{-1} + .2\pi_{-2}. \tag{17-2}$$

Using this model and the price-adjustment equation, with $f = .25$ and $Z = 2.5$, we can look at the effects of several policies.

1. A stimulus that pushes output 3 percent above potential for one year will raise inflation by .75 percent in the second year. Over time, inflation will decrease and will gradually approach zero.

2. A materials price shock, Z, of 2.5 percent for one year. Combined with an accommodative aggregate demand policy so that output does not change, this raises inflation by 2.5 percent in the first year. Over time, inflation slowly falls to zero.

3. A monetary policy that creates a one-year inflation raises output above normal in the first year. Output falls below normal in the second year to bring inflation down, and then gradually rises back to potential.

4. A stimulus that pushes output 3 percent above normal indefinitely cannot be analyzed by this model. Because the sum of the coefficients of lagged inflation, .4 and .2, is less than 1, inflation will not accelerate. This violates the accelerationist hypothesis and illustrates the Lucas critique because the simple model of expected inflation no longer makes sense with the new policy rule. If the government enacted such a policy, the coefficients might change to

$$\pi^e = .5\pi_{-1} + .5\pi_{-2}, \tag{17-3}$$

where, since expected inflation equals actual inflation after two years, inflation will accelerate over time. More generally, no mechanical model of expected inflation (one that can be written as a single algebraic expression) is applicable to all situations. When the economic environment changes, so will the process of expectations formation.

The equations for price adjustment (17–1) and expectations formation (17–2) can be combined with the aggregate demand curve to produce a complete macroeconomic model. A numerical example of an aggregate demand curve might be

$$Y = 3{,}143 + 3.18(M/P), \tag{17-4}$$

where the money supply $M = \$900$ billion. We look at several examples:

1. A **recovery** from a demand-deficient recession describes how an economy, starting below full employment with zero expected inflation, returns to full employment and stable prices. The initial level of output is below potential, causing prices to fall according to the price-adjustment curve. As prices fall, the aggregate demand curve shows that output rises. Eventually, the economy reaches potential output with a lower price level. There is very little overshooting in this example.

2. A **stagflation** is a situation of both high unemployment (caused by deficient aggregate demand) and positive expected inflation (caused by past inflation). A recovery from stagflation describes how an economy, again starting below full employment but now with positive expected inflation, returns to full employment and stable prices. At the beginning of a recovery from stagflation, inflation will be negative if the influence of below-potential output dominates and will be positive if the influence of expected inflation dominates. Even if inflation is initially positive, expected inflation will decline over time and inflation will turn negative. The remainder of the recovery is as described above. The main effect of starting at a point of positive expected inflation instead of zero expected inflation is to delay the recovery.

3. A **boom** is set off by an expansion of aggregate demand. There is higher output at first followed later by inflation. Over time, output falls back to potential at a higher price level. In the numerical example, there is very little overshooting.

4. An oil price shock is an example of a price shock, Z. The economy is initially thrown into stagflation with output below potential and positive expected inflation. The recovery from stagflation proceeds as explained above.

All of the cases considered above display **counterclockwise loops**: The economy tends to spiral back to equilibrium in a counterclockwise fashion. Following a boom, inflation rises and output falls, whereas, following a recession, inflation falls and output rises. Indeed, the combinations of inflation and output for the United States, the United Kingdom, and Germany for the 1970s and 1980s provide evidence supporting the existence of counterclockwise loops.

Self-Test

Fill in the Blank

1. The basic model of price adjustment used in the text is the

   _____.

2. According to the Phillips curve, prices are set as a

   _____ over the costs of production.

3. _____ relates deviations of output from potential to departures of unemployment from the natural rate.

4. Because contracts are staggered, wages respond with a _____ to unemployment.
5. Wages are also influenced by _____ inflation.
6. The proposition that there is no long-run trade-off between inflation and unemployment is called the _____ or the _____ property.
7. Indexing of labor contracts can create a _____ as higher prices and wages reinforce each other.
8. Expected inflation is influenced by forward-looking _____ and backward-looking _____.
9. The _____ is the criticism of macroeconomic models that do not change when policy rules are altered.
10. A _____ describes how an economy, starting below full employment with zero expected inflation, returns to full employment and stable prices.
11. A _____ is a situation where output is below potential and there is positive expected inflation.
12. A _____ is an expansion of real GNP above potential output.

True-False

13. Prices are set as a markup over the costs of production in the Phillips curve.
14. Wages respond immediately to unemployment.
15. There is no long-run trade-off between inflation and unemployment.
16. If labor contracts are indexed, wages are affected only by lagged inflation.
17. A stimulus that increases output above potential for one year will permanently raise the inflation rate.

18. A stimulus that increases output above potential for one year will permanently raise the price level.
19. A stimulus that increases output above potential indefinitely will raise inflation without bound.
20. A recovery begins with unemployment below the natural rate.
21. There is a stagflation if output is below potential and prices are expected to fall.
22. An oil price increase throws the economy into stagflation.
23. Following a boom, inflation rises and output falls.
24. Empirical evidence for the 1970s and 1980s supports the existence of counterclockwise loops.

Review Questions

25. According to the expectations-augmented Phillips curve, what are the three influences on inflation?
26. What does the coefficient f of the price-adjustment model measure?
27. How is Okun's law incorporated into the expectations-augmented Phillips curve?
28. How does indexing change the coefficients of the price-adjustment model?
29. Why are expectations of inflation both forward and backward looking?
30. Why is no mechanical model of expected inflation applicable to all situations?
31. What causes prices to fall and output to rise during a recovery?
32. What causes prices to rise and output to fall after a boom?
33. Why can inflation be either positive or negative at the beginning of a recovery from stagflation?
34. What is the main effect on a recovery of starting at a point of positive expected inflation?

35. What causes a boom?

36. What are several examples of the movements of inflation and output that are described by counterclockwise loops?

Problem Set

Worked Problems

1. Suppose that price adjustment is given by

$$\pi = .2[(Y_{-1} - Y^*)/Y^*] + \pi^e + Z$$

and expected inflation is

$$\pi^e = .5\pi_{-1} + .1\pi_{-2}.$$

a. What are the effects on inflation if, starting from potential output with zero expected inflation, policy-makers increase output by 10 percent for one year?

b. What are the effects on inflation, again starting from potential output with zero expected inflation, of a 3 percent materials price shock that lasts one year if aggregate demand policy keeps output equal to potential?

a. *There is no inflation in the first year because, with no materials price shock, inflation depends only on lagged output and inflation. Inflation is 2 percent in the second year because of the output gap and continues because of the influence of expected inflation. Over time, the inflation rate decreases until it reaches zero.*

Year	π
1	.000 (0 percent)
2	.020 (2 percent)
3	.010 (1 percent)
4	.007 (.7 percent)
5	.005 (.5 percent)

b. In the first year, inflation is 3 percent because of the shock. Thereafter, it is determined by expected inflation and slowly decreases to zero.

Year	π
1	.030 (3 percent)
2	.015 (1.5 percent)
3	.011 (1.1 percent)
4	.007 (.7 percent)
5	.004 (.4 percent)

2. Consider the following macroeconomic model:

$Y = 750 + 1.5(M/P)$ (Aggregate demand)
$\pi = .25[(Y_{-1} - Y^*)/Y^*] + \pi^e + Z$ (Price adjustment)
$\pi^e = .4\pi_{-1} + .2\pi_{-2}$ (Expected inflation)

with potential output $Y^* = \$1,500$ billion and the money supply $M = \$500$ billion.

a. Suppose the economy starts out at a position with the price level $P = 1.25$, but with zero actual expected inflation. Describe the path of the recovery to full employment and stable prices.

b. How is the recovery affected if the economy starts out at a position of stagflation, with inflation equal to 25 percent.

a. In the first year, output is below potential at $1,350 billion. The output gap causes deflation of 2.5 percent, which lowers prices to 1.22 and raises output to $1,365 billion in the second year. Starting in the third year, expected deflation begins to contribute lower prices, and prices fall while output rises until employment with stable prices is attained.

Year	π	P	Y
1	.000 (0 percent)	1.25	$ 1,350
2	-.025 (-2.5 percent)	1.22	1,365
3	-.033 (-3.3 percent)	1.18	1,386
4	-.037 (-3.7 percent)	1.14	1,410
5	-.036 (-3.6 percent)	1.10	1,432
6	-.033 (-3.3 percent)	1.06	1,455
7	-.028 (-2.8 percent)	1.03	1,478
8	-.022 (-2.2 percent)	1.01	1,495

b. The main difference between the recoveries is that, at the beginning, the influence of expected inflation is greater than the influence of market conditions, so that inflation is positive. Output falls at first and the recovery takes longer. The first eight years are presented on the next page.

Year	π	P	Y
1	.250 (25 percent)	1.25	$ 1,350
2	.075 (7.5 percent)	1.34	1,308
3	.048 (4.8 percent)	1.40	1,284
4	−.002 (−.2 percent)	1.40	1,285
5	−.027 (−2.7 percent)	1.36	1,301
6	−.044 (−4.4 percent)	1.30	1,327
7	−.052 (−5.2 percent)	1.23	1,360
8	−.053 (−5.3 percent)	1.16	1,394

Review Problems

3. Suppose that price adjustment is given by

$$\pi = .25[(Y_{-1} - Y^*)/Y^*] + \pi^e + Z$$

and expected inflation is

$$\pi^e = .4\pi_{-1} + .2\pi_{-2}.$$

   a. What are the effects on inflation if, starting from potential output with zero expected inflation, policy-makers increase output by 20 percent for one year?

   b. What are the effects on inflation, again starting from potential output with zero expected inflation, of a 4 percent materials price shock that lasts one year if aggregate demand policy keeps output equal to potential?

4. Suppose price adjustment is the same as in Problem 1 but expected inflation is

$$\pi^e = .6\pi_{-1} + .4\pi_{-2}.$$

What are the effects on inflation if, starting from potential output with zero expected inflation, policy-makers increase output by 10 percent indefinitely?

5. Consider the following macroeconomic model:

   $Y = 1,000 + 2(M/P)$ (Aggregate demand)
   $\pi = .25[(Y_{-1} - Y^*)/Y^*] + \pi^e + Z$ (Price adjustment)
   $\pi^e = .5\pi_{-1} + .1\pi_{-2}$ (Expected inflation)

   with potential output $Y^* = \$2,000$ and the money supply $M = \$500$.
   Suppose the economy starts out at potential output with the price level $P = 1$, and with zero actual or expected inflation. If the Fed increases the money supply to 550, describe the path of the boom.

6. Consider the following macroeconomic model:

$$Y = 400 + 1.5(M/P) \quad \text{(Aggregate demand)}$$
$$\pi = .25[(Y_{-1} - Y^*)/Y^*] + \pi^e + Z \quad \text{(Price adjustment)}$$
$$\pi^e = .6\pi_{-1} + .2\pi_{-2} \quad \text{(Expected inflation)}$$

with potential output $Y^* = \$1{,}000$ and the money supply $M = \$500$.

Suppose the economy starts out at potential output with the price level $P = 1$, and with zero actual or expected inflation. Describe the path of the economy following a materials price shock of 10 percent.

7. Consider the following macroeconomic model:

$$Y = 1582 + .90(M/P) \quad \text{(Aggregate demand)}$$
$$\pi = .25[(Y_{-1} - Y^*)/Y^*] + \pi^e + Z \quad \text{(Price adjustment)}$$
$$\pi^e = .6\pi_{-1} + .2\pi_{-2} \quad \text{(Expected inflation)}$$

with potential output $Y^* = \$2{,}500$ and the money supply $M = \$1{,}275$.

Suppose the economy starts out at potential output with the price level $P = 1.25$, and with zero actual or expected inflation. If the Fed decreases the money supply to $\$1{,}020$, describe the path of the recession and recovery.

Answers to the Self-Test

1. Phillips curve
2. Markup
3. Okun's law
4. Lag
5. Expected
6. Natural rate or the accelerationist
7. Wage-price spiral
8. Forecasts and wage behavior
9. Lucas critique
10. Recovery
11. Stagflation
12. Boom
13. True. These include wage costs and the cost of materials.
14. False. They respond to unemployment with a lag.
15. True. The long-run unemployment rate will be the natural rate regardless of the rate of inflation.
16. False. Indexing means that wages are also affected by current inflation.
17. False. Inflation will eventually return to its original level.
18. True. Inflation will first rise and then fall to its original level, permanently increasing the price level.
19. True. This is the accelerationist property.

20. False. A recovery begins with output below potential and unemployment above the natural rate.
21. False. A stagflation involves output below potential and positive expected inflation.
22. True. It lowers output below potential and causes positive expected inflation.
23. True. This is an example of a counterclockwise loop.
24. True. They characterize inflation and output movements for the United States, the United Kingdom, and Germany.
25. Market conditions, expected inflation, and price shocks are the three influences on inflation.
26. The coefficient f measures the sensitivity of inflation to market conditions.
27. Okun's law is used to represent the pressure of labor market conditions on wage inflation by the output gap.
28. Indexing makes nominal wages more responsive both to market conditions and to price shocks, raising the values of f and Z.
29. Expectations of inflation are forward looking because they are influenced by people's expectations of future wage setting. They are backward looking because they are influenced by contracts signed in the recent past.
30. No mechanical model of inflation is applicable to all situations because the model itself will change when economic conditions are altered.
31. Prices fall first because of market conditions and then because of expected deflation. Output rises because prices fall.
32. Prices rise first because of market conditions and then because of expected inflation. Output falls because prices rise.
33. Inflation can be either positive or negative because market conditions and expected inflation exert opposite influences.
34. The main effect of starting at a point of positive expected inflation is to delay the recovery.
35. A boom is caused by an expansion of aggregate demand.
36. Examples of counterclockwise loops are that, following a boom, inflation rises and output falls, whereas, following a recession, inflation falls and output rises.

Solutions to Review Problems

3. a. There is no inflation in the first year and 5 percent inflation in the second year. Over time, the inflation rate decreases until it reaches zero.

Year	π
1	.000 (0 percent)
2	.050 (5 percent)
3	.020 (2 percent)
4	.018 (1.8 percent)
5	.011 (1.1 percent)

b. In the first year, inflation is 4 percent because of the shock. Thereafter, it slowly decreases to zero.

Year	π
1	.040 (4 percent)
2	.016 (1.6 percent)
3	.014 (1.4 percent)
4	.009 (.9 percent)
5	.007 (.7 percent)

4. The policy of keeping output at 10 percent above potential indefinitely raises inflation without bound.

Year	π
1	.000 (0 percent)
2	.025 (2.5 percent)
3	.040 (4 percent)
4	.059 (5.9 percent)
5	.076 (7.6 percent)
6	.094 (9.4 percent)
7	.112 (11.2 percent)
8	.130 (13 percent)

5. In the first year, output rises to $2,100 with the price level unchanged. First market conditions and then expected inflation begin to cause inflation, and prices rise while output falls to potential.

Year	π	P	Y
1	.000 (0 percent)	1.00	$2,100
2	.013 (1.3 percent)	1.01	2,086
3	.017 (1.7 percent)	1.03	2,068
4	.018 (1.8 percent)	1.05	2,049
5	.017 (1.7 percent)	1.07	2,030
6	.013 (1.3 percent)	1.08	2,015
7	.010 (1 percent)	1.09	2,008
8	.006 (.6 percent)	1.10	2,003

6. In the first year, inflation is 10 percent, the price level rises to 1.1, and output falls to $945. This causes a stagflation. The first eight years of the recovery are presented below.

Year	π	P	Y
1	.100 (10 percent)	1.10	$945
2	.046 (4.6 percent)	1.15	921
3	.028 (2.8 percent)	1.18	908
4	.003 (.3 percent)	1.18	908
5	−.016 (−1.6 percent)	1.16	917
6	−.030 (−3 percent)	1.13	933
7	−.038 (−3.8 percent)	1.09	952
8	−.041 (−4.1 percent)	1.05	974

7. In the first year, output falls to $2,316 with the price level unchanged. First market conditions and then expected deflation begin to cause deflation, and prices fall while output rises to potential.

Year	π	P	Y
1	.000 (0 percent)	1.25	$2,316
2	−.018 (−1.8 percent)	1.23	2,330
3	−.028 (−2.8 percent)	1.20	2,350
4	−.035 (−3.5 percent)	1.16	2,375
5	−.039 (−3.9 percent)	1.11	2,406
6	−.040 (−4 percent)	1.07	2,443
7	−.014 (−1.4 percent)	1.06	2,452

PART IV
Macroeconomic Policy

CHAPTER 18 Designing and Maintaining a Good Macro Policy

Main Objectives

The government is run by politicians, not by economists. That may or may not be for the best. Nevertheless, economic analysis can be useful in thinking about policy options. In this chapter we move beyond the macroeconomic model and how it describes the economy's response to disturbances. We look at the policy options that have already been outlined, and think about how they can be mixed optimally. You should learn the trade-offs along the policy frontier between inflation and unemployment stability, and consider how the frontier can be improved.

Key Terms and Concepts

In analyzing macroeconomic policy, economists rely on the following five propositions.

1. People look forward into the future, and their expectations can be modeled by assuming that they have a sense of economic fluctuations and that they use their information to make unbiased (but not error-free) forecasts.

This is the premise of rational expectations. People know that many features of economic fluctuations characterize each business cycle and use their knowledge to form expectations of the future.

2. Macroeconomic policy can be usefully described and evaluated as a policy rule, rather than by treating the policy instruments as exogenous and looking only at one-time changes in these instruments.

This is a consequence of the rational expectations approach. If the government follows a particular policy, people will incorporate their knowledge of the policy into their expectations. Thus the policy instruments become an integral part of the model. For policy evaluation, we can stipulate policy as a rule. These rules can be **activist**, and thus incorporate feedback from the state of the economy to the policy instruments, or **passive**, as, for instance, the fixed growth rate rule for the money supply.

3. In order for a particular policy rule to work well, it is necessary to establish a commitment to that rule.

This follows from the problem of **time inconsistency**. When people are forward looking, there is incentive for policy-makers to deviate from an announced policy rule—they can make things better by being inconsistent. However, once people realize that policy is inconsistent, the policy-makers lose credibility and the outcome becomes inferior to the original plan. Research on time inconsistency suggests that the scope for discretionary policy should be limited.

4. The economy is basically stable; after a shock the economy will eventually return to its normal trend paths of output and employment. However, because of rigidities in the economy, the return could be slow.

Demand and price shocks move output and employment away from their long-run, or potential, growth paths. Because wage and price setting have both forward- and backward-looking components, there are wage-price rigidities. These rigidities prevent the economy from quickly returning to equilibrium following a shock.

5. The objective of macroeconomic policy is to reduce the size (or the duration) of the fluctuations from normal levels of output, employment, and inflation after shocks hit the economy.

Macroeconomic policy rules that respond to shocks in a systematic manner exert considerable influence on the size and duration of the fluctuations caused by the shocks. How these rules should be constructed is the main concern of this chapter.

The **targets** of macro policy are the variables, such as inflation and unemployment, that we care about, while the **instruments** are the variables, such as the monetary base and tax rate, that are used to carry out the policy. The **social welfare function** summarizes the costs of having the target variables deviate from their desired levels. It reflects value judgments regarding the relative importance of the targets.

Whenever the number of instruments is less than the number of targets there is a trade-off between the different target variables. Equality of instruments and targets is not sufficient to avoid a trade-off unless the instruments affect the targets independently. For example, since monetary and fiscal policy both affect the aggregate demand curve, the two are not sufficient to avoid a trade-off between inflation and unemployment variability.

DESIGNING AND MAINTAINING A GOOD MACRO POLICY

The **policy frontier** describes the set of different combinations of employment and price stability that can be achieved. The **squared error** is a simple measure of the loss from having a variable not equal its target value. One example is the **inflation loss**—the average of the squared deviation of the inflation rate from its target, near zero. (If inflation is 3 percent and target inflation is zero, the inflation loss is 9.) Another example is the **unemployment loss**—the average squared departure of unemployment from the natural rate. (If unemployment is 10 percent and the natural rate of unemployment is 6 percent, the unemployment loss is 16.)

The costs of inflation are hard to quantify. They include "shoe-leather" costs of conserving money holdings, distortions because much of the tax system is not indexed, capricious gains and losses by debtors and creditors, and problems caused by the failure of private pension plans to be indexed. Other, probably more important, reasons why people dislike inflation are that they see inflation as a breakdown of the basic government responsibility to provide a stable unit of purchasing power and that some people view inflation as a decrease in their wages relative to prices, rather than as a general increase in both.

The costs of unemployment are clearer. The direct costs of lost GNP, as measured by Okun's law, are very high in a typical recession. In addition, there are indirect costs such as the loss of training when a young worker becomes unemployed and the social costs from the experience of unemployment itself.

The costs of periods when GNP is above potential, and unemployment is below the natural rate, are less intuitive. As long as the labor supply schedule is not perfectly flat, so that the marginal value of time in other uses rises and falls with employment, workers may prefer, during booms, to work less and have more time available for other activities. Another implication of inelastic labor supply is that the marginal social cost of unemployment is higher when unemployment is high.

The policy frontier, or trade-off, between inflation loss and unemployment loss can be described in terms of a policy rule. The price-adjustment equation with expected inflation equal to last period's inflation is

$$\pi = f(Y_{-1} - Y^*)/Y^* + \pi_{-1} + Z. \tag{18-1}$$

Aggregate demand shifts can be offset through a policy that moves aggregate demand back to its original level. The choice of a rule to counter price shocks is more complicated. The policy response function is

$$(Y_{-1} - Y^*)/Y^* = -g\pi_{-1}. \tag{18-2}$$

where g is the **coefficient of response**. If g is zero, the policy response keeps output at potential and fully accommodates inflation. If g is greater than zero, the policy response lowers output in order to stabilize inflation. The effects of different values of g on inflation can be seen by substituting Equation 18–2 into Equation 18–1:

$$\pi = (1 - fg) \pi_{-1} + Z. \tag{18-3}$$

If g is zero so that $k = (1 - fg) = 1$, then the price shock Z permanently raises the inflation rate by Z. If k is zero, the effect of the price shock disappears after only one year. If k is between zero and 1, the effect of the price shock gradually disappears.

A policy of **strict price stability** ($k = 0$) involves a large amount of unemployment loss. A policy of **strict unemployment stability** ($k = 1$) involves a large amount of inflation loss. The best policy will achieve a compromise between the two types of losses, and will have k between zero and 1.

In terms of the empirical evidence presented in Chapter 17, the United Kingdom followed an accommodative policy during the early 1970s that became less accommodative during the late 1970s and 1980s. Germany followed a less accommodative policy throughout the period. The United States was more accommodative than Germany but less accommodative than the United Kingdom before the advent of the Thatcher administration in 1979.

Nominal GNP targeting is an example of a compromise policy that is easy to express. Since aggregate demand disturbances do not initially affect the price level, nominal GNP targeting correctly offsets them. For price shocks, nominal GNP targeting, which sets $g = 1$, favors unemployment stability over price stability. Since a reasonable value for f is .2, $k = .8$. This means that 80 percent of a price shock is tolerated as a continued increase in inflation the year after it occurs.

We have focused on how to conduct macroeconomic policy in order to choose the best point on the policy frontier. These choices always involve a trade-off between output and price stability. If we could move the frontier toward the origin, we could improve the trade-off.

Streamlining the labor market, or making wages more responsive to price shocks, would move the policy frontier closer to the origin. Some proposals to increase the speed of adjustment of wages include better job matching, eliminating government price and wage fixing, reforming unemployment compensation, and legislating the share economy. It is not clear that any of these proposals would be effective or that their benefits would outweigh their costs.

Other proposals to move the frontier toward the origin include improving indexation so that price increases arising from imports and other materials costs would be excluded, avoiding government price

DESIGNING AND MAINTAINING A GOOD MACRO POLICY

shocks, and using controls and incentives, such as tax-based incomes policies, which reward businesses and workers who follow government guidelines for price and wage increases. As with the proposals to streamline the labor market, it is not clear how effective these would be.

Protectionist trade measures, such as tariffs and quotas, raise inflation when they are imposed and lower inflation when they are removed. Avoiding these price shocks keeps the policy frontier as close to the origin as possible.

Self-Test

Fill in the Blank

1. Policy rules are _____ if they involve feedback from the state of the economy.
2. _____ policy is formulated on a case-by-case basis.
3. With wage and price rigidities there is a _____ between output and inflation variability.
4. The _____ of macro policy are the variables that we care about.
5. The _____ of macro policy are the variables that are used to carry out the policy.
6. The _____ summarizes the costs of having the target variables deviate from their desired levels.
7. The _____ describes the set of different combinations of employment and price stability that can be achieved.
8. The _____ is the average of the squared deviation of the inflation rate from its target.
9. The unemployment loss is the _____ of unemployment from the natural rate.

10. Two extreme policies are _____ and _____ stability.
11. An example of a compromise policy is _____ targeting.
12. Tax-based _____ reward businesses and workers who follow government guidelines for wage and price increases.

True-False

13. People use the information available to them to make unbiased forecasts.
14. A fixed growth rate rule for the money supply is an activist policy rule.
15. The economy returns quickly to equilibrium following a shock.
16. Equality of instruments and targets is not sufficient to avoid a trade-off between the different target variables.
17. The target level of unemployment should be zero.
18. The costs of unemployment are not very large.
19. Aggregate demand shifts can be offset through a policy that moves the aggregate demand curve back to its original level.
20. If policy is fully accommodative, a price shock permanently raises the inflation rate.
21. The best policy is normally one of either strict price stability or strict unemployment stability.
22. Nominal GNP targeting is not optimal if there are demand shocks.
23. Moving the policy frontier toward the origin could improve both output and price stability.
24. Tariffs and quotas are examples of demand disturbances.

Review Questions

25. What is the premise of rational expectations?
26. Why does rational expectations lead to consideration of policy rules?
27. What is the difference between activist and passive policy rules?
28. What does research on time inconsistency indicate about the conduct of economic policy?

DESIGNING AND MAINTAINING A GOOD MACRO POLICY

29. Why can monetary and fiscal policy not be used to avoid a trade-off between inflation and unemployment variability?
30. Why is it difficult to compare the costs of inflation with the costs of unemployment?
31. What is the relation between the degree that policy is accommodative and the persistence of price shocks?
32. Why does the best policy normally involve a compromise between inflation and unemployment losses?
33. How did the policies followed by the United States in the 1970s and 1980s compare with the policies followed by Germany and the United Kingdom?
34. What are the implications of nominal GNP targeting for the response to price shocks?
35. What types of policies could potentially improve the trade-off between output and price stability?
36. Why do protectionist measures worsen the policy frontier?

Problem Set

Worked Problems

1. Suppose that price adjustment is given by

$$\pi = .2[(Y_{-1} - Y^*)/Y^*] + \pi_{-1} + Z$$

and the policy response function is

$$(Y_{-1} - Y^*)/Y^* = -1\pi_{-1}.$$

   a. What is the equation that describes inflation?
   b. What type of policy response function is this? Does it favor unemployment or price stability?
   c. Suppose that the policy response function is

   $$(Y_{-1} - Y^*)/Y^* = -4\pi_{-1}.$$

   What is the equation that describes inflation? How is the balance between unemployment and price stability affected?

   a. Substituting the policy response function into the price-adjustment equation,
   $$\begin{aligned}\pi &= .2(-1)\pi_{-1} + \pi_{-1} + Z \\ &= (1 - .2)\pi_{-1} + Z \\ &= .8\pi_{-1} + Z.\end{aligned}$$

b. Since $g = 1$, the policy response function targets nominal GNP. It favors unemployment stability since $k = .8$.

c. The equation that describes inflation is

$$\pi = .2\pi_{-1} + Z.$$

This less accommodative policy favors inflation stability since $k = .2$.

2. Suppose that price adjustment is given by

$$\pi = .25[(Y_{-1} - Y^*)/Y^*] + \pi_{-1} + Z$$

and the policy response function is

$$(Y_{-1} - Y^*)/Y^* = -1\pi_{-1},$$

with potential output $Y^* = \$1,500$ billion.

a. Suppose the economy starts out at potential output with zero actual or expected inflation. Describe the path of the economy for 5 years following a materials price shock of 10 percent.

b. Suppose that the policy response function is

$$(Y_{-1} - Y^*)/Y^* = -2\pi_{-1}.$$

Describe the path of the economy following the same shock, and compare it with the path in Part a.

a. Inflation is determined by substituting the policy response function into the price-adjustment equation,

$$\pi = .75\pi_{-1} + Z.$$

Inflation is 10 percent in the first year and 7.5 percent (.75 times .1) in the second. Output, which is calculated from the policy response function, is $1,350 billion in the first year ($1,500 billion minus the output gap of $150 billion) and $1,388 billion in the second. The first 5 years are presented below.

Year	π	Y
1	.100 (10 percent)	$1,350
2	.075 (7.5 percent)	1,388
3	.056 (5.6 percent)	1,416
4	.042 (4.2 percent)	1,437
5	.032 (3.2 percent)	1,452

b. The inflation equation for the less accommodative policy response function is

$$\pi = .5\pi_{-1} + Z.$$

Inflation is brought down more quickly but the decrease in output is larger:

Year	π	Y
1	.100 (10 percent)	$1,200
2	.050 (5 percent)	1,350
3	.025 (2.5 percent)	1,425
4	.013 (1.3 percent)	1,462
5	.006 (.6 percent)	1,481

Review Problems

3. Suppose that price adjustment is given by

$$\pi = .25[(Y_{-1} - Y^*)/Y^*] + \pi_{-1} + Z$$

and the policy response function is

$$(Y_{-1} - Y^*)/Y^* = -2\pi_{-1}.$$

   a. What is the equation that describes inflation?

   b. What type of policy response function is this? Does it favor unemployment or price stability?

   c. Suppose that the policy response function is

   $$(Y_{-1} - Y^*)/Y^* = -4\pi_{-1}.$$

   What is the equation that describes inflation? How is the balance between unemployment and price stability affected?

4. Suppose that price adjustment is given by

$$\pi = .2[(Y_{-1} - Y^*)/Y^*] + \pi_{-1} + Z$$

and the policy response function is

$$(Y_{-1} - Y^*)/Y^* = -3\pi_{-1}.$$

   a. What is the equation that describes inflation?

   b. What type of policy response function is this? Does it favor unemployment or price stability?

   c. Suppose that the policy response function is

   $$(Y_{-1} - Y^*)/Y^* = 0.$$

   What is the equation that describes inflation? How is the balance between unemployment and price stability affected?

5. Suppose that price adjustment is given by
$$\pi = .2[(Y_{-1} - Y^*)/Y^*] + \pi_{-1} + Z$$
and the policy response function is
$$(Y_{-1} - Y^*)/Y^* = -2\pi_{-1},$$
with potential output $Y^* = \$1,500$.

   a. Suppose the economy starts out at potential output with zero actual or expected inflation. Describe the path of the economy for 5 years following a materials price shock of 6 percent.

   b. Suppose that the policy response function is
$$(Y_{-1} - Y^*)/Y^* = -5\pi_{-1}.$$
   Describe the path of the economy following the same shock, and compare it with the path in Part a.

6. Suppose that price adjustment is given by
$$\pi = .2[(Y_{-1} - Y^*)/Y^*] + \pi_{-1} + Z$$
and the policy response function is
$$(Y_{-1} - Y^*)/Y^* = -1.5\pi_{-1},$$
with potential output $Y^* = \$1,500$.

   a. Suppose the economy starts out at potential output with zero actual or expected inflation. Describe the path of the economy for 5 years following a materials price shock of 10 percent.

   b. Suppose that the policy response function is
$$(Y_{-1} - Y^*)/Y^* = 0.$$
   Describe the path of the economy following the same shock, and compare it with the path in Part a.

7. Suppose that price adjustment is given by
$$\pi = .25[(Y_{-1} - Y^*)/Y^*] + \pi_{-1} + Z$$
and the policy response function is
$$(Y_{-1} - Y^*)/Y^* = -2\pi_{-1},$$
with potential output $Y^* = \$2,500$.

   a. Suppose the economy starts out at potential output with zero actual or expected inflation. Describe the path of the economy for 5 years following a materials price shock of 15 percent.

b. Suppose that the policy response function is

$$(Y_{-1} - Y^*)/Y^* = -3\pi_{-1}.$$

Describe the path of the economy following the same shock, and compare it with the path in Part a.

Answers to the Self-Test
1. Activist
2. Discretionary
3. Trade-off
4. Targets
5. Instruments
6. Social welfare function
7. Policy frontier
8. Inflation loss
9. Average squared departure
10. Strict price and strict unemployment
11. Nominal GNP
12. Incomes policies
13. True. This is the rational expectations assumption.
14. False. It is a passive rule.
15. False. Because of rigidities, the economy returns slowly to equilibrium.
16. True. The instruments must have independent effects on the target variables.
17. False. It should be the natural rate.
18. False. The costs of lost GNP are very high in a typical recession.
19. True. Aggregate demand shifts can be completely offset.
20. True. Fully accommodative policy never lowers output to stabilize inflation.
21. False. The best policy is normally a compromise between price and unemployment stability.
22. False. Nominal GNP targeting completely offsets demand shocks.
23. True. Moving the policy frontier toward the origin improves the trade-off between output and price stability.
24. False. Tariffs and quotas are price shocks.
25. The premise of rational expectations is that people, in making forecasts, use their knowledge of economic fluctuations.
26. Rational expectations leads to consideration of policy rules because people use their knowledge of these rules to form their expectations of future events.
27. Activist policy rules involve feedback from the state of the economy to the policy instruments, while passive rules do not.
28. Research on time inconsistency indicates that, in order for a particular policy rule to work well, it is necessary to establish a commitment to that rule.

29. Since monetary and fiscal policy both affect the aggregate demand curve, they cannot be used independently to avoid a trade-off.
30. The direct costs of lost GNP from high unemployment can be measured by Okun's law. The costs of inflation, such as the cost of conserving money holdings, are harder to quantify.
31. The higher the degree of accommodation, the more persistent are price shocks.
32. Policies of strict price or strict output stability normally involve such large unemployment or inflation losses that compromise policies are better.
33. The policies followed by the United States were more accommodative than those followed by Germany but less accommodative than those of the United Kingdom before the Thatcher administration.
34. Nominal GNP targeting favors unemployment stability over price stability in response to price shocks.
35. Policies to streamline the labor market, improve indexation, and avoid government price shocks, as well as the use of controls and incentives, could potentially improve the trade-off.
36. Protectionist measures impose price shocks, worsening the trade-off between output and price stability.

Solutions to Review Problems

3. a. Inflation $\pi = .5\pi_{-1} + Z$.
   b. The policy response function is moderately accommodative. It favors neither employment nor price stability.
   c. Inflation $\pi = Z$. The policy rule is completely nonaccommodative. The effects of the price shock on inflation disappear after one year.
4. a. Inflation $\pi = .4\pi_{-1} + Z$.
   b. The policy response function is moderately accommodative. It slightly favors price stability since $k = .4$.
   c. Inflation $\pi = \pi_{-1} + Z$. The policy rule is fully accommodative. The price shock permanently raises inflation by Z.
5. a. Inflation $\pi = .6\pi_{-1} + Z$. The policy rule is somewhat accommodative.

Year	π	Y
1	.060 (6 percent)	$1,320
2	.036 (3.6 percent)	1,392
3	.022 (2.2 percent)	1,432
4	.013 (1.3 percent)	1,461
5	.008 (.8 percent)	1,476

   b. Inflation $\pi = Z$. The policy rule is completely nonaccommodative. The effect of the price shock on inflation disappears after one year but the decrease in output is much greater.

Year	π	Y
1	.060 (6 percent)	$1,050
2	.000 (0 percent)	1,500

6. a. Inflation $\pi = .7\pi_{-1} + Z$. The policy rule is not very accommodative.

Year	π	Y
1	.100 (10 percent)	$1,275
2	.070 (7 percent)	1,343
3	.049 (4.9 percent)	1,390
4	.034 (3.4 percent)	1,424
5	.024 (2.4 percent)	1,446

b. Inflation $\pi = \pi_{-1} + Z$. The policy rule is fully accommodative. The price shock permanently raises inflation by 10 percent but has no effect on output.

Year	π	Y
1	.100 (10 percent)	$1,500
2	.100 (10 percent)	1,500

7. a. Inflation $\pi = .5\pi_{-1} + Z$. The policy rule is moderately accommodative.

Year	π	Y
1	.150 (15 percent)	$1,750
2	.075 (7.5 percent)	2,125
3	.038 (3.8 percent)	2,313
4	.019 (1.9 percent)	2,405
5	.010 (1 percent)	2,453

b. Inflation $\pi = .25\pi_{-1} + Z$. The policy rule is less accommodative. Inflation is brought down more quickly but the initial decrease in output is larger.

Year	π	Y
1	.150 (15 percent)	$1,375
2	.038 (3.8 percent)	2,219
3	.010 (1 percent)	2,429

CHAPTER 19   The World Economy

Main Objectives

This chapter deepens our understanding of international macroeconomic issues and extends our analysis of macroeconomic policy-making to the world economy. We consider the international financial and monetary system from a world perspective, describe the history of the system and how it operates now, examine how concern about the exchange rate affects policy, and study the idea of monetary union. You should learn how the international monetary system operates and how international considerations influence the conduct of macroeconomic policy.

Key Terms and Concepts

The **international financial and monetary system** determines how trade and financial transactions are conducted among different countries. Full integration in the world market requires that countries impose few if any restrictions on currency transactions, capital movements, and movements of goods. Over time, the world economy is becoming more integrated.

The system is dominated by four large countries: the United States, Japan, Germany, and Great Britain. These countries, along with Canada and a few others, have **floating exchange rates**, determined in free markets. Eight European countries are members of the **European Monetary System (EMS)**. They keep their exchange rates fixed relative to the deutschemark by **foreign exchange market intervention**, purchases (or sales) of foreign securities with domestic securities.

Other countries maintain some degree of insulation from the world system, usually through **capital and exchange controls**. Many currencies, such as the Soviet ruble, are **inconvertible**. They cannot be bought or sold on open markets. One of the most difficult economic issues of the 1990s will be how to integrate the countries of Eastern Europe, the Soviet Union, and the People's Republic of China into the international monetary system.

Under **fixed exchange rates**, the central bank of a small country, which cannot affect the world interest rate, does not have control of its own money supply. The central bank of an open economy can hold domestic securities, called **domestic credit**, or foreign securities, called **foreign reserves**. The balance sheet of the central bank requires that the monetary base equal the domestic credit plus foreign reserves. If the central bank tries to increase the money supply by raising domestic credit through an open-market operation, it puts pressure on the interest rate to fall. With high capital mobility, investors demand foreign exchange so that they can receive the higher foreign return. This puts pressure on the currency to depreciate, which the central bank resists by intervention, selling its foreign reserves for domestic currency at the fixed exchange rate. The net result is that the monetary base is unchanged.

Sterilized intervention occurs when a central bank sells foreign reserves and buys domestic credit (or vice versa) at the same time in the same amount. This eliminates the effect of intervention on the money supply. With high capital mobility, sterilized intervention does not have much effect on the exchange rate. Many small countries impose capital controls, such as restrictions on the amount of currency that domestic residents can purchase, in an attempt to gain some control over their money supplies.

Until World War I, countries generally defined their monetary units in terms of gold or silver. Under the **gold standard**, exchange rates were determined by the agreement of each country to freely buy and sell gold at a set price. The **Bretton Woods System** was the international monetary system from the end of World War II until 1971. Each of the participating countries agreed to intervene in currency markets to keep the value of its currency against the dollar within a narrow range, called the **intervention band**, around its fixed exchange rate, called the **par value**. A **reserve inflow** or **balance of payments surplus** occurred when a central bank prevented an appreciation of its currency by purchasing dollar securities. When a country defended its currency by selling dollar securities, there was a **reserve outflow** or **balance of payments deficit**.

According to purchasing power parity, if inflation is higher in one country than in another the exchange rate should appreciate by the difference between the foreign inflation rate and the domestic inflation rate. The Bretton Woods System allowed for the par values of exchange rates to be lowered, called a **devaluation**, or raised, a **revaluation**, but such changes did not occur very frequently. One problem with the Bretton Woods System was that when traders expected a devaluation, as with the British pound in 1967, they pushed down the market rate, causing an exchange-rate crisis. Another problem was its vulnerability to mistakes in U.S. monetary policy. The Bretton Woods System was abandoned in 1971 after inflation worsened for several years in the United States.

Since 1973, the dollar has floated in relation to other currencies. While there have been occasional interventions when the dollar reached an extreme high, such as in 1985, or low, such as in 1978, the United States has not had a systematic exchange-rate policy. The major European currencies, through the EMS, are fixed relative to each other but float relative to the dollar.

Macroeconomic policy-making under floating exchange rates introduces some additional complications to the analysis of Chapter 18. In that chapter, the basic issue was the trade-off between price and unemployment stability. **Exchange-rate shocks**, which may have political origins, change the price of imported goods and are therefore a form of price shock. For example, a decline in the currency and an oil price increase both cause stagflation. The more that a country is subject to exchange-rate shocks, the further its policy frontier will be from the origin.

Exchange-rate shocks are less important to the United States than to smaller, more open, economies. Because the United States constitutes such a large share of the world market for many goods, foreign exporters, in order to maintain market share, will often keep the dollar price of their goods from changing when the exchange rate changes. This behavior is not complete, however, and exchange-rate changes do cause price shocks even for the United States.

The commitment to keep exchange rates fixed, as in the EMS, eliminates discretionary monetary policy. The members of the EMS, by fixing their exchange rates to the deutschemark, allow the Bundesbank to determine their positions on the policy frontier. The EMS has been successful because the Bundesbank has conducted a smooth, noninflationary policy that the other members want to follow.

Discretionary fiscal policy is no more used in the EMS countries than in the United States. With fixed exchange rates producing a flat LM curve, one might think that fiscal policy would be very effective. The openness of the EMS countries, however, lowers the multiplier, causing the horizontal shift in the IS curve from a spending increase or tax cut to be quite small. In addition, the general problems of fiscal stabilization, discussed in Chapter 13, also apply to the EMS countries.

In the long run with flexible prices, the behavior of exchange rates, price levels, and monetary policy is determined by purchasing power parity,

$$PE = P_w, \qquad (19\text{--}1)$$

where P is the domestic price level, E is the exchange rate, and P_w is the world price level.

Consider a fixed exchange-rate system from the perspective of a member of the EMS so that E is the exchange rate between the domestic currency and the deutschemark and P_w is the German price level. If the

German price level increases, so must the domestic price level. By pegging the exchange rate, the central bank will automatically increase the money supply to accommodate the increase in domestic prices. If there is steady foreign inflation the domestic inflation rate must adjust to equal the world inflation rate.

A floating exchange-rate system permits different countries to have different inflation rates, even in the long run, as long as the rate of depreciation of the currency is equal to the difference between the home inflation rate and the foreign inflation rate. The behavior of actual inflation rates and exchange rates for the decade following the breakdown of the Bretton Woods System comes very close to this theoretical prediction.

Macroeconomic policy-making in the world economy can be thought of as a game where each country, having a social welfare function that includes both price and output stability, chooses its instruments to minimize a combination of each type of loss. With a **noncooperative policy choice** each country conducts policy without regard for the others. With a **cooperative policy choice** each country agrees to use a policy rule that doesn't have an adverse effect on the other countries.

An appreciation of the dollar, or equivalently a depreciation of other currencies, has two effects. The depreciation is like an aggregate demand shock that increases net exports for the rest of the world. The appropriate response by policy-makers in the rest of the world is to offset this demand disturbance by tighter fiscal or monetary policy. There is no loss of world welfare on this account.

The second effect of the appreciation of the dollar is to raise the price of imported products, to create a materials price shock, in the rest of the world. Since either inflation, unemployment, or both must rise, the appreciation of the dollar results in a loss of welfare in the rest of the world. A cooperative policy would be one in which both the United States and other countries are more accommodative to inflation than they would be under a noncooperative policy. There is little empirical evidence, however, about the size of the difference between the policies.

Monetary union would be the final step of financial integration. In a monetary union, as in the different states of the United States, countries use a common monetary unit and do not have separate currencies. Because it eliminates the possibility of devaluation, it is a stronger commitment than fixed exchange rates. Monetary union is under active discussion within the EMS for possible adoption later in the 1990s.

Self-Test

Fill in the Blank

1. The _____ determines how trade and financial transactions are conducted among different countries.
2. The _____ was the international monetary system until World War I.
3. The _____ was the international monetary system from the end of World War II until 1971.
4. Since 1973, major industrialized countries have had _____ exchange rates against the dollar.
5. The _____ fixes exchange rates among member countries but jointly floats against the dollar.
6. Many countries impose _____ to maintain some degree of insulation from the world system.
7. With fixed exchange rates, countries _____ to keep currencies close to their par values.
8. _____ is when the central bank offsets the effects on the money supply of keeping the exchange rate fixed.
9. The narrow range around the par value within which, under fixed exchange rates, countries keep their exchange rates is called the _____.
10. Changes in par values of exchange rates are _____ or _____.
11. A _____ policy choice is when each country agrees to use a policy rule that doesn't adversely affect the other countries.
12. _____ is the final step of financial integration.

True-False

13. Today's international monetary system is called the Bretton Woods System.
14. Under the Bretton Woods System, devaluations and revaluations occurred frequently.
15. Most major industrialized countries today are independently or jointly floating.
16. The money supply of a small country is endogenous under fixed exchange rates.
17. Sterilized intervention does not affect the money supply.
18. Under the gold standard, exchange rates were automatically determined.
19. Stabilizing the exchange rate has been the most important determinant of U.S. monetary policy since 1973.
20. Exchange-rate shocks are a type of aggregate demand disturbance.
21. Discretionary fiscal policy plays the same role in economic stabilization in the EMS countries as in the United States.
22. In the long run with flexible prices, a small country with a fixed exchange rate cannot affect its price level.
23. In the long run with fixed exchange rates, inflation rates are the same in all countries.
24. In the long run with floating exchange rates, inflation rates are the same in all countries.

Review Questions

25. What must a country do in order to be fully integrated in the world market?
26. Why does a small country lose control of its money supply under fixed exchange rates and high capital mobility?
27. What are the two problems that caused the downfall of the Bretton Woods System?
28. Why are exchange-rate shocks a form of price shock?
29. Why are exchange-rate shocks less important to the United States than to smaller, more open, economies?
30. Why does the Bundesbank determine the position on the policy frontier for all of the members of the EMS?

31. Why have the members of the EMS allowed the Bundesbank to determine their positions on the policy frontier?
32. Under what circumstances does a floating exchange-rate system permit countries to have different inflation rates in the long run?
33. What is the difference between a cooperative and a noncooperative policy?
34. What are the two effects of an appreciation of the dollar on the rest of the world?
35. Why does an appreciation of the dollar lower welfare in the rest of the world?
36. Why is monetary union a stronger commitment than fixed exchange rates?

Problem Set

Worked Problems

1. Consider the following macro model of a small open economy:

    $Y = C + I + G + X$ (Income identity)
    $C = 100 + .8Y_d$ (Consumption)
    $I = 300 - 1{,}000R$ (Investment)
    $X = 195 - .1Y - 100(EP/P_w)$ (Net exports)
    $M = (.8Y - 2{,}000R)P$ (Money demand)
    $R = R_w$ (Interest rate)

    with government spending $G = \$200$ billion, the tax rate $t = .25$, the world interest rate $R_w = .08$, the exchange rate fixed at $E = 1.15$, and the predetermined domestic P and foreign P_w price levels both equal to 1.

    a. What are the values of Y and M predicted by this model?

    b. Calculate the effect of an increase in government spending of $10 billion on Y and M.

    c. Suppose that the equations refer to a small classical open economy in which the domestic price level P is flexible and output is always equal to potential output at $Y^* = \$1{,}200$ billion. What is the effect on P and M of an increase in G of $10 billion?

a. From the income identity,

$$Y = 100 + .8(Y - .25Y) + 300 - 1{,}000(.08) + 200$$
$$+ 195 - .1Y - 115$$
$$= 600 + .5Y$$
$$= \$1{,}200 \text{ billion.}$$

From the money demand equation,

$$M = .8(1{,}200) - 2{,}000(.08) = \$800 \text{ billion.}$$

b. From the income identity,

$$Y = 400 + .5Y + G$$
$$= 800 + 2G.$$

An increase in G of $10 billion raises Y by $20 billion to $1,220 billion. There is no crowding out.

From the money demand equation,

$$M = .8(1{,}220) - 160 = \$816 \text{ billion.}$$

c. From the income identity,

$$Y^* = 100 + .6Y^* + 300 - 80 + 210 + 195 - .1Y^*$$
$$- 100(1.15P)$$
$$Y^* = 1{,}450 - 230P$$
$$1{,}200 = 1{,}450 - 230P$$
$$P = 1.09.$$

From the money demand equation,

$$M = [.8(1{,}200) - 160]\,1.09 = \$872 \text{ billion.}$$

2. Suppose that prices in Problem 1 adjust according to the price-adjustment equation

$$\pi = .5(Y_{-1} - Y^*)/Y^* + \pi_{-1},$$

where π is the rate of inflation and potential output $Y^* = \$1{,}200$ billion. As in Problem 1, increase government spending by $10 billion starting from potential GNP. Starting with a price level $P = 1$, calculate the paths of inflation, the price level, output, and the money supply for 5 years. Describe the long-run outcome of this policy.

In Year 1, with the price level predetermined, Y and M are calculated as in Problem 1a. Over time, prices rise, output falls to potential, and the money supply rises. In the long run, the values are calculated as in Problem 1c.

Year	π	P	Y	M
1	.0000 (0 percent)	1.000	$1,220	$816
2	.0083 (.83 percent)	1.008	1,218	821
3	.0155 (1.55 percent)	1.024	1,215	831
4	.0216 (2.16 percent)	1.046	1,209	844
5	.0255 (2.55 percent)	1.073	1,203	861

Review Problems

3. Consider the following macro model of a small open economy:

$Y = C + I + G + X$ (Income identity)
$C = 300 + .75Y_d$ (Consumption)
$I = 300 - 2,000R$ (Investment)
$X = 500 - .2Y - 200(EP/P_w)$ (Net exports)
$M = (.5Y - 2,000R)P$ (Money demand)
$R = R_w$ (Interest rate)

with government spending $G = \$200$, the tax rate $t = .2$, the world interest rate $R_w = .10$, the exchange rate fixed at $E = 1.0$, and the predetermined domestic P and foreign P_w price levels both equal to 1.

a. What are the values of Y and M predicted by this model?

b. Calculate the effect of an increase in government spending of $20 on Y and M.

c. Suppose that the equations refer to a small classical open economy in which the domestic price level P is flexible and output is always equal to potential output at $Y^* = \$1,500$. What is the effect on P and M of an increase in G of $20?

4. Suppose that prices in Problem 3 adjust according to the price-adjustment equation

$$\pi = .25(Y_{-1} - Y^*)/Y^* + \pi_{-1},$$

where π is the rate of inflation and potential output $Y^* = \$1,500$. As in Problem 3, increase government spending by $20 starting from potential GNP. Starting with a price level $P = 1$, calculate the paths of inflation, the price level, output, and the money supply for 5 years. Describe the long-run outcome of this policy.

5. Consider the following macro model of a small open economy:

$$Y = C + I + G + X \quad \text{(Income identity)}$$
$$C = 400 + .8Y_d \quad \text{(Consumption)}$$
$$I = 400 - 3{,}000R \quad \text{(Investment)}$$
$$X = 114 - .2Y - 40(EP/P_w) \quad \text{(Net exports)}$$
$$M = (.4Y - 1{,}000R)P \quad \text{(Money demand)}$$
$$R = R_w \quad \text{(Interest rate)}$$

with government spending $G = \$100$, the tax rate $t = .5$, the world interest rate $R_w = .12$, the exchange rate fixed at $E = 1.35$, and the predetermined domestic P and foreign P_w price levels both equal to 1.

a. What are the values of Y and M predicted by this model?

b. Calculate the effect of an increase in government spending of $20 on Y and M.

c. Suppose that the equations refer to a small classical open economy in which the domestic price level P is flexible and output is always equal to potential output at $Y^* = \$750$. What is the effect on P and M of an increase in G of $20?

6. Suppose that prices in Problem 5 adjust according to the price-adjustment equation

$$\pi = .25(Y_{-1} - Y^*)/Y^* + \pi_{-1},$$

where π is the rate of inflation and potential output $Y^* = \$750$. As in Problem 5, increase government spending by $20 starting from potential GNP. Starting with a price level $P = 1$, calculate the paths of inflation, the price level, output, and the money supply for 5 years. Describe the long-run outcome of this policy.

Answers to the Self-Test

1. International financial and monetary system
2. Gold standard
3. Bretton Woods System
4. Floating
5. European Monetary System
6. Capital and exchange controls
7. Intervene
8. Sterilized intervention
9. Intervention band
10. Devaluations or revaluations
11. Cooperative

12. Monetary union
13. False. The Bretton Woods System was the international monetary system from the end of World War II until 1971.
14. False. Changes in par values occurred infrequently.
15. True. They float either independently or in arrangements such as the European Monetary System.
16. True. The money supply is determined by the need to intervene in order to fix the exchange rate.
17. True. Sterilization involves offsetting open-market operations to keep the money supply constant.
18. True. They were determined by the agreement of each country to freely buy and sell gold at a set price.
19. False. The United States has not had a systematic exchange-rate policy since 1973.
20. False. Exchange-rate shocks are a form of price shock.
21. True. Discretionary fiscal policy is not used for economic stabilization in either the United States or the EMS.
22. True. According to purchasing power parity, the domestic price level is determined by the fixed exchange rate and the exogenous foreign price level.
23. True. This is also an implication of purchasing power parity with fixed exchange rates.
24. False. With floating exchange rates, different countries can have different inflation rates, even in the long run.
25. Full integration requires that countries impose few if any restrictions on currency transactions, capital movements, and movements of goods.
26. Because high capital mobility requires that the domestic and foreign interest rates be equal, the commitment to fix the exchange rate determines the level of the money supply.
27. The Bretton Woods System was vulnerable to exchange-rate crises and to mistakes in U.S. monetary policy.
28. Exchange-rate shocks change the price of imported goods, affecting the price level.
29. Exchange-rate shocks are relatively less important for the United States because foreign exporters often keep the dollar price of their goods from changing when the exchange rate changes.
30. The members of the EMS fix their exchange rates to the deutschemark. This eliminates discretionary monetary policy for all of the countries except Germany.
31. The Bundesbank has conducted a smooth, non-inflationary policy that the other members want to follow.
32. The rate of depreciation of the currency must be equal to the difference between the domestic inflation rate and the foreign inflation rate.
33. With cooperative policy, each country agrees to use a policy rule that does not have an adverse effect on the other countries. With noncooperative policy, each country conducts policy without regard for the others.
34. The appreciation of the dollar affects the rest of the world like an aggregate demand disturbance plus a materials price shock.

THE WORLD ECONOMY 247

35. The aspect of the dollar appreciation that acts like a price shock requires that inflation, unemployment, or both must rise. This results in a loss of welfare for the rest of the world.
36. A monetary union is a stronger commitment than fixed exchange rates because it eliminates the possibility of devaluation.

Solutions to Review Problems

3. a. Output $Y = \$1,500$. The money supply $M = \$550$.
    b. Output increases by $33 to $1,533. The money supply $M = \$567$.
    c. The price level $P = 1.1$. The money supply $M = \$605$.

4.

Year	π	P	Y	M
1	.0000 (0 percent)	1.000	$1,533	$567
2	.0055 (.55 percent)	1.006	1,532	569
3	.0109 (1.09 percent)	1.017	1,528	574
4	.0156 (1.56 percent)	1.033	1,523	580
5	.0194 (1.94 percent)	1.053	1,516	589

5. a. Output $Y = \$750$. The money supply $M = \$180$.
    b. Output increases by $25 to $775. The money supply $M = \$190$.
    c. The price level $P = 1.37$. The money supply $M = \$247$.

6.

Year	π	P	Y	M
1	.0000 (0 percent)	1.000	$775	$190
2	.0083 (.83 percent)	1.008	774	191
3	.0164 (1.64 percent)	1.025	773	194
4	.0242 (2.42 percent)	1.049	772	198
5	.0314 (3.14 percent)	1.082	769	203